It Happens Here Too

The Shepherd's Daughter

By: Marissa Conklin

PUBLICATION
CONSULTANTS
We Believe In The Power Of Authors

8370 Eleusis Drive, Anchorage, Alaska 99502-4630
books@publicationconsultants.com—www.publicationconsultants.com

ISBN Number: 978-1-63747-140-1
eBook ISBN Number: 978-1-63747-141-8

Library of Congress Number:

Manufactured in the United States of America

Content Advisory

This novel contains detailed depictions of childhood sexual abuse, religious trauma, domestic violence, and their psychological aftermath. While the narrative ultimately moves toward healing and hope, the journey includes difficult and painful revelations that may be triggering for some readers.

The author has crafted this story with care and purpose, drawing from her own healing journey to offer both authentic portrayal of trauma and genuine hope for recovery. Support resources are provided for anyone who may need them.

Reader discretion is advised.

Disclaimer

This is a work of fiction. Names, characters, places, and incidents are products of the author's imagination or are used fictitiously. Any resemblance to actual events, locales, organizations, or persons, living or dead, is entirely coincidental.

This novel contains depictions of child abuse, sexual assault, domestic violence, religious trauma, and their psychological aftermath. The author has drawn on personal experiences and observations to create an authentic narrative. Still, all events have been fictionalized, and characters are composite creations rather than representations of specific individuals.

If you or someone you know has experienced abuse, please get in touch with the National Sexual Assault Hotline at 1-800-656-HOPE (4673) or visit www.rainn.org.

Acknowledgments

To my son Noah—you are my greatest teacher, my brightest light, and my daily reminder that healing is possible. Your laughter saved me more times than you'll ever know. You are the reason I found the courage to transform pain into purpose.

To Faith—my sister, my protector, my fiercest advocate. Thank you for never letting me walk this path alone and for showing me what unconditional love looks like, even when our family was fracturing around us.

To Dr. Ellen Matthews—you taught me that my voice mattered long before I believed it myself. Your patience and wisdom created the safe space where my healing could begin. You helped me separate truth from the lies I'd been taught about myself.

To my chosen family—Malie, Jo, Celeste, and the countless friends who held me when I couldn't hold myself. You proved that family isn't always blood; sometimes it's the people who choose to stay when staying gets hard.

To Pastor Lyle—thank you for being the first to say "I believe you" without asking for proof. Your faith in my truth changed everything and restored my hope that some shepherds are genuine.

To my publisher—thank you for seeing what this story could become and for having the wisdom to suggest fiction when memoir felt too small to hold all I needed to say. Your faith in this project gave me permission to dig deeper and reach higher.

To my therapists, doctors, and healers—you helped me reclaim my body, my voice, and my story. This book exists because you believed I was worth saving.

To the readers who will hold this story with gentle hands—thank you for witnessing, for believing, and for helping break the silence that protects predators and wounds survivors.

To any other survivors who have been through the unspeakable: You are not alone, you are loved, you don't deserve what was inflicted on you, and you deserve to be believed.

And to the little girl I used to be—you survived the unthinkable. You kept us alive until we could learn to truly live. This story is your victory song.

Author's Note

While *It Happens Here Too: The Shepherd's Daughter* is a work of fiction, it is drawn from my own lived experience as a survivor of religious trauma and childhood abuse. At my publisher's suggestion, I transformed my memoir into a novel, and in doing so, discovered that fiction gave me the freedom to tell my truth more completely than memoir ever could have.

Serenity's story is my story, reimagined and reshaped through the lens of fiction. The characters, while inspired by real people in my life, have been fictionalized to protect privacy and allow for the artistic freedom necessary to craft a complete narrative. Names, locations, and identifying details have been changed, but the emotional truth of this journey—the trauma, the healing, the discovery of voice—remains authentic to my experience.

Fiction allowed me to step outside my own pain just enough to shape it into something that might serve others. It gave me permission to imagine not just what was, but what healing could look like. In writing Serenity's story, I found my own.

To the survivors who see themselves in these pages: you are not alone. Your voice matters. Your healing is possible. I know because I have walked this path.

This novel is my testimony, my offering, my bridge back to the light.

Contents

Part 1: The Facade

Part 2: Fractures

Part 3: Reconstruction

Part 1: The Facade

CHAPTER 1
The Perfect Pastor's Daughter

The cursor blinks — patient, relentless. I've typed this chapter's title at least four times now, erased it just as many. *How do you begin to unravel a story built on appearances? Start with the illusion,* I decide. *The polished surface. Before pulling back the veil.*

[AGE 13 – Grace Harbor Fellowship, Sunday Morning Worship]

The stage lights burned against my skin as I stood behind the microphone, eyes closed, voice rising above the congregation at Grace Harbor Fellowship. I was thirteen. I'd been leading worship since I was twelve — young enough then for people to call it "adorable" when my voice cracked, old enough now to carry the full weight of every lyric and note.

"Serenity's so anointed," the women would whisper to my father after the service, their lipsticked smiles glowing beneath the sanctuary lights.

The men would nod, with firm handshakes and approving glances. "You must be proud, Pastor Nathaniel."

My father's hand would settle on my shoulder, firm and practiced. Just enough pressure to make me stand taller. "She has a servant's heart," he'd reply, and they would beam, and I would smile.

No one noticed how his fingers pressed into that tender spot between collarbone and shoulder — a quiet command to keep the act intact.

The final chord faded. I opened my eyes to rows of uplifted hands, tear-streaked faces. In the front row, my father stood — Bible clasped tightly to his chest — nodding, satisfied. Beside him, my mother, Martha, delicately dabbed at her mascara, though it never actually smudged.

This is what they saw: Serenity Shepherd. Eldest daughter of the Pastor. Gifted. Humble. Dutiful. Pure. Always a smile on her face and a compliment on her lips. Living proof of godly parenting and the fruits of a righteous home.

What they didn't see was the knot that lived inside, so constant it had become background noise. The way my eyes instinctively scanned every room for exits. How every word, every outfit, every fleeting thought had to pass through an invisible filter labeled *perfection*.

What they couldn't see: I remembered nothing before I turned thirteen. As if the first decade of my life had been swallowed whole, leaving a blank space where childhood should have lived.

But God saw. I had to believe that. Someone had to see what happened behind the closed doors of the Shepherd house.

The truth is, I was too busy trying to be the perfect Pastor's daughter to think deeply about any of it. Too many commitments filled my time, most of which were unpaid, and all were expected — at least one each night, after working multiple jobs during the day. Sundays were the worst: two services, sometimes serving in the children's ministry, other times leading worship. And always, always, watching my father stand at the pulpit and talk about us. About *me*.

It was cringeworthy when he'd reference my "beautiful blue eyes," as he often recalled the moment he became a father for the first time, but that was nothing compared to the way the congregation's attention would zero in on me. Like I was a specimen under glass, I'd summon a smile while something inside me wanted to scream. He shared what should've stayed private and turned my life into a sermon illustration. And suddenly I was everyone's moral fable — an example or a warning. Each is a double-edged sword, no matter how you perceive it.

Some looked at me with warmth. Others with glee, as if my embarrassment was entertainment. I felt like a joke they all agreed not to laugh at too loudly.

But I noticed everything. I'd been trained to. The flicker of rage in my father's eyes when I decided anything without his permission. The tightness in his jaw when I wasn't the image he wanted to project. And when I saw that look? That thin layer of disappointment stretching across his face like a second skin, I knew it was my turn in the goldfish bowl.

So I did what I'd learned to do. *Smile. Freeze. Fawn.*

I couldn't cry. Couldn't frown. Not when the church was watching. *There is no room for emotion unless it's joy. I am the example, remember?* And still, beneath the surface, pain rose like bile.

Please, God, not now. Not the pain. Not the noises. Just let me be invisible.

But my body betrayed me, and my father was already watching. The noise escaped from within my belly — loud enough. His eyes narrowed, and I knew. I had become a *disruption*. His disappointment wrapped around me, cold and suffocating.

Fight or flight surged, but I couldn't run. Couldn't rebel. Couldn't even leave the pew. *What would they think?*

So I did what I always did. I disappeared — internally.

There was a waterfall I'd never actually seen but visited often in my mind. My sanctuary. I sang a worship song silently and imagined the sound of rushing water, the scent of lilacs, and the sun warming my skin. I picked flowers, laying them beside countless others I'd placed there throughout just this week alone. I came here so often, my escape from the reality that had me so paralyzed. Most frustrating, more often than not, I didn't even understand what scared me. Was it healthy? Probably not. But it was survival.

And then the plunge. The moment I'd dive beneath the water and feel love crash over me — pure, imagined, impossible love. That moment felt like a hug for my soul.

But it never lasted.

A blink, and it was gone. And I was back on that hard pew, aching and exposed.

My father's eyes still held the same judgment. *I am still not enough. Still too much. A disappointment.*

All I'd ever wanted was to be loved. Fully. Genuinely. To be seen as good. So when the man who was supposed to love me unconditionally looked at me with disdain... I shattered. Because if *he* could judge me, ridicule me, what hope did I have with anyone else? With God?

And so I lived by the unspoken commandment — *be perfect.*

Always. Every moment. Never say the wrong thing — better yet, say nothing at all. Never show anger. Never show pain. Be kind, be sweet, be good. Be what they expect. Anything less, and it'll eat you alive in the quiet of the night.

Looking back, I realize I never had the luxury of many things... but above all, I lacked time — that elusive, precious resource. For a long while, I believed it was godly never to stop, never to rest. I'd grown up hearing, *"Idle hands are the devil's workshop,"* and I took it to heart. No one could have accused me of idleness at the time. I was the go-to for anything remotely connected to childcare in the state — Alpha courses, marriage counseling groups, Kids' Church, youth group, worship band, homeless outreach — you name it, I was there.

I worked at my parents' autobody shop for what, five dollars an hour? It was absurd. But that was just the beginning. I was also a full-time teacher, a childcare provider, and in the spaces between all that, I took on nannying jobs and babysitting gigs. There wasn't a moment in my day unspoken for.

And in the rare moments of nothingness, I escaped through books. Always with one in hand, ready to vanish. Reading was my refuge, my therapy. I could slip into other worlds, imagine I wasn't a nervous wreck, pretend I wasn't always on edge. I inhaled literature, fifty library books a week, never missing the deadline. Unless I had a migraine too punishing to see straight, my lunch breaks and any spare moment were spent reading. It was my sanity, my heartbeat.

Stillness, however, was something I couldn't fathom. The idea of doing nothing felt like failure. If I weren't multitasking, I believed I was somehow letting everyone down; that I'd be loved less for even attempting any break.

My fatal flaw — and it remains a struggle even now — was that I didn't know how to say "no." To anyone. About anything. I thought if I just did what people asked, if I made myself indispensable, then maybe, just maybe, I'd be loved, not just liked. *Loved.* Unconditionally. The kind of love I've never truly known.

I want to say my parents loved me. And maybe they did, in their way. But it always felt conditional, laced with unspoken terms. The message was clear: you're loved — *if.* If you don't mess up. If you're the perfect eldest daughter of a respected Pastor. If you serve with a smile and never complain. If you uphold the good name of the Shepherds, no matter the cost.

It was under the crushing weight of those "ifs" that I began to escape — mentally, spiritually. I built that sanctuary in my mind, though I can't remember when it started. It was always *there*, waiting for me when I was overwhelmed. In that space, I spoke with God. I cried, I screamed, I begged. I hurled imaginary stones into the river, demanding answers: *Why do I always feel so sick, so scared, so tense? Why must I constantly battle some intense agonizing pain? Why can't I relax?*

In that secret place, the only space where my darker emotions were allowed to exist, I asked the question that had haunted me for years: *Why couldn't I have been born to a different father?*

I couldn't name exactly what was wrong between us at that age, but my body knew. It refused to relax around him. The hairs on my arms stood up in his presence. My chest would tighten. Sometimes I'd get lightheaded when he walked into the room. I told myself it was the pressure — the impossible expectations, the constant need to perform. *That would explain the nausea that rose at the sight of him. Wouldn't it?*

Sunday after Sunday, I sat through sermons wondering if the congregation would still admire him if they saw the man I knew. Not the polished Preacher behind the pulpit, but the man who lived a different truth at home. The man whose gaze pinned me in place.

Eventually, I began studying his delivery instead. That was safer. Easier. His eyes no longer sought mine out. He spoke with conviction, with fire — and none of it felt real.

His entire body would pour into his sermons — arms raised, voice rich with conviction. He preached often about respect, especially the importance of honoring one's father and mother. *As a layperson, I understand why people admire him. To many, he seems righteous, passionate, even wise.*

But admiration turned to something else entirely for some: glorification. They placed him on a pedestal, and by association, his wife and children were elevated right alongside him. That included me.

High up where everyone could see me. Analyze me. Pick apart every word I spoke, every expression, every choice. They believed their scrutiny was sacred. Like being the Pastor's daughter gave them the license to decide whether I was a worthy reflection of the family name.

I never asked for any of it.

And for someone like me — anxious, eager to please — there was no crueler spotlight than being held up as a model. Living life under a microscope, in a goldfish bowl, was not admiration. It was slow, suffocating pressure disguised as praise.

Worse still, that pressure, unyielding and suffocating, had seeped into my very body and mind. The exact reason for the random pains, the constant undercurrent of unease, remained a mystery, but I knew it wasn't normal. Then again, neither was I. "Normal" always left a bitter taste. Whatever life was supposed to look like for someone else, it was never going to look that way for me.

Maybe it all began the day my father, Nathaniel, took on the title of Pastor — Evangelist, even. Perhaps it was set long before that. *Was my path drawn before I ever opened my eyes to this world?* I didn't know. All I knew was that I longed for one single hour — just one — of peace. Of stillness. A body unburdened. A mind not frantically running from shadow to shadow. A moment where I could *be* — no effort, no masks.

That, I realized, had become the unreachable dream. It loomed like a distant summit, and I stood barefoot at the base, aching and exhausted, wondering if I'd ever climb that high. And yet, as quickly as the desire came, so too did the guilt.

Others have it worse. I have two parents — together, not divorced. I have a roof over my head, food on the table, and money from the multiple jobs I juggle. Sure, my friends and even my parents borrow without returning anything, but surely, eventually, they'll repay me. Won't they?

And so I clung to gratitude like a child clutching a threadbare blanket. It had always carried me through. Even in the darkest moments, when I was curled in on myself, writhing with pain or dread, I whispered it like a mantra: *It could be worse.* That sliver of light — distant and fading — was the only warmth I had in the cold, creeping dark. It had always been enough. Barely.

Yes, I am anxious — chronically so — and yes, I have quirks even I don't understand. But I am not homeless. I am not an orphan. I'm not living in utter ruin. So, how can I justify these emotions? I can't. I buried them instead, convinced they must be from the devil. Surely the Lord didn't make room for this kind of fear.

I forced myself to stay as the sermon dragged on. When the worship team was called back, I summoned what strength I had, walked to the piano, and fixed a smile to my lips that felt like it might shatter. I sang of God's goodness, straining to find it. I closed my eyes — tightly — pretending I was alone, that I wasn't being watched. Judged.

But the illusion cracked under the weight of the lights, the hiss of the sound system, the voices swelling around me. I missed a lyric. Winced. Opened my eyes — and locked, unfortunately, with his.

The last person I wanted to see.

The disapproval on his face was unmistakable. A silent reprimand. He wouldn't dare say anything here. Not in front of others. At home, maybe — but never in front of the congregation. Still, that look said more than words could. And my stomach twisted again, the sound loud and undeniable.

Please, God, I begged silently, *don't let the microphone pick that up.*

It wasn't hunger. It was stress. Ulcers. The invisible price of being the Pastor's daughter. But I couldn't say that out loud. No one wanted to hear that kind of truth. They'd rather say I was under spiritual attack.

No matter the reason, I just knew I couldn't run — not from the stage. Not from this role.

So I didn't.

I kept singing until Pastor Nathaniel returned to the pulpit, and then I played soft, solemn notes that drifted in a minor key. I couldn't fake joy. Not when my body was on the verge of rebellion.

I need the bathroom. Now.

But I stayed.

Because I would never, ever cause a scene.

I willed my father, silently, desperately, to bring it all to a close — bless them, dismiss them, let us go. The lights bore down on me, far too bright, each second intensifying the pounding in my skull. The migraine was settling in. Relentless. Familiar. Ready to unravel what little strength I had left. My windpipe ached, dry and raw, each swallow a careful, concealed effort to coat my vocal cords without drawing attention — *God forbid I become a distraction.*

I need to leave. But where? The bathroom, probably. That is the immediate goal. Beyond that, though... home never brings peace.

What I want — what I crave is an escape, the one from my dreamscape. I don't know where it is or if it even exists outside my mind, but I have a feeling that place holds something real. Something healing. If I could get there — if I could stand beneath its crashing waters — I might finally feel okay.

God, I want to feel okay.

* * * * *

[AGE 13 – Shepherd Home, Later That Week]

They always said our home was beautiful.

"Just like a magazine," whispered one of the deacon's wives, her heels tapping across the spotless hardwood floor like a Morse code of envy. "Your mother has such a gift for hospitality, Serenity."

I nodded and smiled, as trained. But the house — immaculate, sterile — had never felt like mine. Not really. It was a set piece. Every throw pillow, every vase of plastic roses, every scripture decal carefully affixed to the beige walls was part of the Shepherd family performance.

My mother arranged it all like a stage: the cross-stitch verses, the vintage Bibles stacked like props, the word 'blessed' stenciled in cursive over the mantle. Even the air smelled intentional — lavender and lemon-something, like a woman trying to scrub the scent of truth from the walls.

We didn't decorate for comfort. We decorated for perception.

"Serenity, fix your posture," my father would say when guests were near, not bothering to look up from whatever he was cutting in the kitchen. "You slump like someone with no self-respect."

And I would straighten. Immediately. Quietly.

As if my spine had sinned.

It wasn't that he yelled — rarely. No, his voice was buttered steel. Smooth, but slicing. And always with Scripture to support it. A verse for every flaw. A proverb for every perceived weakness. He wielded the Bible like a scalpel, carefully cutting pieces of me away until only the acceptable parts remained.

But no matter how many pieces I surrendered, it never seemed to be enough.

At dinner, my father prayed long, flowery prayers. Not the kind that spilled from a weary soul, but rehearsed declarations—announcements of spiritual superiority. And sometimes, when he got especially passionate, his eyes would flutter open mid-prayer to make sure I was still bowing my head.

"Don't fidget," he'd say afterward once the dishes were cleared and the guests had gone. "You're a distraction when you can't stay still. A godly young woman should know how to be composed."

Composed.

I learned that word young. I carried it like armor. Because to fall apart was to be accused of rebellion. Drama. Worldliness. Attention-seeking.

There was a mirror in the hallway — long, antique, gilded with faux gold. I avoided it most days, but sometimes I'd stand in front of it after dark, when the house had finally quieted. I'd stare at the girl in the reflection and wonder if anyone else could see how tightly she was holding herself together.

Hair curled exactly right. My dress was modest, overly so, but it was also flattering. Eyes wide, lashes curled, lips glossed in a holy pink.

But behind all that? I was a stranger.

I caught a glimpse of myself, mid-limp, clutching my stomach as quietly as I could. Acid reflux again, unrelenting. But I was alone for a moment, unobserved, and I let the pain show on my face.

The girl in the mirror looked like me, but she was not. Her smile was missing. Her shoulders were hunched. She looked... young. Scared. Too tired to be holy.

I hated her.

Because she wasn't good enough, and if I wasn't good enough, it meant the punishment — silent or otherwise — was coming. A tightening grip on my wrist. A scripture flung like a dart. The door slammed hard enough to make me jump.

"You think I enjoy correcting you?" my father once asked, voice gentle, eyes dark. "This is what real love looks like. The Lord disciplines those He loves."

That was his favorite phrase. Said it often. Said it with love in his mouth and power in his hands.

The thing is, sometimes the words didn't sound angry. They sounded... sad, like he believed it... as if this were all some tragic necessity.

And maybe that's what made it worse — that I couldn't label him cleanly right now. Couldn't call him a monster. Couldn't call him safe.

He existed in the in-between — a shadowy figure shaped like a shepherd. And still, I longed for his approval. Needed it like air.

That was the trick of it.

He didn't have to raise his voice. He didn't need to hit me. All he had to do was withdraw. Go quiet. Refuse to meet my gaze — a spiritual timeout with eternal implications.

One week later, I wore mascara on a youth retreat — a single coat. Barely visible. But one of the elders' wives told my mother, who told my father, and that night I was called into the living room like a criminal awaiting sentencing.

"You wear makeup to draw attention to yourself," he said, Bible open, finger sliding across a verse in Proverbs about seductive women. "Do you want to be like her?" His finger landed on the word *adulteress*.

I was thirteen.

I didn't answer. I didn't let a tear fall.

I apologized. And I thanked him for the correction.

Even now, the memory makes me cold.

At church, people always commented on how well-behaved I was. So mature. So polite. "You're raising her right," they told my parents. And I smiled as if their praise didn't feel like another stone added to the pile crushing my chest.

Because I was raising myself. Piece by piece. And every "good girl" compliment felt like a chain.

I wore modest skirts and a soft smile. I kept my voice sweet and steady. I spoke only when spoken to — unless I was onstage, where I poured everything I had into songs I barely believed anymore.

My voice was the only thing I owned. And even that felt on lease.

But the real abuse, the kind you can't report, was always in the half-spoken things. The veiled threats. The "jokes" that weren't jokes. The way my father's laughter stopped when I spoke too confidently. The way my mother's approval vanished if I expressed anything close to anger.

They called it godliness.

But it felt like being erased.

It happened when my questions were dismissed. In how my opinions were met with patronizing chuckles and phrases like, "You'll understand when you're older," or worse, "That's not very submissive of you."

It happened in church, too. When I tried to discuss theology, the older men would smile — a tight, uncomfortable one — and redirect me to the children's ministry. "You have such a gift with little ones." They'd say, as if I'd asked for placement. As if I hadn't just spoken with clarity and conviction.

But in that world, truth only counted if it came from the right mouth. And mine — young, female, too emotional — wasn't it.

So I buried my voice under layers of compliance. I drowned it in harmonies, Scripture, and silence.

And when I got home, I scrubbed dishes until my fingers pruned. I did the laundry. I watched my younger siblings. I listened to my mother sigh over everything I didn't do exactly right.

"You should be more grateful." She said once when I finally spoke up about needing a break. "You have a roof, you have salvation, and you have a purpose. Some girls would kill for that."

And I nodded. *Grateful. Always grateful. Even when it feels like a muzzle.*

The worst part?

I believed it.

Believed I was selfish for needing rest. Thought I was sinful for wanting out. Believed I was bad for being tired, for being so sick and sad, for not loving my life the way they told me I should.

That's how the spiritual abuse worked. It didn't slap you across the face. It taught you to slap yourself — and then repent for bruising.

But no one saw that. Not behind the curtain. Not behind the pulpit. Not behind the perfect facade.

To them, I was radiant.

To me, I was a ghost in a chapel dress, waiting for someone to notice the flickering light inside had long since gone out.

Still, I kept showing up.

Because that's what a good Pastor's daughter does.

Even when she's disappearing.

Perfection was the mask I wore so well, I nearly forgot it wasn't my face. But something inside me — faint, flickering — remembers. There is a girl beneath the performance. And one day, she might find her way back into the light.

CHAPTER 2
You Are Not Unholy for Having Limits

[AGE 14 – Daily Family Life / Sibling Dynamics]

It always starts the same way — tightness in my chest, like someone slowly winding string around my ribs. A flutter in my gut. Dizziness that feels like stepping off a merry-go-round I never agreed to ride.

By the time I was officially a teenager, I had learned to predict it. I couldn't stop it, but I began to anticipate it like weather patterns. My body was the barometer. And the pressure dropped anytime we neared the church. Or when I heard my father's voice in the hallway, calling my name with that particular tilt that meant he wasn't just asking. He was commanding.

"Serenity Grace," he'd say, voice coated in sugar and steel. And my stomach would answer before my mouth did — tightening, twisting, warning me.

The doctors couldn't find anything wrong. Blood tests, allergy panels, scans — they always came back clean. They'd say it was too much stress; give me some anecdotes about how all I needed was to stop worrying, and they were sure I'd do better.

"You're just sensitive," my mother would murmur, folding another washcloth with military precision. "Too in your head. You need more spiritual discipline, less daydreaming."

I tried. God knows I tried. I fasted, I prayed, I laid hands on my own traitorous body and begged it to behave. To let me breathe. But it didn't listen.

The headaches-turned-migraines came next — piercing, white-hot behind the eyes, like lightning trapped inside my skull. Sometimes I couldn't see straight. Other times, I'd stumble, just for a second, while leading worship, and pretend it was nothing. Just the Spirit moving.

People always clapped harder when I swayed like that. Thought it was anointing. But I was trying not to pass out.

No one ever questioned it. Because what does a "good" girl suffer from?

Certainly not anxiety. Not panic. Not chronic, unnamed pain that wakes you at 3 a.m. like a scream stuck in your bones.

That kind of affliction didn't fit the story.

And I was the story.

The mask of perfection wasn't mine alone to wear — it belonged to all of us in the Shepherd family. Pressed onto our faces like a branding iron.

Caleb was next in line. Two years younger, twelve. Street-smart, charismatic. His room was always neat, his Bible dog-eared and full of notes. But he flinched when our father entered a room. He kept his voice low, his posture folded. I saw the exact string pulled tight across his shoulders, like mine: same instincts, different presentation.

He wasn't as obedient. He was watched more closely than I was. He was, above all, a man, and he had potential; therefore, he was more dangerous.

"You're the future head of your household," our father said one night during devotions. "You need to lead in strength. Your sisters will follow your example."

Caleb nodded, but I saw the twitch in his jaw. The crack in his composure. That subtle flick of his thumb across the edge of the couch — his tells were small, but I knew them. I knew them all.

Later that night, when we were alone in the hallway, he whispered, "Lead in strength? What does that even mean? Like — punch walls or cry silently in the shower?"

I gave him a sad look. "Definitely the second one."

He chuckled, bitter. "Great. Good to know. Can't wait to be in charge of everybody's salvation anxiety."

I nudged his shoulder. "You already are. You just don't know it."

"Awesome," he said flatly. "I'm twelve, Ser. I still miss cartoons and Lucky Charms. But sure, let's talk about my sacred duty to shepherd the flock."

There was a long pause. Then, quieter: "I don't think I'm cut out for this."

I didn't say anything. I just leaned my head against his arm for a moment. He didn't pull away.

I sometimes wondered what Caleb would be like if he were allowed to exhale. To laugh without checking the volume. To read novels without being accused of "wasting time."

Then there was Etta.

Ten. Sensitive. Precise. She threw her pain into poetry when no one was watching and tore them up the moment anyone entered the room.

"Don't you want to show Mom or Dad?" I'd asked once, watching her crumple a page and stuff it into the bottom of her sock drawer.

She froze like a deer in headlights. "Are you kidding? Dad would say it's full of 'emotional idolatry'."

I blinked. "Did he actually say that?"

"Not this time. But he would. You know he would." She bit her lip, eyes darting to the hallway. "It's not safe to feel too much. Or write it down. Someone might read it."

She had learned early what took me years — affirmation always came with a leash.

Etta moved like a shadow in the house, silent but always watching. She read emotions better than she read books. She knew when to leave the room before our father got angry and learned how to keep Faith out of the line of fire when things were tense.

Once, I found her in the linen closet, sitting on a folded comforter with a flashlight, scribbling in a new notebook. Her fingers were wrapped in Band-Aids.

"You okay?" I asked gently.

She looked up, startled, then nodded too fast. "Fine. Just... practicing hiding."

She also bit her nails until her fingers bled.

And Faith — baby Faith — was eight. Still innocent enough to twirl barefoot in the living room without consequence. Still the favorite, still small. She could cry without punishment. She could laugh without correction. But we all knew the clock was ticking.

Eventually, she'd become one of us: another performer in the Shepherd family pageant.

She'd learn soon enough that even tears must be curated. That your sadness had to be poetic. Palatable. Easy to forgive, easy to frame.

One Sunday morning, while I was buttoning her dress, she looked up at me with wide eyes and said, "Sissy, if I smile real big, will Daddy not be mad today?"

I felt the constriction as tight as a vice as I tried to speak. I smoothed her hair back and kissed her forehead.

"Yeah," I whispered. "Smile real big, baby."

"Okay," she said thoughtfully, and beamed so hard it looked like it hurt. She reached for my hand. "Will you sit by me in church?"

"Always."

"Good, 'cause when you're there, I don't feel so... floaty."

"Floaty?"

She nodded, solemn. "Like I might go di... disappearable if I do something wrong."

I squeezed her hand.

"Me too."

* * * * *

By the time I turned fourteen, I'd already learned to fake peace so well, even God might've been fooled.

"Children are a heritage from the Lord," my father liked to say in sermons. "And I am blessed, four times over."

He'd gesture toward the front row, where we sat like museum pieces. Smiling. Perfect. Polished.

No one saw the migraines, the vomiting, the panic attacks that I disguised as "low blood sugar." No one heard Etta crying softly into her pillow after he critiqued her tone at the dinner table. No one saw Caleb retreat to the garage and pretend to fix bikes, to avoid eye contact for a while. No one asked why Faith clung to me so tightly on Sunday mornings, why she traced the cross around her neck like a talisman.

But I knew.

The pressure to be his version of holy had twisted all of us into quieter shapes.

And when I say *holy*, I don't mean *good*. I don't mean *righteous*. I mean... *compliant*. Appearing without flaw. Unshakably joyful. Forgiving. Always forgiving.

I learned that lesson the hard way.

One night — one of the worst — I was throwing up for the third time, curled around the toilet in the dim bathroom light, when my mother knocked once, then entered.

She didn't crouch beside me. Didn't touch me.

Just said, softly, "What did you do this time, Serenity?"

As if I had conjured the pain with rebellion.

As if suffering was a sign of sin.

And I believed her. God help me, I believed her.

The shame burned hotter than the fever. I prayed harder. Fasted longer. Taught myself to thank God for the pain, thinking maybe if I could make it holy, I wouldn't feel so defective.

I was a living contradiction — beloved, but never safe. Anointed, but never rested.

People often told me I had "a glow."

What they saw was exhaustion. Hunger. A girl who had learned to weep silently and still show up smiling.

What they mistook for grace was survival.

And what I wanted — truly, desperately wanted — wasn't applause. It wasn't an affirmation. It wasn't even understanding.

It was permission.

Permission to fall apart. To say, "I'm not okay," and not be met with a Bible verse, a lecture, or a sigh. Permission to scream and not be accused of rebellion. Permission to rest.

To stop carrying everyone else's holiness on my back.

And the silence that followed that thought?

It felt like freedom. Terrifying. Fragile. Real.

But freedom, nonetheless.

I remember the first time I whispered it aloud to myself in bed, curled beneath my blanket like it was armor:

I'm tired of pretending.

* * * * *

One of my changes was facilitated when I saw a different kind of kindness.

He held the door open like it mattered. That was the first thing I noticed. Not the hoodie, not the faded jeans, not the distracted way he tucked his hair behind his ear — like he hadn't realized it had grown long enough to fall. Not even the guitar case slung over his shoulder, battered and stickered, like it had lived through more stories than I could imagine. No — it was the way he waited.

He looked right at me, not through me, not over me, not past me. Not the waiting that said, "hurry up," but the kind that said, "take your time." I didn't know what to do with that. So I nodded, murmured a thanks, and walked past him into the community center.

It was the first Thursday night I'd been allowed to volunteer at the downtown music outreach. Technically, it was sanctioned by the church — one of the many "evangelism extensions" my father endorsed as long as I reported everything back in detail. He called it "accountability." I knew it meant surveillance. But I'd fought and begged for this one. Because, for once, it wasn't about my family name. It was just about music. And maybe... freedom.

His name was Myung-bak. I learned it an hour later when someone called to him across the room, and he smiled in that slow, reluctant way that made it feel like a sunrise. As if he wasn't used to smiling, but he did it anyway. Like joy was unfamiliar, but not impossible. He ran the guitar workshop. I ran the sign-in table. That first night, we didn't talk much. But I watched him. Quiet. Intentional. Gentle with the kids who didn't know how to hold a pick, let alone play a chord. He didn't raise his voice once.

When one boy got frustrated and threw his guitar on the floor, I braced instinctively for the snap — for correction, for control, for some lecture about "stewarding what God gives you."

Myung-bak just knelt, picked up the instrument, checked it for damage, and said softly, "You wanna try again? Or sit with me awhile?" No shame. No fear. Just presence. And I swear something in my chest cracked.

I saw him again the following week. And the week after. He started asking small things — how I liked music, what bands I listened to, if I'd ever written my own songs. I froze at first, unsure how much I was "allowed" to say. Every word felt dangerous. But his voice was steady. Curious. Patient. Like he didn't need me to impress him. He never asked about church. He never asked who my father was. He never once quoted Scripture at me, or tried to measure my purity, or use my gifts for his platform. Instead, he asked me what I loved. No one had ever done that before.

* * * * *

Three Thursdays in, he brought me a tea. Said I looked tired. It might help with the headache. I nearly cried because he noticed. Not my posture, not my modesty, not my presentation. But me.

That night, I went home and stood in front of the mirror in my room. I stared at my reflection for a long time. My blouse is high-necked. My skirt is long enough to touch my ankles. My smile, faint and tight and fragile. I didn't know who I was without the performance. Just a costume, a smile, and the memory of a girl under it all. *Is there a real girl under this costume? Is there someone beyond "pure," "polite," and "put-together"? Do I even want to strive for perfection anymore? I look like the girl they raised me to be. But not the girl I am. If she even still exists under all the yeses.* I took off the skirt and replaced it with sweatpants. Sat on my floor and played a single chord on my old keyboard. And whispered, *"God, are You still there?"* The strange thing was — I felt like He was. Not the thundercloud version I'd grown up fearing. Not the wrathful, watching one. But a warmth in the quiet. A presence that didn't need anything from me. A whisper that sounded like: *"You don't have to earn My love."*

Myung-bak didn't save me. That's not what this is. He didn't try to fix me, convert me, or offer me some rescue wrapped in romance. He just made space. For the first time in my life, someone looked at me and didn't see a sermon, a symbol, or a story to exploit. He saw a person. And that changed everything. Because once you've tasted even a drop of real gentleness, the fake kind makes you sick.

I used to believe everything could be healed with obedience. If I just submitted harder, prayed louder, and read longer. If I just repented more thoroughly. Silence every question fast enough, and maybe I could finally be free. But it never worked. And now, I'm starting to see why.

It began with a single question that felt like blasphemy when I wrote it in my journal: *"What if they were wrong?"* I sat with the sentence for hours, just staring. I could hear my father's voice thundering over it, even in my mind:

"Test not the Lord your God. Doubt is the devil's playground. Lean not on your own understanding." *But what if that wasn't the voice of God? What if the voice I'd been trained to obey was just... a man's?*

A man who needed control to feel holy? It was the most minor shift at first — a quiet fracture in the foundation.

Myung-bak told a story about how his church growing up used to preach that tears were holy. That even Jesus wept. That crying wasn't weakness — it was worship. I couldn't stop thinking about that for days. Because, in our house, crying was a correction-worthy behavior. A sign you were "giving in to emotion" or worse, being "manipulative." Even as a child, my tears earned me a raised eyebrow and a flat, sharp, "Dry it up." When I'd sob from pain — emotional, physical — my mother would sigh and say, "You're not a victim, Serenity. You're blessed. Act like it." And I believed that for years.

But what if I *had* been a victim? What if denying that didn't make me strong — it just made me silent? What if my tears weren't weakness? What if they were the only true thing about me?

I started noticing the dissonance everywhere. The way my father preached grace while practicing vengeance. The way my mother taught gentleness, yet walked on eggshells so expertly, she may as well have built the coop. The way we sang about God's love while shaming anyone who showed up in jeans. I knew verses about peace, but I had never actually felt it. None of it added up.

* * * * *

I read Galatians one night in my room. Slowly. Carefully.

"It is for freedom that Christ has set us free. Stand firm, then, and do not let yourselves be burdened again by a yoke of slavery." That verse hit like a match to dry kindling.

Because my life — our lives — were nothing but a burden.

Choreographed godliness. *Smile, serve, suppress.*

The whole theology I'd grown up under was this: *Be small. Be quiet. Be good. Be grateful. Be better. Be best.*

But where was the room to just... be?

* * * * *

I watched Faith one morning before church, struggling to button the collar of her dress. Her small fingers shook as they tried to slip the pearl button through the tight loop. Her lip trembled.

"Too tight?" I asked gently.

She nodded, eyes wide, cheeks flushed. "Yeah. But... Daddy say 'modesty armor'." Her voice was quiet, as if she were reciting something from memory.

"Do you know what that means?" I asked.

She tilted her head. "I think... like a princess shield? So boys don't look wrong?" Her brow furrowed. "But I don't like how it feels. It scratches my neck. Am I still good if I don't wear it?"

I knelt and slowly buttoned it for her. "You're good just because you're you, Ladybug. Armor or no armor."

She looked down at her shoes. "Don't tell Daddy I said that."

Her voice was so small I almost didn't hear it. At eight years old, she was already learning that her body was a battlefield, and her protection lay in pleasing Pastor Nathaniel. She didn't even know what she was protecting herself from. Just that if she weren't careful, it would be her fault.

And Etta — sweet, furious Etta — she'd started sleeping with earbuds in. Blasting music that she knew wasn't "church safe." She claimed it helped her "fall asleep faster."

But when I passed by her room late one night, the lyrics bleeding under the door said otherwise: "I'm not okay, I promise..."

I knocked gently. She paused the music but didn't open the door.

"You alright?" I asked.

A pause. Then, from behind the wood: "Just writing. Don't come in."

"You don't have to hide it, you know."

"I'm not hiding," she snapped, too quickly. Then softer: "I just don't want you to look at me like they do."

The air turned to dust in my mouth. "I wouldn't."

There was silence, then the whisper of paper shuffling. "They say I'm dramatic. But what if I'm just sad? What if I don't want to pretend to be okay for Jesus all the time?" She didn't wait for my answer. Just said, "I tore up the one about Mom. It was too angry. God doesn't like angry girls, right?"

"God's not Dad," I said, but I don't know if she heard me.

She was already plugging her earbuds back in.

* * * * *

Even Caleb was disappearing.

Into books, into sketchpads, into hours alone in the garage where he welded and soldered old bike parts like he was trying to build a way out.

One evening, I found him hunched over a bent rim, hands stained with grease, sweat glinting on his brow.

"Thought you were doing your Proverbs memorization."

"Yeah, well." He tightened a bolt with more force than necessary. "Proverbs won't fix the derailleur."

I leaned against the doorframe. "You okay?"

"I'm great," he said flatly. "You know, just out here being the next spiritual leader of the family. While I try to turn two junk bikes into one that actually works."

"Is it working?"

He looked at the frame, then back at me. "Better than most of the theology Dad pushes." He blew a breath out his nose, then muttered, "You ever feel like... like you're supposed to be a hammer, but they only ever let you be a nail?"

I didn't answer. I just walked over and handed him the wrench he'd dropped.

* * * * *

We were building secret worlds in the cracks.

Because the real one — the Shepherd faith — was a cage disguised as a castle, it was a fortress of rules masquerading as righteousness.

I wanted to set the script they wrote for me on fire. But I only had matches and no map.

So I started small.

I wore jeans to the store one Saturday and didn't explain.

I skipped morning devotion once and didn't apologize.

I let the worship song play and didn't sing.

I let the question live in my chest without killing it: *What if they were wrong?*

My body, too, began to betray the lie.

The headaches. The chest pain. The nausea. The shaking hands. The hot-cold sweats that came from nothing but being perceived.

No one ever called it trauma.

They called it spiritual warfare. "The enemy knows your calling." "Don't give him a foothold."

"Maybe fast a few days — realign your spirit."

But I wasn't possessed. I was drowning. And I didn't need deliverance. I needed someone to listen. Someone to hold my hand and say:

"It makes sense that you're hurting."

"It makes sense that your body keeps the score."

"It's not rebellion to question abuse dressed up as authority."

"It's not a sin to want to breathe."

* * * * *

Myung-bak said something the night I finally told him I wasn't sure I believed in God anymore. He didn't flinch. Didn't try to fix it. No verses. No altar call. No redemption fast-tracked by fear. Just a pause. And presence. He looked at me, real quiet, and said, "You don't have to believe everything they told you to still believe in something real." And then, "Sometimes, the first real faith we ever exercise is the courage to say, *this doesn't look like love.*"

I don't know what I believe right now. Not fully. Not clearly. But I know what I no longer think. I don't subscribe to the thought that love looks like fear. I don't believe obedience is the same as healing. I don't think perfection earns peace. I don't believe silence makes you holy. I don't feel God would rather see me suffer than see me free. And I don't accept that my father gets to be both my warden and my savior.

* * * * *

[AGE 14 –Grace Harbor Fellowship]

Grace Harbor Fellowship was where obedience had a spotlight. And I was expected to shine on command.

I was fourteen the first time I said "no." Not the soft kind. Not the type whispered under breath when shoes pinched or sermons scraped. This was a "no" that cracked the silence. A "no" that didn't sound like me.

It was a Wednesday night, just after our prayer meeting. The sanctuary was mainly dark, with the faint glow of exit signs illuminating a red hue against the pews. I was cramping so badly I'd doubled over behind the piano after service. My voice had trembled through every worship set, each breath like dragging glass through my ribs. I was exhausted. Not tired — spent. Hollowed. But that didn't matter. Because the chairs in the fellowship hall hadn't been stacked yet. And Pastor Nathaniel didn't like disorder.

"You'll finish before you leave," he said flatly as he handed me the keys to lock up. He wasn't angry. Not visibly. No one else was around. He'd kissed my mother, patted the heads of Caleb and Etta, kissed Faith's cheek, and said, "Drive safe." But when he looked at me, his eyes told a different story. This wasn't about chairs. This was about obedience. This was about me forgetting my place during prayer when I hadn't bowed my head fast enough. About the whisper of rebellion he thought he saw in the slope of my shoulders.

Be small. Be grateful. Be useful. These were commandments I knew better than Scripture — carved deeper than stone tablets, etched right into my skin.

But something inside me that night, quiet, aching, caged, rose. Possibly it was the pain. Maybe it was the fact that no one else stayed to help. Indeed, it was the weight of a thousand yeses pressing on my chest. All I knew was I couldn't do it. I wouldn't. "I'm not staying," I said. Out loud. Voice hoarse, but steady.

The words didn't fit yet. They clunked in my mouth like borrowed shoes. Like a name I wasn't sure I deserved.

But I said it anyway. I didn't take them back. My father's head turned slowly. "Excuse me?"

"I said no." My hands shook. "I'm not staying to clean. I don't feel good."

Silence stretched between us, long and taut. He didn't raise his voice. That would've been easier. Instead, he smiled. That smile. Tight, closed mouth, the kind that never reached his eyes. "You're tired," he said. "That's why your spirit is weak."

"I'm sick." I corrected.

Pastor Nathaniel stepped closer, no longer a father (if he ever was), in full sermon mode. "You're selfish. You want to be seen as holy, but you don't want to serve when it's inconvenient. That's pride, Serenity. That's rebellion."

I remember the way my throat closed. The dizzying flash of heat in my face. His words weren't new. I'd worn them since birth. But this time — for the first time — I felt the seam tear.

I didn't believe him. I knew I wasn't perfect. Of course, I knew that. But I wasn't proud. I was hurting. And he wasn't seeing me — he was punishing me for being human. "I said no," I repeated, softer. "I'm going home." And I walked out. I walked past the stack of chairs. Past the row of fluorescent lights humming overhead. Out the side door.

The air hit my face like absolution.

I didn't let my emotions out.

I didn't even shake.

I just walked toward the car.

Each step heavier — and yet somehow... lighter.

I didn't look back.

* * * * *

My father didn't speak to me for three days. He told my mother I needed "spiritual realignment." I was "entering the age of temptation." My attitude was "a foothold for the devil." But he didn't yell. He iced me. Taught the rest of the family to do the same.

Caleb wouldn't look at me — his loyalty torn between truth and obedience.

Etta offered confused smiles, like she didn't know whose side she was supposed to be on.

And Faith... Faith sat across from me at the table, staring at her mashed potatoes like they might answer her questions.

Still, I didn't apologize. I was terrified. But I didn't repent. Because deep in my bones, I knew — if I repented for needing rest, I would vanish for good.

* * * * *

The following Sunday, I stood on the stage as usual. Microphone in hand. Voice steady. But I didn't smile the way I used to. Not with my whole face. Not with my entire soul.

And when Pastor Nathaniel referenced me from the pulpit, he said, "My firstborn — so obedient, so devoted," something in me curled into a fist. Because I knew what it had cost him to say that. And I knew it wasn't true. I had broken the rules. And I wasn't sorry. I had said no. And the world didn't end.

That night, alone in my room, I wrote a new commandment in my journal:

You are not unholy for having limits.

It wasn't written in red letters. But it saved me anyway.

CHAPTER 3

Beneath the Surface

Kitchen table. Monday afternoon. Late summer heat curling through the window. A half-empty mug of mint and chamomile tea sits beside me — my failed attempt at calm. The mug is sweating slightly against the wood. I trace a circle in the condensation with my fingertip, round and round, until the paper beneath it curls at the edge.

The screen glows in front of me, bright, expectant. The page is blank. The cursor blinks with mechanical patience, taunting me with every flicker like it knows. Like it's counting down.

I hate that blink.

It feels like pressure and emptiness at the same time — the weight of something I can't quite reach pressing down on the hollow place where words should be. Thoughts swirl, too fast to hold onto. It's not that I have nothing to say.

It's that I don't know how to say it. Or worse — I don't even know what "it" is.

This is supposed to be easy. A school essay. Just a couple of paragraphs about "who I am."

But how do I answer a question like that when the very foundation of who I am feels... uncertain?

[AGE 16 – Grace Harbor Fellowship]

I stare at the instructions again.

Write about your life — your childhood, your family, and a memory that shaped you.

Seems simple. For most people, anyway. The kind of thing they'd fill out in fifteen minutes, maybe less. They'd smile while typing about that one trip to Disney, or the summer they broke their arm climbing a tree. Something warm. Personal. Maybe funny.

Me? I've got nothing.

When you first meet someone, what do you notice? A smile, a hairstyle, and posture. Surface stuff. But real friendship — that takes a story. Memory. History.

And what if you don't have those?

When I try to recall my childhood, it's like tuning an old radio. Static. Distortion. Silence. Occasionally, a flicker. But never long enough to hold.

My memories feel locked behind glass. I can see they're there, but I can't feel them. And I don't know why.

I scroll through old photos, hoping for a spark of recognition. Me at three, squinting into the sun on a beach I don't remember. Me at six, blowing out candles on a cake I didn't choose. Me at nine, stiff smiling in matching Sunday clothes beside my siblings.

The faces are familiar — mine, my parents', and my relatives'. But the moments feel like strangers. Like scenes from someone else's life. I recognize the shapes and colors, but I don't understand the meaning. Like reading a book in a language I've never learned.

That's the unnerving part — the silence where memory should be. A childhood I know I lived... but can't reach.

How do you explain that to someone? How do you build a future when your past is a locked room with no key?

The harder I try to remember, the more the headache builds. If I stare at the images too long, I swear they move, just for a second — a flicker of film. Maybe my brain is trying to cooperate. But it vanishes. And I'm left wondering if it was real or my desperation manifested.

Am I imagining these flashes because I want a past worth remembering?

Why is everything before thirteen shrouded in darkness?

I know I existed. The pictures prove that. But they don't feel like *me*. I study my face like it belongs to a stranger. My past feels like a story someone else lived.

What kind of person doesn't remember their childhood?

It's not amnesia. I didn't hit my head. There wasn't one big event — at least not that I remember. That's the irony. I don't remember, *not* remembering.

The blankness is too familiar now. Like background noise, I've learned to live with it until someone asks me to explain.

Like this essay.

I've asked before. My mom waves it off. "You were quiet." She says. "Kept to yourself," like that explained it.

My dad? I wouldn't dare ask. He'd call it "drama." Or "rebellion." Or worse — "disrespect."

But I know something's not right. I feel it. Like I was kept in a windowless room for years, and someone just cracked the door — and now the light hurts my eyes.

Maybe that's dramatic. But what else am I supposed to think when the past feels like fiction?

Even if others could tell me what happened, how would I know what's true? How can I trust memories that aren't mine?

I hate this. I hate *this.*

I close the laptop. It's no use. The page is still blank.

I press my fingers into my temples. The headache is coming back. It always does when I think about this too long. My body doesn't want me to go there.

But if I don't go there — if I don't write something — I'll fail the assignment. And I can't afford to fail anything. Not with Covenant starting in a few months.

I already feel the weight of this place draining what little energy I have.

* * * * *

I know what people expect when they hear "church school." Clean hallways, wholesome kids, teachers who pray before class, and mean it. And maybe that's true for some. But for me, Covenant Academy means more of the same. More rules. More expectations. More eyes to watch me, measuring me against a standard I didn't choose.

I definitely don't want to go to Covenant Academy.

Homeschool was bad enough, but now my parents want to enroll me full-time in both homeschool and Covenant, which is housed here, in the very church that already smothers me. I'm here constantly: for babysitting gigs, worship practice, volunteering, and church. And now, every single day for school, too?

Do I ever get to leave this place?

I might not love home, but this building... it drains me. It's like it's alive — feeding off my fear, sapping my energy through the too-bright fluorescent lights. The moment I pull into the parking lot in that busted car my father sold me — a total lemon — I feel the panic rise — fight or flight. But I'm never allowed to flee.

I'm always stuck. Trapped.

It's like they're building a life for me entirely within these walls — walls I never asked for. Walls I can't breathe inside.

The church is meant to be a place of comfort and solace. Maybe the church once felt safe. Maybe. Before the smiles turned brittle. Before I noticed how my dad's voice changed depending on who was listening.

Now, it's a cage — a holy cage — polite, gilded, lined with scripture.

* * * * *

The weight of the assignment followed me even into the church office that afternoon. Fluorescent lights buzzing overhead like flies.

Martha, my mom, leaned against the door frame, tapping at her phone with her impossibly long nails. Click. Clack. Click. The sound grated on my nerves.

"Mom?" I said, my voice barely above a whisper.

She didn't look up. "Hmm?"

"Could I possibly... please... not go to Covenant Academy?"

She paused mid-click. Her eyes finally met mine, but they were flat, distracted.

"Serenity, we've been over this."

"I know. It's just... I'm already doing homeschool, PACES, and nannying..."

"And you need the help," she cut in, her tone edging toward impatience. "Especially with math. It's more than homeschool can give."

"But I'm already working so hard—"

"It's in our church. It'll be great." She said it as if reading from a brochure. Like maybe if she said it enough times, she'd believe it too.

Then came the voice that always made my spine lock up.

"Serenity." My dad. Sharp. Loud. Unmistakable.

I hadn't even heard him come in, but now he was there — arms crossed, jaw tight, anger radiating off him like heat.

"That tone is disrespectful to your mother. Apologize. *Now.*"

I flinched, instinct kicking in before thought. "I'm sorry," I said, eyes downcast, like always.

A beat of silence. Heavy. My mom stared at her phone again, as if it were a shield.

"What is she going on about?" he asked.

"She just doesn't want to go to school at the church," she said lightly, like it was funny. It felt like just another one of my silly ideas that would fade away if ignored long enough.

"What?!" His voice cracked through the air like a whip. I barely stopped myself from shrinking into the corner.

"After everything we did to get her in? Unacceptable. This is a fantastic opportunity. You will make the most of it."

My lungs started to close. I knew where this was going.

"You will go to Covenant Academy. You will rise to the occasion. I expect nothing less."

I didn't respond.

"What is our family motto?" he asked.

I didn't want to say it. But I did. "I can do all things through Christ who strengthens me."

"Philippians 4:13," he said, like he was reciting a military creed. "That's what our family is built on. So enough with the attitude. Are we clear?"

My body reacted to the stress like it always did. But I couldn't let him see that. He'd think I was being dramatic. Manipulative.

"Yes, sir."

And just like that, the discussion was over. At least in his mind.

But something in me refused to lie down this time.

"I think I can graduate with the homeschool program," I said, my voice small but steady. "I'm already doing PACES, and my teaching job, and nannying... Please. I'm just asking not to add one more thing."

His jaw clenched tighter.

My skin buzzed, like a thousand ants crawling just beneath the surface, and my head began the dull warning ache at the base of my skull. I looked at my mother, hoping she'd say something. Defend me. Acknowledge that I wasn't being lazy. That I was trying.

But she didn't even lift her head.

"Listen to your father, Serenity. He knows best."

The words were soft. Empty. As if she were reading a script she no longer believed in. The pain in my head intensified as I tried to continue breathing normally.

And that's when I felt it — that profound, sinking realization that maybe mom was just as trapped as I was.

Maybe she didn't speak up because she'd forgotten how.

The migraine that had fully taken hold wasn't just pain. It was a protest. My body knew what I wasn't allowed to say. I wanted to scream. Or run.

Instead, I swallowed it all — the frustration, the hurt, the panic. A dull ache throbbed beneath my ribs, just enough to make me shift in my seat, restless and uneasy, but I didn't move. Not with both their eyes on me.

* * * * *

The knock on the door was a reprieve. For a moment, I let myself hope it would be someone nice.

It was Mezicah.

Kindness radiated off him like sunlight — the kind that makes flowers bloom without asking permission. "Nathaniel!"

The sudden cheerful voice sliced through the tension, a lifeline. My father transformed in an instant — anger gone, smile on, like a magic trick. He turned toward the newcomer, a genuinely kind man from our church who was here after hours, all warmth.

"Mezicah! Great to see you! How's the car?"

"Still running like a dream!" The man beamed, then turned to my mom and me. "And this must be your lovely wife. And your daughter?"

Nathaniel puffed up with pride, gesturing to me. "This is Serenity — our oldest. We've got four kids. She's just thrilled to be starting school here, aren't you, Serenity?"

I forced a smile, lied with my face. "Yeah, we were just talking about the school."

A half-truth. But it stuck in my vocal cords like sandpaper.

Mezicah grinned. "You'll love it here! Yearbook, Bible class, girls' basketball — are you athletic?"

I shook my head with a genuine grin — *no, absolutely not* — answering, "I once tripped on a flat rug. If that counts." I was only partially joking, but my humor caused a warning flash in Nathaniel's eyes, so I quickly changed my tune, all mirth evaporated in an instant. "Uh... I don't know. I haven't really tried."

"Perfect place to start, then!" My father added. "Try it all. Find your gift."

I had to bite my lip to stop my face from betraying how terrible that sounded. I hated sports. My body was clumsy. My joints hurt. My brain never moved fast enough to react. How could I thrive in a place that demanded even *more* from me?

My mother faded into the background, as usual. She echoed bits of agreement but never stepped forward, never spoke up for me. And somehow, that hurt more than Nathaniel's anger. Her silence was a kind of abandonment all its own.

He bragged about me, of course. "Our Serenity — sings, plays piano, she's the perfect representation of our family."

I don't know how he did it — switched masks so quickly.

I couldn't pivot like that. I couldn't forget the things he'd just said. Couldn't pretend I didn't notice how often kindness made him uncomfortable.

The door clicked shut behind Mezicah. And just like that, the warmth drained from the room. My father let out a sharp sigh, a sound that oozed contempt. His voice followed, loud and clear — too clear.

"Nice guy. Shame he's a fag."

I gasped — couldn't stop it. The sound escaped me before I could think better of it. I'd always known his feelings on the subject; he'd never been subtle. But hearing him say it out loud, in the church, about someone from our congregation? That felt different. Worse. Cruel.

It wasn't a shock, exactly. My father had a notoriously foul mouth (not around church people, of course)! He wielded judgment like a weapon, cutting deep, even when smiling. He preached often about the Lord's love and grace, but it always rang hollow, like a rehearsed line in a play he'd long since grown bored with. Truthfully, he struck me as more of an Old Testament Preacher — fire, brimstone, wrath — than one who rejoiced in the radical, inconvenient kindness of Christ.

"Serenity," he snapped, drawing me back. "Cut it out. We're not done talking about the school."

Here we go again.

"You *are* going," he continued. "You'll get the scholarship. You'll go to the college *we* picked. And you'll show everyone what it means to be a Shepherd. Understood?"

Understood? Sure. What I want? Not even close.

But I nodded, because arguing rarely led to anything but a headache and that awful, hollow feeling in my chest that lingered for days. "Understood," I said quietly. Then, cautiously, "But... Dad..."

"What." He said. Flat. Sharp. Not a question — more a warning.

I hesitated. Swallowed hard. Tried to steady my voice. My hands curled into fists in my lap as nails dug into skin. A scream rose in my throat, hot and wild — but I swallowed it. Again.

I could disappear. That was the safer rebellion.

I asked — begged — to take a break from some of the endless pile of things.

"Could I maybe drop some of the other responsibilities? Just a few things. Like babysitting for Alpha, or helping with the Marriage Course? That way, I could use that time to study. I'm already homeschooling full-time, and Covenant Academy will be full-time too, right? It's just... I want to do well, but I don't know how I'm supposed to fit everything in."

He didn't even blink. "We'll discuss it later. I'm sure you can handle it all. You're a Shepherd. It's in your blood."

Right. Because being a Shepherd apparently means I'm some superhuman machine who doesn't need rest, or boundaries, or basic emotional support.

That word — Shepherd — feels less like a name and more like a prison sentence!

But of course, I didn't say any of that.

And as was the norm, Mom said nothing. Just sat there in silence, like always, compressing into the background while Dad filled the room with his expectations, his certainty, his voice.

So I sat still, clinging to the only freedom I had left — my thoughts. Because silence is safer than defiance, they were the one place where I could speak freely, where I didn't have to worry about being called disrespectful or disobedient. *If only thinking something counted for anything.*

In my mind, I screamed.

You terrify me.

You preach love, but you use it like a leash.

You act like God is on your side, but I wonder — if He stood in this room right now, would He even recognize you?

I hate the performance. Smiling, nodding, playing the good daughter while I quietly suffocate. That I'm sixteen and still treated like a child — worse, like an employee who hasn't earned trust or autonomy. When, exactly, will that change?

Eighteen? Twenty-one? Will it ever?

Because I can't picture a future where they see me as my own person. Someone with thoughts. Opinions. Dreams that don't align with theirs.

I'm not sure they'll ever let me become who I am.

* * * * *

The cursor blinks on the screen again.

Still waiting.

Still blank.

I type a few words, then delete them.

I sit back, the silence pressing in like fog, thick and suffocating.

There's a name on my birth certificate, but it doesn't feel like mine.

My identity is the question I keep circling, like a wolf pacing the perimeter of a trap it doesn't know how to escape.

They say stress is invisible — a ghost that sneaks into your bones, that sleeps in your spine, and wakes up in your gut. But my stress isn't invisible. It lives in me. Tangible. Bruising. It leaves fingerprints across every system in my body.

Perhaps it's a result of years of being watched, measured, and weighed. Being told that God Himself was disappointed if I didn't fold the towels right or flinched when the paddle came down. Maybe it's the church walls closing in, every pew splintered with memory.

Perhaps it's waking up each day in a body that remembers more than my mind ever wanted it to.

Or maybe it's this: never once being believed when I said something felt wrong inside me.

Because my pain didn't come with a cast or a wound to show, it came in waves and warnings, in the way I'd sit too carefully or wince at a certain touch. And when I tried to describe it, the adults in my life nodded like they were listening — but they weren't hearing. "Oh, honey, that's normal."

"You're just hormonal."

"Maybe drink more water."

"Have you tried praying more?"

Yes. I prayed. I prayed until my throat was raw with it. And when the pain didn't leave, I didn't stop praying — I just stopped believing my voice reached past the ceiling.

Sometimes I wonder if that's when the real damage began. Not with the first hit, or the first humiliation, but the first time I realized I wasn't allowed to call it what it was. That if I spoke the truth, it would be labeled rebellion. If I named the pain, I'd be called histrionic. Bitter. Ungrateful.

So I stopped naming it. I just... endured it.

And the stress from that — from swallowing the truth over and over until it soured in my belly — became a permanent resident in my body. It lodged itself in my neck. In the coils of my intestines. In the heat that blooms between my legs without warning. It lives in the migraines that explode like broken glass behind my eyes. In the dizzy spells. The numb hands. The burning joints. It's all real, even when no one believed me.

Sometimes I lie in bed and imagine what it would feel like to be safe in my own skin. To not flinch at sudden noises. To not second-guess every word that comes out of my mouth. To not constantly monitor the volume of my voice, the length of my skirt, the curve of my smile.

To not be on guard — always, always on guard.

I've never known what that feels like. Even now, in my room, with the door closed and no one watching, I still feel the need to perform. To be fine. To be grateful. To be "above reproach." That phrase — it haunts me. It was one of Dad's favorites. *Be above reproach. Be blameless. Be the example.*

But I wasn't a child. I was a product. A presentation. And the cost of that performance? A body in revolt. A soul in hiding. A girl who learned to let her tears loose in silence because tears made people angry.

This pain isn't just physical. It's historical. It's the history of every time I was told I was too emotional. Too sensitive. Too much.

It's the weight of years of invisible labor — emotional, spiritual, physical — carried on a back too young to bear it.

Sometimes, the pain is so consuming, I wonder if I'm imagining it. If I've been gaslit so completely, so thoroughly, that even my nerve endings lie. But then it comes — the spike, the rush, the searing edge of it — and I know.

My body isn't lying. But someone did.

Someone made me believe I didn't have the right to feel what I feel. To hurt. To question. To name what happened.

And I think... that's the stress.

Not just the memories. Not just the church. Not just Nathaniel's rage or Martha's silence.

It's the war between what I was told and what I know to be true.

That war never stops. Not when I'm laughing with friends. Not when I'm leading worship with my voice shaking. Not even in moments of joy, because the voice still creeps in: "This isn't real. You're not allowed. You don't deserve this. God is watching."

That's what is causing me to lose so much sleep: the ongoing battle for ownership of my own life.

* * * * *

I was still contemplating these thoughts when my father called my name.

The living room felt too small, the air thick and stale, like it hadn't been breathed in properly for years. The worn Bible lay closed on the coffee table, its leather cracked, a silent witness to the arguments that echoed through these walls.

I stood near the doorway, clutching my arms to stop my hands from trembling. He paced slowly, every step deliberate, his eyes sharp and cold beneath the heavy weight of his collar.

"Cut the theatrics," he said, voice flat as stone. "I'm your father. Not your audience."

I flinched but said nothing.

"You want a stage? This isn't it. This is discipline. And you will receive it."

I wanted to tell him how hollow that sounded, how his guidance felt like chains, not comfort. But the words caught.

"God gave you a spirit of peace, not this tempest of complaints," he continued, voice hardening. "You act like every problem is a tragedy worthy of a stage, but I see through it. You want to stir the flock, to make us doubt, to unravel what I've built. But this overblown sorrow is nothing but noise. You will not make a mockery of the church. Whining is not acceptable."

His presence loomed closer, and I shrank back instinctively. The man who preached love now felt like a judge, a shepherd turned wolf.

"You need to learn restraint," he said, eyes narrowing, voice tightening. "Stop turning every wound into a spectacle. I won't have my house torn apart by your incessant, overemotive storms. You think you're hurting? Serenity, you don't know pain."

A silence fell, thick and suffocating. I fought the rising tide of tears and the rage that bubbled beneath them. He shook his head slowly, disappointment dripping from every movement.

"I'm here to lead you," he said quietly, "but you keep throwing these flamboyant fits. Enough. Be still, be quiet. Be the daughter God intended — not this firecracker of chaos."

I closed my eyes, the weight of his words crashing down like a sermon gone wrong, and I realized: *This isn't love. This is control. This is pain masquerading as faith.*

He stepped back, but the sharpness in his eyes never softened. "You think I'm harsh?" His voice was almost gentle, but the weight behind it crushed the room. "Remember what Proverbs 13:24 says: 'Whoever spares the rod hates their children, but the one who loves them is careful to discipline.' I discipline you because I love you."

He paused, letting that settle like a stone in my chest. "You confuse love with indulgence, but God's love isn't soft. It's firm. It's correction. You need to repent of this rebellious Jezebel spirit, this drama that tempts you away from the path."

His gaze bore into me. "Jesus said in Luke 9:23, 'If anyone wants to follow me, they must deny themselves and take up their cross daily.' Are you willing to carry your cross, or will you continue to play the victim?"

I opened my mouth to speak, but he raised a hand, silencing me. "I don't want excuses. I want obedience. God's work is hard. So is being a daughter of His. Stop this performance. Stop twisting Scripture to justify your feelings. This isn't about you. It's about His will."

He folded his arms, the finality of his words sealing the room like a tomb. "Pray on it. And maybe, just maybe, you'll find the peace you say you're searching for."

He left the room, leaving me reeling, and I decided then and there: *Every day, I will write. Not because it's easy. But because I have to. Not just to get the emotions out... but maybe... eventually... I will feel brave enough to speak the truth.*

Because silence was his favorite scripture, and I'm not quoting it anymore.

Every word I write is one less I'll swallow.

CHAPTER 4
When the Mask Cracks

[AGE 16 – Grace Harbor Fellowship]

It happened on a Tuesday night in late October. I was sixteen, and I hadn't yet started my sophomore year. Midweek revival service. The kind with too much noise and not enough air.

The sanctuary at Grace Harbor Fellowship was packed tighter than usual — there was a guest speaker. Prophetic worship. Something about a breakthrough. It didn't matter. They all blurred together eventually. A carousel of holy fervor and frenzied hands, constantly spinning, never still.

I'd worked all day — cleaning the shop, grading homeschool assignments, and wrangling two toddlers during a nanny shift. I hadn't eaten and hadn't slept the night before, either. My body had started speaking louder than I liked, but I kept quiet. There was no room for weakness in the house of miracles.

"You're leading tonight," my father had said after dinner, adjusting his tie in the mirror with the calm assurance of a man who expected to be obeyed.

I nodded, as a wild drumbeat echoed inside me, out of rhythm with everything else. I didn't even ask what songs he wanted. I knew the drill. Knew what he liked — what "invited the Spirit." And what didn't.

The sanctuary lights were brighter than usual. Too bright. They hit my skin like interrogation lamps. I swallowed down the bile, the spinning room, the tightness in my ribs that felt like my very breath was being siphoned. *Was this still worship, or had it become just a performance now?* I didn't know anymore.

Fake it. Smile. Sing.

The worship team launched into the first song — upbeat, crowded with harmonies. I clutched the microphone, blinked against the lights, and prayed my knees wouldn't give out. My voice cracked on the second verse. Barely. No one else noticed. But he did. I felt it — the flick of his eyes from the front row. That flash of tension in his jaw: a message, silent but deafening.

Get it together.

I kept going. Muscle memory. Training. Terror. Whatever you want to call it, it carried me through the set like a ghost in a glittering dress. But somewhere in the third song — right before the key change — something gave. I don't know what it was. The lights? The heat? The hundredth time pretending I wasn't breaking? One moment, I was singing. Next, the words were scattered. Notes slipped through my fingers like dust.

I stared at the screen. Knew the lyrics. Couldn't form the sounds. And then the tremble started. First in my hand. Then down my arm. Then my jaw. My knees buckled slightly — I caught myself against the keyboard stand, my knuckles white against the plastic. My vision swam. I heard a gasp — maybe mine. Maybe someone else's.

The music faltered.

The room didn't.

People continued to sing, their hands still raised, lost in their encounters with God. But I stood frozen like a statue, half-carved and abandoned, unfinished, unformed, unchosen.

* * * * *

Etta told me later she saw it first. Saw my shoulders stiffen from her seat in the first row.

"I knew something was wrong," she whispered that night, curled at the foot of my bed.

"You don't breathe like that when you're okay. You do this little... thing. Like you're holding in a scream."

She hugged her knees to her chest and mumbled, "I wanted to go to you. But Mom would've said I was being dramatic. So I just... sat there. Watching you disappear."

* * * * *

I tried to speak into the mic — anything at all. A verse. A transition. A prayer. But I couldn't seem to swallow. That familiar ache: like knives in the gut, pulsed hot and sharp, and I knew what was coming.

Not here, God. Please. Not here. But it didn't matter.

The mask cracked.

A silence bloomed inside me first — cold and aching — then my body followed, quivering like leaves in invisible wind.

My legs gave out.

And in front of the entire congregation — beneath lights, behind a microphone — I collapsed to my knees. Silence bloomed, slow and stunned. Music faded into confusion. Someone said my name. A few rushed toward me. But the only face I saw was his. Pastor Nathaniel Shepherd. My father. Expression unreadable. Arms crossed. A muscle twitched beneath his eye. Not concerned. Just... stillness. Like the silence before a verdict.

It stung more than any fall.

Someone helped me up — I think it was Caleb. "Let's go," he murmured under his breath. His voice was tight, panicked beneath the calm. He gripped my arm with both hands — too gently to hurt, but firm like he didn't trust me not to fall again.

But my father stepped forward. He took the mic. "Let's take a moment to pray for Serenity," he said, voice thick with fake compassion.

"She's under heavy spiritual attack. The enemy targets those with great callings."

Murmurs of agreement rippled through the room. A few "Amens." Someone even clapped.

Spiritual attack. Of course. Because anything else — exhaustion, sickness, trauma — would make the <u>shepherd</u> look like a <u>wolf</u>.

He placed his hand on my head as I shivered beside the pulpit and began to pray. Loud. Commanding. Scripture-laced. As if volume could cast out what was never demonic to start with. His hand was heavy. Too heavy. Something cold slid down my spine, in that tiny place where my soul used to live.

I didn't close my eyes. I stared at the floor. Frozen. Drifting.

The safe place in my mind began to appear — but faint this time, like it too was afraid to show up here.

I barely made it off the stage. Caleb guided me down the hall to the back stairwell, where the lights flickered and the tile was cold to the touch. I collapsed onto the bottom step, my dress pooling around my legs like water. I couldn't speak. Couldn't think.

We sat in the half-dark, the air buzzing with the hum of the fluorescent lights.

"Why didn't you tell someone?" Caleb whispered after a long silence. His voice cracked. He looked at me like I'd betrayed him by being in pain without letting him carry it.

"You're always in pain," he said. "And you never say anything."

I wanted to laugh, but all I could manage was a shuddered breath. "Who would I tell?" I asked.

His silence was answer enough.

We stayed there for a while, in the half-dark. Just two Shepherds trying not to drown. Both too old and too young for the weight we carried.

And I realized — maybe the mask didn't crack just for me that night.

Maybe it cracked for him, too.

For the first time, someone had seen me fall apart — and hadn't looked away.

Caleb didn't pray.

He didn't quote Scripture.

He didn't fix it.

He just stayed.

And in that moment, I wasn't the Pastor's daughter. I was just... Serenity.

Shaking. Broken. Seen.

And for the first time in years, I let myself cry.

No lights. No altar. No script.

Just a girl on a stairwell, weeping her way toward something that looked like freedom.

* * * * *

The next morning, I woke to silence. Not the peaceful kind. The kind that creaks. That waits. Downstairs, dishes clinked gently. My mother. The way she moved in the kitchen always sounded like an apology — precise, careful, almost invisible.

I stared at the ceiling fan above my bed, watching it spin in lazy circles. My body ached like I'd run for miles, though I'd barely made it off the stage. My first thought: *Is he angry?* My second: *What has he already told them?*

I sat up slowly, every muscle heavy, every nerve buzzing. I half-expected to find oil smeared on my forehead, a prayer cloth on my night-stand, or a note — some holy chastisement wrapped in "I'm praying for you."

But there was nothing. Just silence. And that, more than anything, unsettled me.

The church reacted in predictable ways. The ones who didn't like me whispered that I was having a breakdown. That I'd been too proud, too busy, too worldly. They tossed around words like *burnout* and *backsliding* with a kind of hushed delight, the way people at potlucks gossip between bites of casserole.

The ones who adored me turned it into a miracle. "She's under attack because she's chosen," they said. "God is purifying her through trial." One woman even gave me a homemade journal with the words *Beauty for Ashes* hand-painted on the cover. She smiled as she passed it to me, as if she were giving me a medal for enduring it well.

No one asked if I was okay. They offered casseroles and claps, but not questions. They just wrapped scripture around my silence and called it healing.

My father, of course, made it a sermon. The following Sunday, he stood at the pulpit and addressed the congregation with a solemn face and a lowered voice, as if something tragic had occurred. "My daughter," he said, "has been enduring a spiritual battle. The enemy sees her gifting and wants to extinguish it. But we will not let him. Amen?"

"Amen," they echoed.

"She's strong," he continued, hand pressed dramatically to his chest. "I've never been more proud of her faith."

And there it was. My collapse, repackaged into a parable. Sanitized. Safe. Marketable. A story he could use. People lined up after the service to hug me. To cry with me. To say things like, "You're going to come out of this stronger," or "I saw Jesus all over you when you fell to your knees." Margaret hugged me so tightly I thought my ribs would crack as she stated, as if it were a fact: "God's just refining you, baby girl, gold only shines after fire."

No one noticed that I flinched when touched. That my body tensed beneath their affirmations. That my smile was stitched so tight it hurt my cheeks.

I was still wearing the mask. Only now it was heavier. Because now they expected more. Deeper holiness. Deeper gratitude. I wasn't just the Pastor's daughter anymore. I was the girl who suffered for the kingdom. They needed me to be strong. To be brave. To be anointed. But I wasn't any of those things, and sleep wouldn't help. Not when it was my soul that ached.

* * * * *

[AGE 16 –Shepherd House -After Service]

The house creaked like it always did after services, old bones shifting in the quiet. The air held that familiar post-church hush, not peace, exactly, but performance cooling on the edges, like steam on glass.

I had showered. Or maybe just stood under the water long enough to convince myself I was clean. My skin still buzzed with leftover nerves. My body felt foreign, like I'd been stitched back together in the wrong order. I curled up on the floor beside my bed instead of climbing in. The carpet was scratchy, but solid. Something unmoving. Something real.

My dress from earlier lay crumpled across the desk chair, still carrying the weight of that stage. I couldn't touch it. Couldn't even look at it. There were tear stains on the collar. Sweat along the sides. The faintest smear of anointing oil at the hem. It smelled like stage lights and someone else's expectations.

I stared at the ceiling. At the uneven plaster lines I used to trace when I was little, pretending they were rivers on a map. I used to imagine God's finger drawing them, carving routes toward something sacred.

But tonight, they just looked like cracks. Like evidence of something that had held too much for too long.

Somewhere in the hallway, I heard my parents' bedroom door click shut. The sound felt final, like a judgment passed.

No one had come to check on me. Not really.

Earlier, I'd walked through the living room wrapped in a blanket. My father had looked up from his study chair and nodded, like he was proud of me. As if collapsing on a church stage was a rite of passage, like my pain had somehow made *him* more holy.

"You were brave," he said, smiling softly. "The Spirit moved. That was powerful, sweetheart."

And I wanted to scream. Or maybe vanish. *No one asked if I was okay.*

I reached for the Bible on my nightstand and pulled it into my lap. It felt heavier than it used to; it knew too much.

I didn't open it.

Instead, I pressed it to my chest and whispered into the quiet, "Was that You?"

Silence.

Not absence. Just... stillness. Thick and aching.

"If You were there," I said slowly, "why didn't You stop me from falling?" I hadn't meant to sound angry. But I was. A little. A lot.

Not just at God.

At myself. At my father. The audience that had watched me fall and called it worship. At the part of me that still wanted their approval and that still called this place *home*.

My stomach growled. I hadn't eaten since morning. But the thought of food made my lungs close.

Instead, I whispered again, smaller this time: "Do You even see me?"

The silence answered in echoes — air through vents, distant pipes, the creak of Faith's door opening down the hall. But no voice. No thunder. No vision.

Only the faint sound of my breath.

And then, unexpectedly, I felt something — not warmth, exactly. Not presence. But permission.

Permission to not understand.

Permission to be angry.

Permission to *doubt*.

It didn't make anything better. But it made it bearable, like the air had cracked just wide enough to let something else in.

Not answers. But possibility.

I slid under my blankets, still trembling. That night, I didn't dream of the waterfall.

I dreamed of standing on the edge of a cliff, barefoot, the ocean roaring beneath me. The sky was vast and gray. No stage. No spotlight. Just wind. Salt. And space.

A voice in the distance — not booming, not even clear. Just a whisper.

Not *go back.*
Not *be better.*
Just: *"You are not what they say."*
And for the first time in a long time, I believed it.

* * * * *

At home, the weeks after the fall caused the silence to shift. It wasn't anger. Not quite. It was a strategy. My father treated me like something sacred and fragile. A vase with cracks — but still displayable. He spoke to me with the solemn tone reserved for the sick or the spiritually suspect. Asked if I was "reading the Word." If I'd forgiven "whatever door you may have opened."

And when I asked, gently, what he meant by that — what door — he just shook his head with that look of spiritual superiority that makes you feel like dirt wrapped in sin.

"I'm not blaming you," he said. "I'm just saying the enemy only has access if we allow him." And just like that, it was my fault again. The pain. The collapse. The entire incident. I had "let something in." Some invisible darkness. Some unspoken rebellion. And I believed him until Etta came into my room late that night.

She crawled into bed beside me without asking, her face tight, hair damp from a shower.

Etta, now twelve, pressed a glass of water into my hand. Her eyes were red. "They're saying you fainted from fasting. That it was... noble." She scoffed. "They don't know what it costs to be their version of holy."

She sat beside me on the floor. "You looked like a ghost," she said. "Like you were trying to disappear, but God didn't let you finish."

Then, under her breath, "I wanted to scream at all of them." She waited a beat, then whispered with a worried tone, "Are you okay?"

I couldn't answer. Instead, I asked vulnerably, "Do you think I'm weak?"

She looked at me, wide-eyed, like I'd said something obscene. "What? No. Are you — Serenity, no."

She shook her head hard, her damp curls clinging to her cheeks. "You're the strongest person I know. That's why it scares me. Because if you can break..."

Her voice cracked on the last word.

We lay in silence for a long time, the fan humming above us like static. Then she whispered,

"He's using it."

I blinked. "What?"

"Dad. He's using what happened to you. To look holier." Her voice was tight, angry, and careful all at once. "He told the youth leaders you were 'battling in the Spirit.' Said your 'humility was inspiring.' Like it was some testimony."

And something in me, something that had been curled up and silent for years, woke up.

It wasn't a rebellion. Not exactly.

It was recognition.

I had been broken on the altar of his image. And he was parading my pain like a trophy.

I hadn't fallen apart because I lacked faith.

I had fallen apart because I'd been carrying a weight no human was meant to take.

* * * * *

And Faith — Faith crawled under the pew when I collapsed. She told me that as she was curled under the blanket next to me.

"Everyone got loud," she said. "And I didn't know if you were dead or just... gone." Her little hand found mine under the quilt. "I prayed God would make you invisible so Daddy wouldn't be mad. Was that wrong?"

I shook my head and pulled her close.

"No, Ladybug," I whispered. "It was brave."

That night, while Faith stayed curled beside me under the blanket, I heard a soft knock on the door. Then it opened slightly, and Caleb peeked in.

"You good?" he asked, voice almost too soft to catch.

I nodded. *Sort of.*

He didn't step inside. Just stood there in the half-dark. "Mom asked me to read the devotional tonight. I told her I had homework. She looked at me like I was spitting in the communion cup." A pause. Then: "I didn't mean to leave you up there. I couldn't move. It was like my feet were glued."

I sat up. "Caleb, you didn't leave me. You carried me off the stage."

He shrugged. Wouldn't meet my eyes.

"I should've said something. Before. About how bad it was getting." Another pause. "I see it in your face sometimes. Like you're holding your breath in a place that doesn't let you breathe."

He rubbed the back of his neck. His voice dipped lower.

"Sometimes I think about wrecking something on purpose. To feel like I exist outside of him. But I know what will happen. They'd just turn it into a testimony."

He left without saying goodnight. Just nodded once and closed the door quietly behind him.

* * * * *

My youngest sister seemed to be hit the hardest by this unfortunate turn of events. She lingered in corners, quieter than usual, hugging her doll tighter, watching me the way kids do when they don't have language for what they're feeling.

That next morning, Faith came and stood beside me while I brushed my hair. She didn't say anything at first. Then: "Are you gonna sing again?"

I paused mid-stroke. "I don't know, Ladybug."

She kicked the floor with her bare toe. "I liked when you did. Even when your voice was shaky. I still liked it."

I turned to face her. "Were you scared?"

She nodded, looking sad as she admitted in ten-year-old logic, "I thought maybe God made you fall 'cause you weren't being perfect.

Like that time I spilled grape juice on my dress and Daddy said I wasn't careful with holy things."

My chest squeezed. I knelt and took her hands.

"No, sweetie. That's not what happened."

She tilted her head. "So... did God make you fall, or did Daddy?"

I didn't know how to answer that. Her question didn't come with judgment — just the soft ache of someone too young to understand how belief turns into a burden. So I just hugged her tight. She smelled like shampoo and dryer sheets.

"Can we live somewhere else someday?" she mumbled into my neck. "Somewhere without loud noises."

I couldn't answer that either. But I wanted it, too.

In the shadows, my siblings were shouldering their versions of what had happened. Caleb, quieter than ever now, barely speaking at dinner. Etta, restless and jittery, hid poems under her mattress. And Faith, watching everything, absorbing the script before she even knew she was cast in the play. We were all dying beneath the weight of glory we never asked to bear. And no amount of prayer or fasting could fix what wasn't ours to hold.

* * * * *

That night, I dreamed of my escape again.

But this time, I wasn't alone.

Etta stood beside me, silent but solid. Her blonde hair floated in the breeze, her hands loose at her sides — free.

Caleb leaned against a tree in the background, his eyes soft, watching the water like it made sense to him now.

And Faith came running barefoot through the grass, giggling, light, whole, and wild.

We were safe.

Real.

Whole.

No lights.

No pulpit.

No masks.

Just water. And wind. And lungs that finally remembered how to fill. A silence that didn't shame us. A sky that didn't stare.

* * * * *

The Bible on my nightstand hadn't been opened in weeks, not since the day of the fall. It sat there, worn and fraying at the corners, pages curling like overworked hands. It used to comfort me — it felt like home. Now, just looking at it made my stomach somersault. Not because I hated it. Because I didn't trust the person who taught it to me.

For most of my life, Scripture had been a tool, a scalpel in my father's hands: cutting, precise, and always sharp enough to wound. There was a verse for everything, so I needed to obey without question. Why I was not allowed to question his tone. Why my body didn't belong to me, and so I needed to keep it hidden so that men wouldn't stumble. Why rest was dangerous. Why saying no was rebellion.

I had memorized entire chapters by the time I was nine. Recited Psalms while brushing my hair. Whispered Proverbs while washing dishes. But somewhere along the way, the Word stopped being bread and became a leash. And I was starving.

That Sunday afternoon, I found myself sitting on the edge of my bed, holding the Bible like it might explode. A part of me wanted to throw it across the room. Another part wanted to open it — desperately — like it might tell me something different this time. Something real. Something kind.

Instead, I opened a notebook. And I wrote this at the top of a blank page: "Who is God when no one is watching?" I stared at the question for a long time. My pen trembled.

Not who is God in church. Not who is God to my father. But who is He — truly — when the lights are off, when the pews are empty, when I'm curled on the bathroom floor because I can't keep food down again? Because the God I've been handed is suspicious. Distant. Quick to anger. A God who loves order more than honesty. A God who demands perfection and punishes pain. A God who requires me to be useful before I can be loved. That God sounds more like my father than my Father. I want a God who doesn't loom from pulpits, but one who lingers quietly in stairwells, beside shaking daughters. I am beginning to wonder if I've confused the two. I had been told God was fire and judgment. But what if He was the quiet voice that never made it into the sermon?

I didn't say these things out loud. Not yet. Doubt wasn't safe in the Shepherd house. Questions were seen as doorways to deception. "Leaning on your own understanding" was practically a curse word.

But inside, something had started to unravel like the first loose thread in a tapestry. I began watching the sermons differently. Listening not to what he said, but how he said it. The manipulation hidden in the cadence. The way he wept on cue. The message often conveniently circled back to honor, obedience, and submission. It wasn't always what he said. It was what he skipped. What he never preached about. Tenderness. Lament. Doubt. Trauma. Safety. God was always a judge, never a comforter. Continually refining fire, never refuge. And that silence was louder than anything else.

Etta caught me reading a different Bible one night — one I borrowed from the church library. It had commentary in the margins from authors my father would disapprove of. Bold ones. Those who asked questions out loud.

She peeked into my room, her steps hesitant, socked feet making no sound on the hardwood. Her brows pinched, like she wasn't sure if she was interrupting or intruding.

"What's that?" she asked, voice low but curious.

"A study Bible," I said carefully, like it was contraband. Because in our house, it kind of was.

She walked in without asking — not cautious, just comfortable. Sat cross-legged on my bed and leaned over the book, her blonde curls brushing the edge of the page. She scanned the notes, the scribbles in the margins, the circles and arrows someone had drawn, as if they were trying to map their way out of something.

"It looks... different," she said.

"It is." I hesitated. Then added, "It's softer."

Etta didn't respond right away. She just ran her finger slowly along the underlined verse in the corner of the page:

"Come to me, all you who are weary and burdened, and I will give you rest."

Her fingertip paused over the word 'rest' as if it hurt to touch it.

Then she whispered, without looking up,

"Do you think God sees us?"

The question sliced something open in me — because she didn't say 'Does He see me'? She said 'us.' And I knew exactly what she meant.

"I think He sees more than they want Him to," I said.

She nodded, barely. Like she wanted to believe that — needed to. But didn't know how yet.

That week, I started praying again. But not the way I used to. Not loudly, not with folded hands and rehearsed lines. Just small prayers. Raw ones. *If You're really there, show me who You are. If You love me, I need it to be different than this. If I was made for joy, help me believe that. If You're angry, I don't think I can survive it.*

And now and then, when the pain eased just long enough for me to breathe deep, I imagined Him there, not judging and just sitting beside me. Quiet. Steady. Not like my father. Not like anyone I'd ever known. And for the first time in my life, I wondered if God wasn't angry at me at all. Maybe He was just heartbroken by the way His name had been used. Perhaps He never asked me to earn love. Maybe love had always been the starting point, not the prize.

* * * * *

It was small things at first — slivers of rebellion so quiet they looked like normal teenage behavior.

I let Faith choose her own worship songs one morning while we got ready. She scrolled through my phone, lips pursed in concentration.

"Do they have the one with the drums?" she asked. "The one that sounds like a thunderstorm? Daddy says it's too emotional, but I like it."

"Play it," I said. "We won't tell."

She grinned — a real one — and hit play. The beat filled the bathroom like a pulse. She twirled once in her socks, then whispered, "If Daddy asks, we just listened to the instrumental."

She didn't wait for permission. She just knew it was safe with me.

I gave Etta my hoodie when she came downstairs in a long skirt, tugging it every five seconds like it was shrinking by the minute.

"You want it?" I asked, nodding to the oversized hoodie slung on the chair.

She hesitated. "Dad said—"

"I didn't ask what Dad said."

She looked at me, then pulled the hoodie over her head and sank into it, as if in relief.

"I'm tired of being cold," she muttered. Then, after a beat: "And tired of pretending I'm not."

And Caleb — he skipped youth group on Wednesday, and I covered for him without question. Said he was in the garage fixing the mower. He wasn't.

I found him downstairs later, sketchpad in his lap, earbuds in. Drawings of hands — not folded in prayer, just open. Holding nothing.

I knocked once on the wall to let him know I was there. He pulled one earbud out.

"I know it's not holy art," he said, already defensive.

"Who said that?" I asked.

"You know who."

I sat beside him on the floor. Looked at the page again.

"You made that?"

"Yeah." A pause. Then softer: "It felt like something was trying to get out of me. I don't know."

I didn't tell him to put it away. I didn't quote Philippians or guilt him with calling.

I just said, "It's beautiful."

He blinked. Nodded once.

Didn't say thanks. Didn't have to.

Tiny freedoms.

I didn't even know I was offering liberation until I saw how their shoulders dropped, how their eyes lit up, how they looked at me like I might be something other than the enforcer.

They were watching me.

And I was changing.

Maybe slowly. But surely.

One ripple at a time.

Like my waterfall — quiet at first, then unstoppable.

CHAPTER 5
Being A Shepherd

Like a pulsing heartbeat on a hospital monitor, the cursor blinks. I've been staring at it for an hour. Fingers frozen. *This is the moment I stop burying the truth.*

[AGE 16 – Shepherd Home, Two Weeks Before Covenant Starts]

I've said it before, and I'll repeat it: I hate the Shepherd House.

Some of my friends, the ones who knew the darker undercurrents behind the smiling façade, had their own name for it — *Shepherd Island.* A place isolated not by geography, but by fear. Some even called it a cult. And honestly? They weren't far off. Especially when it came to the art of "practice."

That's what my parents called it. A neat little euphemism. Clean enough to say in public. A coded threat dressed as discipline. A word so sterilized it could be spoken aloud in public without raising suspicion. "Keep it up," my father would say with a smile, "and you'll get a little *practice* tonight." The people around him would laugh, assuming it was some inside joke. We knew better.

It wasn't a joke. It was a warning.

When we were in trouble — according to his standards — he would call us in, one at a time. Nathaniel — my father — would call our names with a voice like thunder. Face tight with fury, lips pressed into a line, eyes cold. When he was like that, there was no reasoning with him. No mercy. We were forced to strip. Not just a belt over clothes. No. Pants down. Underwear off. Until we stood there, bare and trembling. Shame and fear clung to me like smoke — impossible to wash off.

And then he would reach for the paddle, a crude piece of wood he'd shaped by hand — less a tool, more a weapon. We knew the drill. Tears would fall before the first strike, because if we didn't, he'd keep going until we did. To him, repentance didn't count unless it was loud. Wet. On display. So we learned to perform.

We discovered how to cry on cue. Forced sobs, real pain — it didn't matter. What mattered was that he saw our suffering before the paddle even made contact. Our father believed that proved repentance. Anything less meant more punishment.

* * * * *

Practice meant pain. Agony. The kind you couldn't forget, no matter how hard you tried.

And we *knew* what was coming.

I remember, too vividly, how the panic overtook me — how my breath would catch, how I'd start to wail before he even lifted his arm. My hands would shake. My knees would buckle. I would beg. Plead. Whisper apologies through my sobs, hoping — praying — that he might stop. That something inside him would soften.

It never did.

If anything, my emotions made it worse. It angered him more. My fear seemed to fuel him.

"Bend over," he'd order, voice like gravel.

And I would because there was no other choice. I'd freeze, even as my body twitched with terror, my skin buzzing with shame and helplessness. My bare skin would be red and stinging for hours after. Sometimes, depending on how serious he claimed the offense was, or how foul his mood had been, he would spank me again. And again.

We weren't allowed to dress until we'd "repented."

That word always made me feel sick. Not because I didn't understand it, but because I *did*. They'd taken something sacred, something spiritual, and twisted it into a requirement for obedience. Repentance wasn't about growth in the Shepherd house. It was about submission. Control.

They said it was love. That correction was godly. That discipline was biblical.

But I've never known love to feel like that.

For me, it meant doing everything in my power to avoid being "practiced." That fear of pain, of exposure, of losing control — that shaped everything. I tried to be perfect. Obedient. Invisible, if I could manage it. It was a trauma-born perfectionism, and it burrowed deep.

My sisters and I adapted. We learned the rhythms of survival. But my brother... Caleb was different. He was stubborn. Brave in ways I never dared to be. He wouldn't cry.

No matter how many times the paddle fell, no matter how loud the smacks echoed, he would grit his teeth and hold his silence. I don't know if it was pride, or protest, or a desperate bid for dignity, but he refused to give our father what he wanted. It drove Nathaniel mad.

He would hit Caleb over and over again, until his arm gave out. I remember one time — I wish I didn't — that he walloped him, so many times, that the wooden paddle *snapped* in half. Splinters cut into Caleb's skin. Only then did my brother cry out — not from weakness, but because his body had finally betrayed him. I can still hear the sound he made. It wasn't just pain. It was a betrayal. Like something inside him had cracked, too, and through it all, my mother stood by. Silent.

Sometimes she was in the room, and sometimes she wasn't. Her presence, or absence, made no difference. It was like she lived behind a pane of glass, unreachable. Whenever we screamed, she buried her head in her phone, in a book, in a chore — anything to avoid eye contact, to avoid responsibility. I used to imagine she had some hidden world in her mind that she escaped to. A secret place where none of us was being hurt. Where the reality of what was happening didn't exist, I had my mental escape, and I so desperately needed to make up an excuse for her behavior. Or lack thereof.

It was easier to think that than to believe she simply didn't care. I used to wonder if she was trapped, too. But the older I got, the more it looked like a choice.

One of my sisters once said something that has stayed with me. She was trying to explain the horror of it to our mother. I'm paraphrasing, but the words were something like this:

"If someone were stripped naked and beaten in front of others, people would call that abuse — sexual abuse, physical abuse. Even if you take the audience away, it *still* is what it is. You can't strip a kid naked, beat them, and call it 'practice.' That's not holy. That's abuse."

Our mother just shook her head. "You're only remembering the bad things," she said one day. Other times, she'd claim none of it happened at all.

But it *did* happen — all of it.

Each of us dealt with the trauma differently. I had panic attacks. My body was always tight, clenched like I was preparing for another hit. I lived in constant dread of the next "practice."

Caleb rebelled. He pushed limits, tested boundaries, and paid dearly for it. But he didn't give in. Not unless his body was forced to.

I remember finding him after a "practice," sitting on the basement stairs. His lip split. His hands curled into fists.

He looked up, eyes dark but steady. "They want me to cry," he said, voice quiet, "but I'm not giving them that."

Etta — our middle sister — was dramatic. Always was. But her screams weren't theater.

They were terror: high-pitched, raw, helpless.

I remember one night she banged her fists on the wall, shouting, "This isn't love! This isn't God!" Then she broke down, shaking with sobs.

Then there was Faith, the youngest. Fierce from the start. Even as a little girl, she argued with Dad like a tiny hurricane.

She talked in circles until he was red-faced and exhausted.

She refused to bend over when told to do so.

And though she got punished, she kept her fire.

Her voice. Something I'd already lost — a kind of fire even his rage couldn't drown.

For me, every spanking chipped away a piece of my spirit. Hollowed me out, one blow at a time.

Each of us found our own language for pain: silence, fire, performance, protest... but none of us were spared.

* * * * *

We all carried the bruises — some visible, most invisible. But the pain didn't just live in our skin; it settled deep in the way we moved around each other, the way we spoke, the way we avoided certain rooms or topics.

The Shepherd house was more than walls and rules. It was a prison we shared. And the man who was supposed to guide us, Nathaniel — our Pastor, our "shepherd" — he was the one who kept the gates locked tight. We continued to splinter with each "practice" session:

Me: I started to feel like a cracked vessel, half full but fragile. I was the oldest, so the weight landed on me the heaviest. I tried to hold everyone together, but the cracks within me began to leak.

When I looked in the mirror, I didn't see a daughter or a sister — I saw a battleground. Between who I was and who I was supposed to be, between the quiet voice inside begging for mercy and the loud one screaming to be perfect.

I was supposed to lead by example, to be the "good child," the one who carried the family's faith on her shoulders. But inside, I was breaking.

Caleb: My brother spoke even less than he used to. When he did, it was blunt, clipped — sometimes angry, always guarded.

One night, I found him sketching in the basement again, surrounded by his scattered drawings. I asked, "Why don't you ever come to youth group anymore?"

He didn't look up. "It's not for me," he said, voice flat. "And I don't need him watching me."

He didn't say who, but I knew. Dad, the shepherd, was watching, judging, and waiting for the subsequent failure.

Caleb's rebellion wasn't loud. It was silent resistance — retreating into his art, shutting out the church and all its rules.

Etta: My middle sister's fire flickered but never went out. She's dramatic, yes, but there's truth behind it.

She'd slam doors, throw herself into her poems, and sometimes burst into tears when no one was watching.

One evening, after another tense dinner, she whispered to me, "He's not a shepherd. He's a predator in sheep's clothing."

Her words hit me like a fist.

But I couldn't argue. I didn't know how to fix her, or me, or... any of this.

Faith: My baby sister's fierceness was both a gift and a curse.

She challenged Dad openly — more than any of us dared. She'd argue scripture with him, call him out when his tone turned harsh.

But every time, she paid a price.

I remember one afternoon when she came to me, her eyes blazing but her lips trembling.

"I don't want to be like this," she said, "but I can't just be silent anymore."

Faith's rebellion was loud — maybe too noisy — but it was the only way she could keep her soul from cracking.

And then there was Dad, the man who wore the mantle of shepherd like armor, or a weapon.

He preached about love and grace, but his hands dealt out fear and control.

The pulpit was his throne, the Bible his sword.

He spoke about leading his flock, but all he did was herd us into submission.

He broke the sheep, then blamed them for bleeding.

But he never led us to safety.

Only to silence.

How it all tangled us up:

We were siblings, supposed to be each other's refuge. But under Dad's reign, we became fractured.

I tried to be the anchor, but I faltered. Caleb pulled away, his silence a wall. Etta flared up like wildfire, burning hot but vulnerable. Faith fought fiercely but was weary from the constant battles.

We loved each other, yes. But there was fear of Dad, of judgment, of shattering the fragile peace by speaking too loudly or too honestly.

We were bound by blood and broken by fear.

And in the middle of it all, I questioned who I was.

Was I just another cracked vase on display?

Or could I be something else?

* * * * *

In the Shepherd household, rules were everywhere — some spoken, many not. Respect and obedience were demanded, especially toward Nathaniel. Anything he interpreted as "disrespect" was met with fury. Martha, meanwhile, just... existed. Present in body but often gone in spirit. She turned away, as if hiding from the truth could erase it.

And then there were the strange rules — those wrapped around Nathaniel's personal vices. One summer, he smashed the Nintendo 64 because *he* couldn't stop playing *Zelda: Ocarina of Time.* Said it was a distraction. An addiction. So he destroyed it instead of dealing with his own lack of self-control. Later, he flipped all the TVs around to face the walls, declaring we'd had too much screen time —even though he was the one watching.

We were told, "Work hard, play hard." But it was mostly work. Fixing up cars to fund family trips. No TV, no distractions, just tasks. Just control.

And at church... oh, we had to be perfect.

Everyone knew our family. Nathaniel had made the rounds in so many congregations across the state, and people seemed to remember him.

I, unfortunately, looked just like him, so I was told, so often it felt like needles piercing my skin. That meant wherever I went, people recognized me. I had to behave. *Smile. Serve. Shine. Be a beacon of Christlike obedience.*

Even now, the word repentance tastes like ash in my mouth. Like something you're forced to say so someone else can sleep at night.

And if we slipped up — even just a little — there it was again. That word. That lie. That warning. *Practice.*

A threat dressed in piety.

* * * * *

[AGE 33 -Present Day]

Some pains you can't leave in the past. They follow you.

No one ever heard it — the screaming inside me. I was polite, smiling, and quiet. But silence was my scream. Every time I didn't speak, didn't fight back, didn't release my shame, I thought I was being strong. But I was breaking, quietly. Every word I write feels like pulling splinters from my soul. But I have to do it. I have to get it out. The pain, the shame, the parts of me I left in locked rooms. This story is mine now — even the ugliest chapters.

Have you ever woken up fine, only to be ambushed by pain that grows until it swallows you whole? A typical day, hijacked by something invisible, relentless, and cruel.

You wake up, and the day starts like any other. You're not feeling great, but you're not feeling awful either. There's no significant pain, no overwhelming fatigue. You're looking forward to what's ahead, motivated to tackle whatever comes your way.

But then, almost without warning, something shifts. It's subtle at first, the discomfort creeping in without a clear source. You can't quite place it — just a vague sense that something's off. The sensation starts small, almost like an itch in the background — a whisper of discomfort that you try to ignore. But as the hours pass, it grows. It's not sharp, but it's persistent — a gnawing, dull ache that settles deep in your stomach. There's pressure building at the base of your skull, and an odd, subtle burning between your legs, like a fire you can't extinguish.

You acknowledge these small, frustrating signals, praying for relief, and pushing through. Life doesn't stop for your discomfort. The day continues, ebbing and flowing like the tides. There are moments when you feel strangely energized — enough to be productive, to do the chores, to play with the kids, to get things done.

But then, like a freight train barreling down the tracks, exhaustion hits you with a force that's almost impossible to ignore. You yawn endlessly, even as you try to fight it. It's not even afternoon yet, but all you want is to crawl back into bed, to let sleep erase the weight pressing down on you.

But you can't. You have a job. You have responsibilities. There's no time for rest. So you push forward, even as your insides churn with more intensity, and that familiar discomfort evolves into something much worse.

It becomes a sharp, stabbing pain — intermittent but piercing, like acidic bubbles bursting inside you, each one sending shockwaves of agony. It's like shards of glass tearing through your insides. You can feel the acid swirling, wreaking havoc on your body. The cramps hit with violent intensity, and for a moment, you're helpless. You try to double over, curl into a fetal position, but nothing stops the onslaught. The pain keeps coming.

Then, without warning, an urgent need arises — an overwhelming, pressing demand to use the restroom. There's no time to waste. You rush to the nearest bathroom, praying for relief but dreading what's to come.

Will it be diarrhea, constipation, or something equally humiliating and painful? As you struggle through the process, you know that the skin between your legs — the perineum — will burn with a searing, tearing sensation, a pain that feels unbearable.

And it doesn't stop there. The pressure that began at the base of your skull has now crawled upward, enveloping your entire neck, and somehow, it's found its way into your left ear. The tension builds. Your trapezius muscles tighten like a vice, sending waves of pain down your back. It feels as if everything in your body is protesting, each sensation adding to the crescendo of pain, the headache growing worse by the second.

You finish in the bathroom, but the relief is fleeting. You look at yourself in the mirror. The tears are there — tiny, pinprick tears, betraying the toll the pain has taken on your face. Your brows are furrowed, your eyes squinted in a futile plea for the pain to stop. You find yourself silently praying, begging God for relief, for healing, for restoration. Your forehead is tight, as though your entire face is carrying the weight of the pain, and as the headache intensifies into a migraine, you feel like you're sinking into a fog, drowning under pressure that makes every breath a struggle.

Your body feels out of control. The migraine pounds relentlessly on the left side of your head, radiating down your back. Pinpricks race down your arms. Your fingers go numb, then suddenly sharp, like tiny sparks under your skin.

You hear the rumble, loud and persistent, as the acid bubbles within you continue to crescendo, each burst more painful than the last. The sensation inside your abdomen is no longer just discomfort. It feels as though something alive, something frantic and forceful, is twisting and turning within you, pushing against your insides.

You try to find a position of relief. You sit on the couch, but a sudden sharp stabbing pain in your private area forces you to rethink your choice. You stumble to your bed, praying for relief, praying for this relentless torment to cease. But as you lie there, you feel the battle raging inside you.

So many sensations, so many sources of pain, it's impossible to focus on just one. It's the migraine, the unbearable tension in your neck and shoulders, the searing cramps — each one vying for your attention. And yet, amid this torture, eventually, it begins to subside.

Slowly, imperceptibly, your body starts to calm and lighten. The pain, although still present, becomes more manageable and bearable. You breathe a little easier, though you can still feel the weight of exhaustion settling over you.

You lie there, spent, wondering what caused this latest episode, when the next one will come, and why, despite everything you've tried, it never truly goes away.

I've lived through this cycle many times. Even as I write this, I'm in the midst of it. The pain is still with me, gnawing at my insides. I just took half a pill of morphine prescribed for my chronic pain, but it didn't help. It just made me dizzier and more exhausted without offering any relief. It's not a solution; it's just a temporary escape that doesn't change anything.

I've prayed for answers, for healing. I've searched for anything that might explain this nightmare. My medical team has run a seemingly endless series of tests and procedures, and I've received a multitude of diagnoses. But none of them provides a permanent solution. The treatments I've tried offer only short-term relief at best.

Each time, I beg God, asking Him to take away the pain, to heal me, to restore my body. And each time, the answer is the same: stress.

Stress is the culprit, they say. Stress affects my body in ways that are both devastating and unpredictable. *But stress from what?*

I don't have answers. Not yet. But I've stopped pretending this pain doesn't exist.

I'm learning to name it.

And in naming it, I'm finally reclaiming something that was stolen from me:

My voice.

Part 2: Fractures

CHAPTER 6

The Park

Mornings have become a ritual. Tea or energy water. A deep breath. Then I open the journal. I never used to write. I didn't think my voice mattered. But silence was slowly killing me.

When I think about the moments that defined my past, this one in particular stands out, even though it's shrouded in mystery, clouded by the fog of memory, to this day.

[AGE 16 –Park, One Week Before Covenant Starts]

Deloris told me to wait at the park. Said she'd forgotten the decorations — "the good ones" — and would be right back.

I believed her.

I sat on the swings, dragging my feet in the dirt, trying to guess what kind of setup she had in mind. *Streamers? Balloons? A banner with our names in glitter?* Then, I blinked, and the trees blurred at the edges. My head felt strange, like it was floating a few inches above my body.

I tried to chalk it up to the heat, but the air wasn't warm. Just still. Too still. The kind of quiet that should've felt peaceful... but didn't.

The trees were motionless. No rustling, no birdsong. Like the world was holding its breath.

That's when the car pulled up.

Not hers. Sleek. Slow. Intentional.

The driver stepped out — tall, messy-haired, walking like he owned the pavement. Connor Reeves. I recognized him. He'd hovered near us before, when I was with Deloris.

She'd said his name with a smirk, like it was a joke I wasn't in on.

Now he was walking toward me.

My limbs lagged behind my brain, slow and unresponsive. I stayed on the swing, my fingers clenched too tightly around the chains. He said something — a joke maybe — but I didn't catch it. I couldn't answer. My voice was buried beneath a rising weight on my chest.

He kept approaching.

The park was empty. Just us and the silence. And the sick realization that Deloris wasn't coming back.

The moment I saw him, I felt off — not just uneasy, but physically wrong. The ground felt uneven. My thoughts were slow. It wasn't just fear. It was something else. A softness in my limbs. A blurring at the edges of sound.

He reached me. His stride was deliberate, not relaxed. Predatory.

I gripped the swing's chains, suddenly aware they weren't comforting — they were trapping me. I waited, praying Deloris would pull up any second, laugh it off, say it was all some dumb prank.

But she didn't come.

Only Connor did.

He started talking, words spilling out of his mouth in a tone that was too familiar, too casual for someone I barely knew. He made jokes, tried to tease. I didn't laugh. I didn't even speak. I barely nodded. Talking to guys was already hard for me — awkward, anxiety-ridden. But with him, it wasn't just shyness. It was something colder. Deeper.

His eyes tracked every movement I made. Every shift in posture, every shallow breath. The park was wide open and completely empty, yet I felt like I was trapped inside a box. No one was around. No one could help me.

I used to give people the benefit of the doubt. I assumed kindness. But with him, every instinct rebelled. Something about Connor was wrong.

Still, I stayed frozen.

He started talking in a way that immediately made my skin crawl — low and suggestive, like we were in on some sick joke together. Only, I wasn't laughing. I wasn't speaking.

He leaned in a little, watching me with that same twisted smirk as he asked, completely unprovoked, "So, what's your favorite position?"

Like he was asking about favorite pizza toppings.

I said nothing, just sat frozen on the swing, trying to stay small. Trying to become invisible.

Then he chuckled to himself and added, "Bet it's missionary, huh? You look like the type. All quiet and modest. Good little church girl." He leaned closer. "Bet you've got a good figure under all those clothes. Maybe I'll find out."

It wasn't just offensive — it was a violation. His words wrapped around me like something rotten, something invasive, seeping into my ears and under my skin.

The way he said "good little church girl" didn't feel like a compliment.

It felt like a threat.

That was the moment my panic finally kicked in. Every nerve in my body lit up like a flare, screaming *run.*

I launched myself off the swing and bolted — not toward safety, not toward the road or an exit — but instinctively toward the playground equipment, the only thing in sight with any cover. I think some part of me still thought I could hide, like a child playing a game of tag. But this wasn't a game.

I didn't even make it halfway.

He caught up fast, grabbing me from behind and slamming me into the climbing frame. My shoulder hit with a dull thud. Then his hand — just one — pinned both my wrists above my head. Like I weighed nothing.

My mind screamed. My body didn't obey.

I felt... wrong.

Not simply scared and not just frozen. My thoughts were warped. My limbs detached. The world tilted, distorted at the edges. At the time, I told myself it was just panic. But now?

I'm convinced I was drugged.

Maybe I'll never be able to prove it. But I believe Deloris slipped something into the punch earlier. Something tasteless. Designed to soften resistance. Make me easier to control.

Then she left me there.

Like a gift.

Like a party favor wrapped in silence.

What kind of person does that? What kind of friend?

I don't know if it was cowardice, cruelty, or fear. Maybe she was trying to please someone with more power than I understood. Perhaps she thought it was funny.

I'll never know.

But that was the moment the world changed.

It wasn't just fear anymore. It was a betrayal. Sharp. Quiet. Deep.

The betrayal of a friend saying, *"Wait here. I'll be right back,"* while knowing full well she wasn't coming back.

And there I was, pinned against splintered wood by a man I barely knew, panic sweeping over me like a tsunami, impossible to outrun — too dizzy to scream, too slow to fight back, and too confused to understand how I had gotten there in the first place.

His hand tightened around my wrists — too tight — and I winced, but no sound came out. My voice had vanished, swallowed by the fear and the fog clouding everything around me. I couldn't scream. I couldn't even speak. The only thing I could do was breathe, and even that felt like a struggle; shallow, uneven gasps, like my lungs were forgetting how to work.

I remember the texture of the wooden beam behind me — rough and sun-warmed, pressing into my back, biting through my shirt. I remember how he leaned in close enough that I could feel his breath on my neck, hot and sour. I remember the gleam in his eyes — not passion, not desire, but power. Cruelty. He enjoyed seeing how helpless I was.

His free hand moved without hesitation, fingers grazing places they had no right to touch, as though he were inspecting an object, not a person. I tried to move, but my body barely responded. Every part of me felt far away.

Somewhere nearby, a child laughed. It was faint, probably blocks away.

It cut through me like broken glass.

How could laughter still exist in a world where this was happening?

I was there, but drifting — my mind stepping backward from a body I could no longer control. Yet try as I might, I couldn't retreat to my waterfall. It seemed far away, as I grew more dizzy, more out of it.

He whispered things. I'll never forget that part. Not the exact words at first — just the tone. Mocking. Intimate. As if we were lovers sharing secrets, not predator and prey.

But then one sentence cut through everything else, slicing through the fog with perfect clarity:

"If any guy gives you attention, it's because he wants this."

He said it as if it were a universal truth, like I should've known it already.

"If he's nice to you, buys you things, opens doors — it's not because he likes you. It's because he's waiting to get inside you. That's all you're for. Sex."

The words carved themselves into my brain. I didn't understand it fully then — what that moment was doing to me — but I felt something fracture. Not physically. Internally. A quiet, almost imperceptible splinter in the way I saw the world, in how I would come to know every man after him.

And then — nothing.

I don't know when I blacked out. It wasn't dramatic like in movies — no slow fade to black, no final scream. Just... a sudden, yawning silence in my memory. One moment I was pinned, too dizzy to move, and the next—

Nothing.

A blank space.

[AGE 16 – Aftermath]

Then I was walking.

Barefoot, I think. Or maybe I'd kicked my shoes off somewhere. My legs felt like they belonged to someone else. My surroundings were blurry; the sun was glaring too brightly through the trees, and my ears were filled with a high, constant ringing.

I don't remember streets or traffic. I don't recall looking for signs or landmarks. I just kept moving.

My clothes were wrinkled and dirty at the hem. My bra strap was twisted awkwardly over my shoulder, and I remember tugging at it without really understanding why.

The next clear image I have is the bathroom mirror.

I was standing in front of it, staring at my face, unable to process what I was seeing. My cheeks were pale. My eyes were dull, unfamiliar, and sunken. I looked like someone else. Someone used up. Like the wind had been knocked out of me, and it hadn't come back.

And still, tears didn't flow.

I wanted to. I could feel the pressure in my chest, the ache behind my eyes. But nothing came. My body was stuck somewhere between fear and numbness, like it didn't know how to react.

I didn't tell anyone.

Not that day.

Not the next.

Not for a long time.

Because how do you explain something you can't fully remember? How do you say, *"Something terrible happened,"* when you don't know where the line was crossed? When all you have is a feeling — a horrible, sinking certainty that you were betrayed, used, and discarded?

I wanted to pretend it hadn't happened.

I tried to erase it, rewind time, and walk away the moment Deloris first said she forgot the decorations. But I didn't.

I stayed.

I waited.

I trusted.

And Connor taught me what a mistake that was.

After that day in the park, something in me broke — subtly at first, like a crack in glass that you barely notice until it starts to spread. It was like someone took a mirror I didn't know was whole and slammed it to the floor. The world still looked the same, but now I could only see it in shattered pieces.

I didn't immediately think, *I've been traumatized.* I didn't have the language for it. I just... changed.

Quietly.

Internally.

In ways I didn't understand at the time and wouldn't have been able to explain to anyone even if I had tried.

Most people wouldn't have noticed it, not unless they looked closely. I still smiled when I had to. I still nodded along in my homeschool classes, still walked the same hallways, and sat at the same lunch table. But inside, everything felt altered. Foreign.

Especially when it came to boys.

Before that, I'd always been shy around them — awkward, unsure. But after... I became something else entirely. Hyper-aware. On edge. Suspicious of even the most innocent gestures.

Every compliment sounded like a setup.

Every smile felt laced with a hidden motive.

Even small things — like a guy holding the door open or offering to carry something — would send my abdomen into knots. I could never tell if they were being genuinely nice or if it was the start of something darker. And the terrifying thing was... I believed Connor.

I believed that if a guy was nice to me, it was only because he wanted something from me.

It didn't matter that I knew, logically, that it wasn't true of all men. The damage had already been done, especially considering both Connor's assault and even more Blake's daily bullying/groping/teasing (which I'll go into detail about in the next chapter). My gut reaction had been rewired, and logic rarely wins when fear has taken root.

I flinched when people touched me, especially if it was unexpected. Even a casual pat on the shoulder from a classmate or a nudge in a crowded hallway could make my body tense up like a trap snapping shut.

And flirting? Forget it.

If someone tried, I didn't blush or giggle like the girls around me. I froze. My brain would spiral with questions I didn't want answers to: *What does he want? Why is he looking at me like that? Is this going to turn into something I can't control?*

It didn't matter how nice they seemed. I didn't trust any of them.

And the worst part? I hated that about myself.

I hated how I saw monsters where there might have been decent people. I hated how I second-guessed every guy's intentions, even the ones who gave me no reason to. I hated how the words he whispered in my ear had taken root so deeply that they started growing thorns around my ability to connect with anyone.

* * * * *

[AGE 18 – College – Flash forward]

The weeks turned into months, the months into years — but the swing still creaked in my memory. When I eventually tried to get to know my crush — years later, in college — it was a disaster.

The first time I let someone get close at Langs Baptist College, it went badly. He was patient. Kind. But he didn't understand why I pulled away when he reached for my hand.

Why did I jump when he brushed against me? Why did I turn cold when he complimented my body?

He thought I didn't like him. I did. My heart did.

But my body didn't feel safe, not even with kindness.

His gentle gestures triggered something else. Not because he did anything wrong. But because I still heard Connor's voice. Still remembered Blake's bullying hands (but that's next chapter).

Eventually, he stopped trying.

And I couldn't blame him.

I didn't know how to explain: *It's not you. It's the part of me still trapped on that swing.*

After that, I didn't let anyone in for a long time.

Even now, trust is hard.

Some days, I wish I could be the kind of girl who flirts easily, who believes compliments, who doesn't see danger in a smile.

But that version of me — the girl who waited on the swing, believing her friend was coming back?

She's gone.

And maybe that's what survival means.

Still, sometimes, I miss her.

I miss trusting without fear.

I miss believing someone could care without wanting something in return.

I miss walking through the world without a target painted on my skin.

That day didn't just hurt me. It rewired how I see the world, especially those who smile easily and say, *"I'd never hurt you."*

Because those are usually the ones who do.

* * * * *

[AGE 16 – Leaving the Park]

I don't remember the walk home.

I don't remember if I took a sidewalk, if I cut through backyards, if I cried, or just kept my head down. There's a strange kind of blankness that sets in after something like that — a fog that makes everything feel dreamlike and far away. I must've looked normal to anyone who passed by. Just a quiet girl walking home from the park, nothing to see here.

But inside, I was hollow. Detached. Like my body had returned before my mind caught up.

I closed the door behind me and made it to my bedroom without a word. No one stopped me. No one asked why I was home early. The house was quiet — too quiet. I wanted someone to ask. I wanted someone to notice something was off. But I also didn't want to talk. Didn't want to explain what I didn't fully understand myself.

I collapsed on my bed and stared at the ceiling, clothes still on, shoes still laced.

And then it started.

Not the sobbing — that didn't come for days. But the shaking. This full-body, uncontrollable quiver that crawled beneath my skin like it was trying to tear its way out. I wrapped myself in a blanket and tucked into the corner of my bed like I was trying to meld into the walls.

My thoughts were scattered, looping the same few fragments over and over.

What if Connor had done more?

Why didn't I scream?

Why did Deloris leave?

Was it my fault?

That last question latched on hardest. I didn't have words for it at the time, but I knew the shame was already blooming inside me, staining everything it touched. I hadn't fought hard enough. I hadn't run fast enough. Maybe I should've known better. Perhaps I should've seen it coming.

I couldn't stop picturing his face, those cold blue eyes, the mocking tone in his voice like he was teaching me some life rule I'd been stupid not to know already.

If a guy is nice to you, it's because he wants sex.

It etched itself into my brain like a curse. Even knowing it wasn't universally true didn't matter. It had rewired something. Permanently.

Every kindness became a red flag.

Every smile is a trap.

I didn't talk about it. Not then. Not for a long time.

There were days when I almost convinced myself that nothing had happened. Maybe I imagined it. Perhaps the drug-like feeling was just some weird reaction to heat, stress, or dehydration.

But then I'd wake up in the middle of the night in a cold sweat, my insides hammering, the smell of the playground — sun-warmed wood and dust and stale cologne — still thick in my nostrils. And I'd know. I'd *know*.

He touched me. He whispered those words into my ear like a secret promise. He looked at me like I was nothing.

And Deloris never came back.

She wasn't just a casual friend. She once made me feel seen. Said I was, *"Different in a good way."*

That's why I waited.

That's why I trusted her.

But she vanished. Never texted. Never called, gone like she'd never existed.

Sometimes I wonder if she felt guilty.

Other times, I wonder if she enjoyed it.

Either way, the message was clear:

I wasn't safe.

Not with friends.

Not with boys.

Not in my body.

Something in me folded. Clothes got looser. My voice got smaller. I ducked my head when any boys looked at me.

And I never sat on a swing again.

Some things, once broken, don't get put back together.

Some places.

Some people.

CHAPTER 7
Marked for Predators

[AGE 16 –First day of Sophomore year at Covenant Academy]

The moment I stepped into the school of Covenant Academy at Grace Harbor Fellowship, I knew I was prey. No one had to say it out loud. The air told me everything — too quiet, too watched. A church dressed as a school, or maybe the other way around. And in the hierarchy of holy boys and perfect daughters, I already knew my place.

I could feel it, like walking into a room and instinctively knowing who holds the power and who gets picked apart for sport. I was the latter.

I was sixteen the first time Blake Wilson decided I belonged to him.

It started small — not with blows, but with precision. A glance that pinned, a smirk that unsettled, a whisper that landed exactly right to make me question my footing. Blake was the kind of boy who dismantled you without ever raising his voice.

I was clutching Pride and Prejudice like armor when it happened. My name was barely signed on the office forms. First day, scarcely a breath in this new world. And then: "Well, well. What do we have here, boys?"

Five of them. All eyes, all teeth. But only one stepped forward, like the others were just backup dancers in his performance. Blake. Lean, sharp-eyed, hungry. He looked at me like I was already his.

The others were watching, but only Blake studied me as if I were a challenge. He grinned — sharp, knowing. "Tell me about yourself, pretty thing."

I muttered, "No, thank you," and stepped back.

He laughed like I'd flirted. "You think you have a choice?" Then he called out to someone behind me. "You know her?"

I turned — and my insides dropped. *Caleb.* My brother. The one person I thought might be safe ground in all of this. For a split second, I thought he might defend me. That he'd step between us, laugh it off, pull me out of the spotlight.

But instead, Caleb swallowed hard, glanced away for just a moment, then forced a tight, shaky smile. "Yeah, she's my sister," he said, voice low, like he was trying to sound casual but couldn't quite hide the tension.

Blake's grin widened. "Perfect. What's her name?"

"Serenity," Caleb said, the word hanging in the air longer than it should. His eyes flicked briefly to mine, like he wanted to apologize without saying it. "Serenity Shepherd."

Blake repeated it like a promise. "We're going to have so much fun together."

By the time I arrived at class, I was shaking. And there he was again — of course he was. Front row seat, directly across from me. Blake leaned in, voice soft but unmistakable:

"You're so cute when you're scared."

I gritted my teeth. I wanted to say something sharp, but fear was a hand over my mouth. When we were dismissed, I tried to vanish into the crowd, but his shadow stayed close. "Please leave me alone," I said.

He smiled. "I like your voice."

"I'm boring," I tried. "Find someone else."

"Not a chance," he murmured, stepping in close. "You're mine."

That was the shift — not teasing, not attraction. It was possession. Blake didn't see people. He saw territory. And in that moment, I realized I wasn't being courted. I was being cornered.

* * * * *

Pre-Calculus. New class. Same orbit. Blake slid into the seat beside me like it had been reserved. "You'll enjoy my company eventually." He kept brushing the border of my space — an elbow here, a foot there. Nothing loud. But it was the quiet pressure that made it worse. A slow siphoning of control I didn't even realize I was losing, until I felt hollow.

I imagined my mental barrier — roaring, foaming, drowning out his voice. Every poke, every breathy comment, dulled behind the noise in my head. It was the only way I managed to make it through.

But the last class of the day broke me.

At my locker, he slammed the door shut with his palm — loud, jarring. My anxiety lurched. "What was that for?" I snapped.

He lit up. "Ooh, you've got fire. I like feisty Serenity."

"Leave me alone!"

He grabbed my arm, not hard but deliberate. "You'll come around. They always do. My friends and I run this place."

I drove Caleb and me home in silence. Not because I didn't have words, but because I was afraid of what would come out if I let myself go.

Caleb broke the quiet first, his voice low but steady. "You're making this bigger than it is."

"You told him I was scared of guys and sex," I said softly, the awful jokes still ringing in my ears — all spun from what Caleb had said.

He shrugged, avoiding my eyes. "I was just being honest."

"You gave him a map," I whispered, voice tight. "You gave him me."

He hesitated, fingers tapping his seatbelt. "It's just words. Doesn't mean you're not more than that." He looked away, chewing the inside of his cheek like he knew. Like he hated himself, but not enough to stop.

I blinked hard, swallowing the sting. I was his sister. I would never have thrown him to the wolves just to fit in. But maybe I was the only one still trying to play by that rule.

* * * * *

[AGE 16 – Same Day, at the Shepherd Home]

The dread settled in my chest like a stone as I climbed the stairs, each step heavier than the last. The soft creak beneath my foot sounded like a warning, urging me to turn back — but I kept going, toward the living room and my parents' bedroom beyond it. My hands were clammy as my mind slipped its leash, causing me to sprint toward chaos. I stopped at the closed door, terrified.

Find your calm. You have to be calm.

I stood there, frozen in place, whispering encouragement to myself. *Just ask. Be respectful. Show them you're serious. You can do so much better in homeschool, you'll do anything you need to get the scholarship to the college they want so badly — just explain that. You can do this. You have to do this.*

I reached out to knock.

But my hand hovered inches from the door, trembling. My fingers twitched, but I couldn't make contact. It was as if something invisible was holding me back, draining my nerve with every passing second. Finally, from somewhere deep inside, I summoned the tiniest sliver of courage and tapped once.

The knock echoed far louder than I'd intended. The sound rang out like a shot, and I cringed.

A moment later, Nathaniel's voice pierced the silence, sharp with irritation. "What?"

I flinched. It felt like a slap.

Forget this. I can't do this. I'm going to be sick. Panic surged up my throat like bile. My body reacted instinctively — I needed to run. *Just get away. Hide.*

I barely turned before the door creaked open behind me. "What do you want?" His voice was flat, annoyed. No patience. No warmth.

I turned, my eyes wide, my mouth dry. "I... school. It didn't go well, Dad. Please, I want to withdraw. I promise, I'll work hard; harder than ever. I can do the homeschool curriculum. I can earn a scholarship. ... please don't make me go back. They're mean. I'm being bullied. Please."

He exhaled sharply through his nose, the sound thick with frustration. His expression darkened — not angry, exactly. Worse. Disappointed.

"Shepherds don't quit," he snapped. "That's not the attitude we raised you to have. What's the family motto?"

I looked away, too ashamed and too exhausted to repeat the scripture. I knew it by heart, but my mouth wouldn't open.

He didn't wait. He spat the words out for me, his voice rising as he added, "We endure. We excel. We do not complain."

I winced. "I'm not exaggerating..."

"You are," he said, his tone sharp, final. "You have to stop being so dramatic, Serenity. Focus on your studies. You'll go to that school until you earn a scholarship to *Langs College*. That's the goal. So get straight A's. And don't bring this up again."

The door began to close, slowly, deliberately — conversation over.

His voice was firm, but his face haunted me more than his words did. The Parkinsonism was slowly stealing his expressions, softening his features into a kind of impassive mask. For someone like me — a people-pleaser who lived for smiles, for approval — it was devastating.

His face told me nothing. And that, more than anything, broke me. All I knew was that he wasn't proud of me.

My gut twisted violently. I clutched it with both arms, trying to will it away. *Not now. Please. Not now.*

Because if I lost control in front of him — if I cried, got sick, or pushed back — I didn't know what would happen. He might yell, he might practice me, even as old as I was... he might do worse. The possibilities, vague but terrifying, kept me quiet.

I swallowed it all. But my body paid the toll.

* * * * *

Back then, I didn't know it yet. But I'll never forget that doctor who failed me in high school — a man whose cold dismissal left a lasting scar. I was in constant pain, unable to keep food down, rapidly losing weight, and terrified. But instead of listening, he dismissed me with a glance and labeled me with an eating disorder I didn't even understand.

When I asked questions, he mocked me. He didn't examine me, didn't ask how I felt — just assumed I was starving myself to be "prettier." I tried to explain the nausea, the pain, the helplessness. He didn't care.

Worse still, my mother sat silently beside me, flipping through a magazine, offering no defense. I felt invisible.

Eventually, she listened. We found a new doctor — one who *did* listen, who tested and diagnosed me with severe ulcers caused by stress. He gave me the care I'd been begging for.

I often wonder: *if someone had believed me sooner, how much suffering could I have been spared?*

* * * * *

[AGE 16-18 –Covenant Academy]

For three years, I lived in a theater of humiliation — snickers in the halls, sideways glances that weren't subtle, laughter that wasn't kind. Blake orchestrated it all, always flanked by boys who echoed his cruelty like a chorus. He made me feel like I was on display — too small to matter, too exposed to ignore.

At first, Blake's torment looked like typical bullying — mocking my voice, my clothes, the way I walked. But it didn't stay there. The cruelty darkened, sharpened into something calculated. His jokes became graphic. The sexual innuendo started as sarcasm, then grew grotesquely detailed, spoken loud enough to wound, quiet enough to be denied. I stopped trying to steel myself. The words still cut... every time.

Alone, Blake shifted tactics. No audience, no theatrics — just a low, claustrophobic kind of menace. He'd trap me against cold metal or frame me in doorways with nowhere to go. His touch masqueraded as casual, but his eyes betrayed the truth: he was studying fear, collecting it like a favorite pastime.

My panic was fuel. He didn't want a scene. He wanted my collapse. Quiet. Complete.

During those years, I survived on slivers of escape. Most of the others left me alone outside their scheduled moments of cruelty. But Blake lingered. He was relentless — his presence a threat that stalked the edges of every space I entered. I half expected him to follow me into the girls' bathroom to prove he could. And honestly, I wouldn't have been surprised if he had.

But I had two places where he couldn't follow.

The first was worship band. For whatever reason — school rules, divine mercy — he wasn't allowed near. That space became sacred. Playing music, surrounded by people who didn't flinch at my presence, who didn't mock or sneer... it was a breath of clean air in a smoke-choked world.

The second was one I carved for myself. I begged one of the elementary teachers to let me be her TA. I didn't give her details — just offered to scrub tables and sort crayons if she'd give me somewhere to go. She said yes. And that little classroom became a haven. The kids — tiny, joyful, unguarded — made me feel human again. Needed. Safe.

That's where my love for working with children took root. In the middle of my own unraveling, I found purpose in their laughter.

* * * * *

[AGE 17 –*Spiritual Emphasis Camp via Covenant Academy*]

There was this school-mandated camp trip — Spiritual Emphasis Camp — one of those forced kumbaya weekends where we were expected to come back "changed." Closer to God, closer to each other. I hated it before we even arrived.

But what truly etched that weekend into my memory was a game they made us play. They called it *Blind Leading the Blind*. Meant to build trust, to teach us something about listening to "the right voices." What it really taught me was that the people in charge didn't recognize danger, even when they handed it a title and called it leadership.

The rules were simple, or so they said. We were blindfolded and scattered across the woods. Our job? Find "angels" — fellow students assigned to guide us kindly — and avoid "demons," who would try to mislead or sabotage us.

It was supposed to be metaphorical. They thought it was a lesson about good versus evil. But they didn't know evil wears charm, cologne, and smiles in front of adults.

When a teacher tied the fabric over my eyes, it stopped feeling symbolic and started feeling like a trap.

Immediately, I was disoriented. Sound came from everywhere — shouts, laughter, rustling leaves, feet snapping twigs underfoot. I stood frozen, trying to find my breath in the dark.

Blake.

You learn the sound of a predator the way you know the heat of a stove — once is enough. His voice didn't rise above the chaos. It sliced through it.

"Come with me," he growled, and I flinched when his hand closed around my upper arm, demanding and possessive. His grip bruised. His breath was hot against my cheek. "Don't be stupid," he said, low and cold. "You'll wish you hadn't."

My body locked up. It was déjà vu in my bones — the same helpless stillness from every stairwell, every corridor where he'd backed me into silence. I couldn't see him, but rage simmered just under the surface, hidden behind that same fake charm he always wore when teachers were watching.

And then — another hand.

This one slid into mine — gentle, firm, grounding. *Hàoyú.*

One of Blake's sidekicks, sure. But softer. A flirt, not a threat. Wrong in his own way, but he didn't make me feel like prey.

"Don't go with him," he said quietly. "An angel wouldn't hurt you like this."

I couldn't see either of them. But I felt Blake's agitation like a pulse in the air. His grip on my arm tightened, fingers digging into my skin. Hàoyú's hand didn't move. He just waited.

And for once, I made a choice that felt like defiance. "I'm going with Hàoyú," I said, voice low but steady.

Blake exploded behind us as Hàoyú pulled me gently away. Cursing, shouting, and calling me a fool. He screamed that I was wrong, that I'd chosen a demon, that I'd failed the whole point. I didn't care. Hàoyú's arm around my shoulders kept me upright. Kept me moving.

When Hàoyú told me I could remove the blindfold, I ripped it off like it was suffocating me.

Hàoyú was calm. Still. Watching me with a kind of softness that didn't match the chaos we'd just left. Behind him stood a teacher holding a sign that read hell.

Figures.

Blake had been assigned as an "angel." Hàoyú, the "demon." *So I failed. But how could I not? Blake is a demon, not in some spiritual sense, but in every real, human way that matters. Hàoyú might've crossed boundaries, but he doesn't try to break me. And today, he didn't let Blake hurt me.*

I remember Hàoyú turning to him, calm but firm. "Maybe if you wanted her to trust you, you should've treated her like a person instead of a punching bag."

Blake said nothing. Just glared like a child denied a toy he thought belonged to him.

Later, walking back to the main lodge, he found me alone. His fury had cooled, replaced by something unfamiliar in his eyes, something like confusion. Maybe even pain.

"I wasn't going to hurt you," he said quietly, almost to himself. "Why didn't you trust me?"

"Because you always hurt me," I said. "You grab me when I try to pull away. You jab my stomach at random. You make me a punchline in front of your friends. You talk about my body like it's a game. Like I'm supposed to laugh along."

He looked down. Silent. And then, almost like an afterthought, he said: "My dad hits me. A lot. My house is hell."

And for one second, something flickered. Not pity. Just a grim kind of recognition. I knew what it meant to feel small, to feel powerless in a place that was supposed to keep you safe.

But pain doesn't justify cruelty. I still don't know why I became his target. Maybe because I wore modest clothes, because I didn't fight back, because I looked like the kind of girl who would break easily. Maybe I did. Perhaps that was the point.

What I do know is this: whoever thought *Blind Leading the Blind* was a good idea had never truly been unsafe in the dark. Because that night, the game followed me home. And it never left. That moment in the woods when my breath caught, my skin burned under his grip, and the only thing louder than my fear was the voice in my head screaming *run*.

* * * * *

[AGE 18 – Light on a Hill Church Daycare]

By the time we graduated, I hoped I'd never see him again. But Blake didn't fade away. He followed.

The church daycare I worked at after school was far from where we'd gone to high school. No one knew I was there. Not unless they'd looked for me. It was the first place that felt like home. The toddlers adored me, and I loved them back. Their laughter softened something jagged in me. For the first time in years, I felt like I could breathe.

But somehow, one Monday, Blake showed up. Strolling the hallway like he belonged. He leaned against the wall outside my classroom and grinned through the door.

"Public church," he shrugged when I asked him why. "Everyone's welcome."

He never stepped inside. Never touched me. But he didn't have to. His presence was a contamination — an echo of past trauma dropped into the one space I'd believed was safe. He came often after that. No schedule. No explanation. Just... there.

Every time I looked toward the door, I half-expected to see him grinning nearby.

He would lounge in the lobby, arms crossed like he belonged there. Watching and listening, he made comments under his breath, loud enough to carry.

* * * * *

I told someone. Then a few more. But the answer was always the same: "It's a church. Everyone's welcome. He's not doing anything wrong."

Except he was. He was breaking something sacred — quietly, expertly. He wasn't a safe individual. I lost track of how many times he'd jabbed my stomach, pulled me flush against him by my arm or waist, veiled threats about what he and his friends would do to my body... yet no one wanted to believe me. I'd learned that lesson already: telling the truth only made people look at *me* differently.

* * * * *

And then there was Ryder.

He was the only man I didn't flinch around. Kind. Steady. He never asked why I panicked when someone raised their voice — he just adjusted his tone. If Blake hovered in the hallway, Ryder would stand in the door-way. No grand gestures. Just enough to make me feel seen. Protected.

Sometimes I wondered if I should've fallen for someone like that — someone safe. But safety wasn't something I trusted yet. Not fully. Not then.

* * * * *

Then came the day Blake pushed too far, after he'd been torment-ing me at my workplace for over six months.

We were in the middle of free play — toddlers giggling over pup-pets, Ryder stacking blocks with one of the little ones. Blake appeared again in the hallway, loud enough to be heard, quiet enough to claim innocence.

"You're ignoring me again? That's not very Christian of you."

I flinched. He saw it. Fed off it.

"You look tired," he added lazily. "Is this job getting to you? Or is it me?"

Before I could respond, Ryder stood. Calm. Solid. He walked to the door and placed himself between us, a silent wall. "You need to leave," Ryder said.

Blake raised an eyebrow. "The babysitter's got a guard dog now?"

"She works here," Ryder said evenly. "You don't. Take the hint."

Something in Blake's eyes cooled. He wasn't used to being called out, especially by someone who wasn't afraid of him.

"I'll get the Director," Ryder added. "And the Pastor. Or you can walk away."

For a second, Blake just stared. Then he muttered, "This isn't over," and turned.

Ryder waited until he was gone, then gently closed the door and looked at me. "You okay?"

I could barely breathe. "Thank you," I whispered.

"You never have to deal with that alone again." He didn't say it like a promise. He said it like a fact. Ryder never pried. Never asked me to relive the *why*. He just kept showing up — quietly rearranging the room so I'd be in the back, near the youngest kids. Always with a reason. Always subtle. I didn't realize it was intentional until much later.

He didn't need to understand everything about Blake. He saw enough to know something wasn't right. And he responded with the kind of steadiness that asked for nothing in return.

Ryder didn't need to own me to care about me. And that's how I started learning the difference.

* * * * *

But Blake wasn't done. When I was only months from my nineteenth birthday, he visited again.

One quiet afternoon, the toddlers were napping, and I was alone in the classroom; no Ryder. No backup. Blake appeared again, leaning in the doorway like he had every right.

"Tell you what," he said, voice syrupy with false charm. "I'll leave... if you agree to something."

The air left my lungs in a rush. "Agree to what?"

His grin turned sharp. "Be mine."

I blinked. He already had a girlfriend. I'd seen her around. A quiet girl. I pitied her more than I feared her.

"You have a girlfriend," I said.

"She's boring, not like you. You've got fire. Fear. Makes things interesting."

He leaned closer, voice dropping like a secret: "You're supposed to be mine. I know it. And I think... You know it too."

I stepped back, the half-door between us feeling suddenly paper-thin. "This isn't funny."

"It's not a joke."

The air went still. "I said no," I whispered.

His smile fell. Something shifted behind his eyes — something hollow, like he couldn't compute rejection. "You're really gonna say that to me after everything?"

"You've done nothing but torment me," I replied, my voice trembling but clear.

He scoffed. "I call that chemistry." I didn't answer. "If you don't say yes, I'll kill myself."

Just like that. Flat. Empty. No hesitation. Time stopped. I felt cold all over.

"Blake, don't say that." My voice was unsteady despite how hard I tried to control it. "That's not okay. That's not fair. You don't threaten someone just because they won't give you what you want!"

"I'm serious," he said, eyes locked on mine. "I'll do it. Tonight. I'm done. You don't understand what you do to me."

I looked at him, really looked at him, and what I saw wasn't love — it was obsession. It wasn't about me. It was about control.

And I was done being afraid.

"I will never be your girlfriend," I said, the words solid and dry. "You will never touch me again. And if you come near me, I will file a restraining order. Don't ever speak to me like this again."

For a long time, he didn't move.

He stared for a moment, then turned and left, without slamming doors. No scene.

I saw the muscles in his jaw tighten before he disappeared down the hall. As soon as he was far enough away, I collapsed to the floor, silently sobbing so as not to wake up the thankfully still-sleeping kids, my knees weak and useless.

But I knew it wasn't over. Blake never exploded. He corroded. Quiet. Strategic. Persistent. And in the silence he left behind, I understood something terrifying: this wasn't about affection. It was about domination. And the moment I said no, I stopped being fun — and started being dangerous.

For two days, I let myself feel safe. I laughed again. I slept. I stopped checking over my shoulder.

* * * * *

Then came Thursday.

The youth group buzzed with casual chaos. People arriving late, someone spilling lemonade on the carpet. I was seated in the second row, just a few chairs away from Evander, the man I had a crush on. For the first time in weeks, I felt a sense of calm. Even a little happy.

Then the youth Pastor stepped up front, looking pale and stiff in his blazer. "If I could have your attention for a minute," he said, clearing his throat. "I have something difficult to share."

The moment the words left the youth Pastor's mouth — "He took his own life" — something broke inside me.

Everything in me churned violently, bile rising, hot and bitter. The floor fell out from under me; all my organs seemed to drop six inches lower. Heartburn ignited behind my ribs, spreading like wildfire. And then my whole body started to convulse — uncontrollably, violently, as if my bones no longer belonged to me.

I couldn't stay in that room.

Without thinking, I bolted from the auditorium, pushing through the double doors and stumbling into the hallway. The air outside hit my lungs like icy shards. The world shimmered, too bright, too loud, almost cruel.

I collapsed into a sobbing heap near the stairwell, unable to catch my breath. Panic blurred my vision. And through the chaos of my thoughts, a singular, sharp belief began to carve its way into my chest: *I did this.*

It's my fault.

That's when she found me, one of the female leaders, a gentle woman with warm eyes and a voice like a lullaby wrapped in prayer. I had always known her to be a quiet force of compassion, someone who prayed as if God were sitting right beside her.

I barely managed to whisper his name before I broke. The sobs tore out of me with more force than I thought possible. And she held me. Not tightly, not in a way that made me feel trapped — but open-armed, calm, safe.

"I think I made him do it," I cried. "I said no. I told him I'd never be his. I told him I'd file a restraining order if he came near me. I thought it was over. I thought I was protecting myself. But now he's — he's gone."

She didn't interrupt. Didn't correct or console with clichés. She just listened. And when I was finally quiet, her voice came like warm rain after a long drought.

"You are not responsible for the choices he made," she said softly. "You did what was right. You protected yourself. That's not something to feel guilty for. That's survival."

I nodded, exhausted, the storm inside me settling into a quiet ache. But deep down, guilt still ate me alive. Because even though Blake had a girlfriend — someone else he'd been with basically the entire time — he kept choosing me... tormenting me... turning my life into a waking nightmare.

He had reinforced every fear I'd ever carried about men. And yet, I still wondered... *could I have stopped him?* That question never really left me. It dug its way into the corners of my mind and lived there, quietly gnawing, even when I told myself the truth. *I didn't kill him. I said no. And saying no shouldn't come with a body count.*

Eventually, I returned to the auditorium, my face blotchy, my eyes swollen, my limbs heavy with emotional fatigue. The room felt different now. Dimmer. Quieter. A strange, reverent stillness had settled in, like everyone was holding their breath.

My crush, Evander, was no longer sitting in his seat. Gravity shifted inside me for a moment until I noticed the folded piece of paper resting on my chair.

I picked it up, hands still shaking, and opened it.

It was from him. A note, kind and gentle, the words chosen with care. He said he was sorry I was hurting. That he hoped I was okay. At the bottom, he'd written his phone number.

Just that small gesture... it was enough to send a flicker of light through the darkness that had wrapped itself around me.

I remember clutching that note to my chest, something fragile and beautiful amid the chaos. A part of me swelled with quiet happiness, the possibility that maybe — maybe — Evander cared. Perhaps I wasn't invisible.

But the happiness came tangled in a knot of other emotions.

Because I didn't know how to trust men, not after Connor, not after Blake, and I'd felt terrified of men even before them. But especially not after years of being stalked, pressured, manhandled, and threatened. And certainly not on the heels of someone using the most final act imaginable to manipulate my refusal.

I was scared of what a simple act of kindness might mean. So I folded the note carefully and tucked it into my Bible, right between the Psalms. I still have it, even now. But I've never shared what it said — not fully. I don't want to risk anyone tracing it back to him. It was his kindness, freely given. And mine to quietly keep.

It remains a strange moment of grace in a storm I'm still learning to navigate.

The youth group said Blake's death was a tragedy. They didn't know the half of it. *The real tragedy? That no one saw him for what he was until it was too late. And by then, he'd already carved his name into the softest parts of me.*

CHAPTER 8

A Degree of Separation

Looking back, it began with a whisper, not a roar. Not a bold declaration or a grand revelation. Just a slight shift in thought, a gentle nudge of possibility. *What would it look like to actually have control over my own life?* At eighteen, it was high time I found out for myself.

[AGE 18 – Langs Baptist College]

That first college? It wasn't truly my choice. Not in the way that mattered. On paper, it looked like my decision — I'd earned a scholarship from both the Christian school and even homeschool, after all. But when I took a step back, I realized I'd been swept into it more by momentum than conviction.

My parents had always told me what was best, what was right, and what was expected. And for most of my life, I'd complied — quietly, obediently, never asking if it was what *I* wanted.

It was the practical path — the one with the scholarship, the safe bet. My parents nodded approvingly. The numbers made sense. The papers were signed. They enrolled me. And that was that.

But a part of me, buried deep under layers of compliance and caution, had hoped for something more. Something mine.

Things on campus unraveled in their own quiet way. I showed up to every class, sometimes thirty minutes early, my anxiety convincing me that on time was already too late.

I pushed through seven courses, a full-time daycare job, nannying gigs, and lab work — even while recovering on crutches. I aimed for straight A's, held on through exhaustion, pain, and the weight of proving myself.

I showed up. I worked hard. But they didn't see me.

I was quiet, not defiant. Respectful, not passive. But somehow, invisible.

When internship applications came around, I asked for recommendation letters, and what I got instead was a slap in the face. "You have an attitude."

"You're not reliable."

"You're not cut out for this field."

The words felt like a closed door slamming shut. I remember asking, politely, vulnerably, "Why? What can I improve?"

One professor reminded me of the time I had challenged an exam question about how saying "no" supposedly damaged children's creativity. I had offered a different perspective — politely, I thought. It hadn't sat right with me, so I had to say something. "I don't believe telling a child 'no' is inherently harmful," I'd said, carefully choosing my words, "Boundaries help children feel secure. It's all in the way we deliver them. Instead of just saying what not to do, we can redirect: 'We walk with scissors' instead of 'Don't run.' That teaches safety and builds autonomy."

The room had gone quiet.

The professor gave a tight smile and said, "Well, that's one way to look at it." But I could see it in their eyes. I had challenged the unchallengeable. To them, disagreement equaled defiance.

It stunned me. I'd shown up every day, even injured, even after car accidents. I limped through lectures, worked double shifts, and chased straight A's. But none of that mattered.

They had already decided: I was too much. Or not enough. A risk. A burden.

And so, the weight of their verdict settled over me: I wasn't wanted here. Maybe I didn't belong. Maybe I had dreamed too big. I cried for two days straight, my pillow soaked and my voice hoarse.

But even through the hurt, something stubborn stirred in me. A quiet, flickering voice I'd never really let speak before. *This place isn't for me. And that's okay.* It felt radical. Defiant. Freeing. Somewhere in the haze of rejection and humiliation, a new thought emerged:

Maybe I'm not the problem. Perhaps this place isn't right for me.

And with that revelation came a sense of terrifying clarity. *I have to leave.*

Telling my parents felt like trying to cut a wire connected to a bomb. I knew the explosion was coming, and still, I did it anyway. I knew Nathaniel would be furious. I knew walking away from the scholarship would make me look ungrateful. Lazy. Lost. And I was right.

"I don't think this college is the right fit for me."

My father's face darkened, his voice rising before I finished. Suddenly, he exploded; his anger was volcanic, red-faced, spitting fire, veins straining.

"So you're quitting? Is that it? You're walking away from your future because what? You got a little criticism?!"

"It's not that," I began, but he didn't let me finish.

"You're on the devil's path now," he screamed. "I could die any day — and you're throwing away your future? Your degree? How are you going to survive?! How are you going to make something of yourself?!" He thundered about how he knew what was best, how I was his daughter, and his daughter would not be a quitter.

I froze.

Screaming that I wasn't quitting on my dreams — refusing to let someone else define them — felt impossible. I wanted to find a place where I could grow and thrive, not just survive. But I knew none of that would reach him.

Underneath the fury, I recognized something else for the first time: fear. He was scared. Scared of losing control, of me making choices outside his influence. Scared of death, maybe. Afraid that without him, I'd fail. But perhaps, even more terrified that I was finally standing up for myself for the first time in my life, now at eighteen years old.

Here's the thing — his fear couldn't dictate my path anymore. For the first time in my life, I didn't shrink away. I didn't retreat or apologize to keep the peace. I listened to him. I absorbed his pain. But I didn't change my decision. I chose for myself.

I didn't cave.

For once, I didn't back down. I let him rage, let him hurl every accusation and fear. And when he was done, I was still standing.

I had chosen something for myself. And it was terrifying.

But it also felt... right, like taking a deep breath after being underwater for too long. I had always been "daddy's little girl," a role I never wanted, and in that moment, I wasn't her anymore. I was becoming someone else. Someone who could say no. Someone who could say yes to herself.

* * * * *

That night, after the shouting stopped and the house fell back into its brittle, aching quiet, I sat on the floor of my bedroom with the lights off, staring at the moonlight crawling its way across the hardwood like a slow escape.

The walls felt too close. Like they knew things I hadn't said out loud yet. The air smelled of dust and cedar from the hope chest by the door, filled with old church programs and purity pledge cards — relics of a version of me I was already outgrowing.

My suitcase was half-zipped, open like a wound on the floor. My fingers hovered over it, trembling. Not from fear, exactly. From release. From the shaking that comes when your body realizes the cage door is open, but your wings haven't stretched in years.

I had never made a choice this big on my own. Never crossed a line I wasn't invited across.

And the guilt came fast, as it always did. Thick. Familiar. Like a second skin.

Ungrateful. Rebellious. Worldly. Selfish.

Those words echoed with the sound of sermons and slammed doors. With the sharp edge of my father's disappointment and the weight of every Sunday spent trying to prove I was good enough.

But beneath all of it, that flicker again.

Small.

Unapologetic.

Mine.

I sat there in the dark for hours, hugging my knees to my chest, forehead pressed to bone. Every so often, I'd hear footsteps downstairs — the soft tread of my mother, maybe, or the creak of the front porch under my father's pacing. He always paced when he was spiraling out of control. Always looked for control when things slipped from his hands.

I didn't let it out. Not yet. I just breathed. Slowly. Quietly. Like I was learning how to do it for the first time.

And then — something shifted.

I stood up, walked barefoot to the mirror, and looked at myself — really looked. Not for flaws, not through the filter of how he might see me, but for something else. A trace of who I was becoming. My reflection was tired. My eyes were dull at the edges, like a candle that had been burning too long. But there was something else there, too. Resolve — a quiet kind of strength that didn't come from confidence, but survival.

My voice, when I finally spoke out loud, barely registered above a whisper.

"I'm not going back."

The words hung there, unfamiliar. Unsteady. And then they grew stronger.

"I'm not going back."

My voice cracked on the last word — but it didn't break me. It set something free.

* * * * *

The next morning was heavy with silence. The kind that folds itself into breakfast plates and avoids eye contact at all costs.

My father sat in his usual seat at the kitchen table, reading something — probably a devotional and probably underlining passages about obedience or prodigal children. His presence filled the room like smoke. My mother moved around him softly, setting a mug down without meeting his eyes, retreating to the stove as though avoiding fault lines.

I poured my tea and didn't speak. My hands were shaking just enough that I had to grip the mug with both of them.

When I sat down, he didn't look up. Just flipped the page and muttered, "You're making a mistake."

I nodded once, like a confirmation. Not defiance. Not agreement. Just... acknowledgment.

"I know that's what you think," I said and took a slow sip. The heat burned my tongue, but I didn't flinch.

His eyes narrowed. "And you don't?"

I met his stare. For the first time in my life, I didn't drop my gaze.

"I think I'm finally listening to something that isn't fear."

That did it. His chair scraped back against the tile — sharp, jarring — and he stormed out the back door without another word. The door slammed like punctuation.

But even after the echo died, I sat there. I kept sipping. Kept breathing.

It didn't feel victorious. It felt like grief.

But grief can be holy, too.

* * * * *

That week, I packed up my dorm room. Quietly. Carefully. Each item held a strange mix of shame and defiance. My textbooks, still pristine, marked by notes no one had cared to read; my planner, full of crossed-out goals. The "God is good" magnet from my dorm fridge, its chipped corner a perfect metaphor.

I turned in my student ID. Strolled across the campus quad one last time, beneath trees turning gold with early autumn.

Leaves crunched underfoot like whispers of goodbye.

It felt like walking away from a version of myself I'd been told to be — the perfect Christian daughter. The tireless worker. The girl who never said no, never broke down, never failed.

And even though I left with no plan, no applause, no clean ending... it was still the beginning of something sacred.

I drove home alone with the windows down. Let the wind tangle my hair. Let myself sing along to a song I wouldn't have been allowed to listen to a year ago. Let my voice shake and crack and fill the car anyway.

I was alive.

I was choosing.

Not perfectly.

But finally.

It would take years to fully understand what I had done that day — and what it had opened in me.

* * * * *

[AGE 22 –Flashforward]

Later, after I was married in my early twenties, I did return to college — on my own terms. I re-enrolled in a different college and earned both my associate's and bachelor's degrees in early childhood education. I found a school that saw me — professors who welcomed my voice, who praised me, who didn't see disagreement as defiance.

They saw my heart and praised my dedication, my deep love for children. Called my compassion a strength. Told me I had a gift. And I believed them — not because they said it, but because I finally *felt* it.

And the children I worked with believed it, too. In their sticky-fingered hugs and trusting eyes, they saw something I had hidden away — even from myself.

Every laugh, every question, every tiny hand in mine whispered back the purpose I had clung to in the dark.

And now, when I look back, I realize that choosing to leave that first college wasn't a failure. It was a beginning. The first time I stepped away from my parents' predestined path and dared to draw my own. If I can give the children in my care what I never had — safety, love, and the freedom to speak and explore — then everything I endured, every detour and heartbreak, will be worth it.

Because the truth is: the first person I had to say yes to... was me. And that yes — after all the rejection, the trauma, the detours — led me home.

To heal.

To purpose.

To the life I chose.

And now, every time I look into a child's eyes, I make them a silent promise: *You are safe. You are seen. You are loved. You will never have to earn that. It's already yours.*

After everything, after the detours, healing, the classroom, and the children with sticky hands that wrapped around mine with wild trust, I found myself in the middle of a naptime lull, sitting at a tiny desk with paint on my jeans, watching soft-bellied toddlers breathe in unison.

And I whispered, "Thank you" — not to the past, not to the pain. But to the version of me who had been brave enough to walk away.

She didn't have answers. But she had a flicker of truth. And that flicker lit the way home.

The childhood I never had? I'm building it now, one student at a time.

CHAPTER 9
Heartbeats and Heartache

[AGE 18 – Baptist College, Fall Semester: The Almost-Love]

The first time I even *considered* the possibility of a relationship, I was eighteen, freshly graduated, newly enrolled, and wide-eyed in that particular way you are when the world still feels like a storybook waiting to be written.

It happened in the most offhand way, over half-finished conversations, and flickers of shared laughter. I said it like a joke, a soft dare tossed to the wind: "You should come to college with me."

A smile played at the corner of my lips, part teasing, part testing. I didn't think he'd take it seriously — not really. It was the kind of thing you say when you're half dreaming, half terrified. A wish, barely whispered, quickly buried under nervous laughter.

But he said yes.

Just like that. No hesitation. No dramatic pause. Just a quiet, steady, "Okay."

And suddenly, the air felt thinner. I felt dizzy as if on a roller coaster, where thrill and fear are indistinguishable for a moment. I hadn't expected him to show up, but he did. Backpack slung over one shoulder, sunlight in his hair, walking beside me like he'd always belonged there.

And the ground shifted beneath my feet.

I couldn't breathe.

This boy, this beautiful boy I had imagined from a distance, safe behind the barrier of fantasy, was real now. Present. Smiling at me like I mattered. As if I were someone worth following.

And in that moment, my body betrayed me.

It went cold. My hands turned to ice, my shoulders tensed, words snagging like thorns. I could barely look at him. Could barely *speak*.

I tried to stay near the other girls — safer terrain. Laughter and light conversation were easier with them, like clinging to a floating raft when the ocean underneath felt too deep. They must have thought I was standoffish. Maybe he did, too. And maybe, in some ways, I was.

But not out of cruelty.

Out of fear.

Because even though he was gentle — the gentle that made you believe in good men — he was still a man. And my body didn't know how to separate safety from threat, tenderness from danger.

He hadn't done anything wrong. But my nervous system didn't care.

To my trauma-wired brain, his nearness registered like a fire alarm: *danger*, *danger*, *danger*. Every step he took closer made me want to become one with the wallpaper. Every kind glance sent panic sprinting through my veins, as if it had been training for this moment.

He couldn't have known about the men: Blake, Connor, Nathaniel, Caleb, whose names still echoed in my mind like curses.

He didn't know about the park. The time my voice froze and never quite returned to its original state.

No way for him to realize that when he offered a handshake, or reached for a side hug, and I recoiled — it wasn't rejection. It was reflex — a trauma response disguised as distance.

Even though the memories were fragmented and blurry, my body remembered the language of fear. It remembered how to flinch.

And God, how I *hated* myself for it.

I hated that I couldn't explain. That I didn't have the words. That I was too afraid of scaring him off to be honest about why I pulled away every time he reached out.

I wanted to tell him.

I wanted to say, *"You were the one I watched from across the room. The one whose voice softened the sharp edges of the world. You were the daydream I returned to when everything else felt like a nightmare."*

But I didn't say it.

Fear stole my voice again.

And slowly, inevitably, he stopped reaching.

The space between us widened, quietly, like a tide pulling back. Not with drama. Not with pain. Just silence.

And in that hush, something hopeful dissolved — not in rejection, but in retreat.

A love that never got the chance to begin.

A future I couldn't bear to hold.

A heartbeat swallowed by heartache.

* * * * *

[AGE 18 – Summer Youth Group Camp: The Revelation That Shattered Me]

But the ache I carried wasn't just about almost-love. It ran deeper than romance — it was a wound lodged inside my bones. And that summer, it finally surfaced.

It happened at youth camp — one of those glossy, mountain weekends filled with worship music, bonfires, and calls to repentance. We were meant to get "right with God." To be washed clean by spiritual fervor and acoustic guitars.

I hadn't expected anything from it.

I only went because Caleb asked me to. Begged, really. Something about how "God moves in places like this."

And a part of me, the part that still whispered *maybe*, went along.
Perhaps something will shift.
Maybe I'll finally feel light again.
Maybe God can reach even *me*.

The service that night was held in a large tent strung with fairy lights, filled with the scents of wet grass and wood smoke. The air was cool, damp with dew, clinging to my skin like a cold reminder. At the front, a young Preacher's voice rose and fell with urgent passion, talking about "past wounds" and the power of confession.

And then he said it — "God can't heal what you hide."

And suddenly, I was sixteen again.

Frozen on a rusted playground.

Connor's hands gripping my thighs, his laugh sour and mean in my ear. The pressure of his body pinning mine. The panic. The confusion. The unbearable stillness — because I didn't know what else to do.

I hadn't screamed. I hadn't said "no."

I'd just... stopped moving.

I felt the heat of shame crawl up my spine like fire ants.

My limbs danced with involuntary shudders as my vision blurred.

I bolted out the back of the tent, past the glowing string lights, into the shadowed trees. The cold night air slammed into my lungs like ice. I collapsed onto the dirt, curling behind the worship tent, and sobbed — not soft tears, but guttural, wrenching cries, as if my body was trying to vomit up the memory itself.

I was still trembling when Caleb caught up with me behind the worship tent. His face was tight with worry, his usual easy confidence replaced by something raw, like he was carrying a weight too heavy for him to handle.

"Hey," he said softly, crouching beside me. "What's going on? Talk to me."

I swallowed hard. My mouth felt like it was full of gravel. After a long pause, I whispered, "Something bad happened... when I was sixteen. I never told anyone. I couldn't."

His jaw clenched, and for a moment, I thought he might say nothing. Then he said, voice low and urgent, "Serenity... you *have* to tell Mom and Dad. They have to know."

I shook my head violently. "No! You don't get it. They won't believe me. You know how Dad is."

Caleb ran a hand through his hair, eyes flickering with regret and helplessness. "I know. But hiding it won't make it go away. I'm sorry I didn't protect you in high school. I should have. I'm so sorry."

I looked at him, the brother I thought would shield me from everything. "You didn't protect me," I said quietly, not angry, just crushed. "But... maybe we can fix it. Together."

He nodded, voice cracking, "We'll fix it. I'll be with you. Every step."

Caleb wouldn't let it go. He meant well, but his insistence ripped open a wound I hadn't agreed to reveal. His urgency forced me to hand my story over before I was ready. "You have to say it, Ser. I'll be right here." He handed me his phone and made me call them.

I dialed. My hands shook like I was holding a live wire.

My fingers felt like lead. Anticipation twisted my insides in a slow, punishing spiral with every ring.

When my father answered, I could already hear the suspicion in his voice.

I told them, every syllable scraping against my throat, forced out through trembling lips as if dragging my soul across broken glass.

The playground. The pressure. The violation I hadn't had the language for.

How I hadn't said yes.

How I hadn't screamed. The possibility that I was drugged.

How I hadn't understood anything except that something *broke* that day, and I never got it back.

There was a long pause on the line.

Then my father's voice came through — sharp, clipped, that cold pastoral tone he used from the pulpit when he was condemning someone from behind a Bible.

"I want you to search your heart and tell us the truth," he said, "Did you invite that boy there? Did you want him to do those things to you... And now you feel guilty?" Caleb's grip tightened on the phone, looking shocked.

I couldn't even speak. I felt like someone had knocked the wind out of me. The world spun. "I didn't — I never —" I tried to say, but my voice crumbled.

"Serenity," he continued, colder now, "You've always had a flair for dramatics. Always the emotional one. This isn't new. You take something small and twist it into a crisis. And this? This sounds like one more lie you've built for attention."

I sat there fighting tears as Caleb's face went pale. He looked like he wanted to yell at Dad, to protect me, but no words came.

I bit my tongue to keep from screaming. My hands were shaking. My brother looked like he didn't know what to do anymore. I sat in the dirt, clutching my skirt with shaking hands while my father dissected my pain like a prosecutor.

And my mother?

Silent.

Utterly, devastatingly silent.

Not a word. Not a breath of defense.

She let him rip me apart with scripture and suspicion. Let him say the sentence that would live in my bones for the rest of my life: "No one is going to believe you if you keep making things up."

I thought my mother would surely step in then. That she would interrupt and defend me. *Just say something.*

But she didn't, while I sat on the ground of a youth camp, too ashamed to look at anyone.

That was the night I stopped hoping to be seen — and learned that speaking the truth doesn't always set you free.

Sometimes it just shows you who never wanted to hear it in the first place.

I felt the weight of the world crashing down, not just on me, but on Caleb, too.

When the call ended, Caleb didn't say anything at first. He just pocketed his phone and looked away, his shoulders shaking like he was holding back a storm.

Finally, he whispered, "I'm sorry. I thought telling them would help. I thought I was doing the right thing."

I reached out and touched his arm. "You did what you thought was right. We'll figure this out — together. You're not alone."

He looked at me then, eyes wet. "I'm scared, Ser. Scared I'll lose you too."

I swallowed the lump inside and nodded. "We'll hold on to each other. That's all we have."

And in that moment, beneath the stars and broken promises, we found a fragile kind of hope — a tether that maybe, just maybe, could pull us through.

I sat in the dirt, clutching my skirt, my breath shallow. Somewhere, a cricket chirped — oblivious to the storm raging inside me.

When I finally left Caleb for some time to myself, I didn't tear up anymore. I'd already emptied everything.

Some wounds don't bleed. They calcify.

And the scar?

It's still there — a quiet ache beneath the skin.

But maybe it was the first mark of survival.

The first piece of armor.

The beginning of the end of pretending I was okay.

* * * * *

After that night, everything between Caleb and me changed. The walls we'd built to survive the Shepherd house — walls of silence, distance, and unspoken fear — started to crumble, brick by brick.

Before, he was the brother who sometimes felt like an ally, sometimes like someone trying to fit in so badly he'd forget the rest of us, and at still other times, unsafe and unhinged when he got high on whatever drugs he could get his hands on to escape. Now, he became someone I could lean on in the darkest moments. Not because he had all the answers — far from it — but because he showed up, even when it hurt.

We started talking more, quietly and carefully. About what we'd seen. What we'd felt. About the things we'd buried deep because saying them aloud was like opening a wound that never fully healed.

Caleb admitted his regrets — the times he wished he'd been braver, louder, more protective. He admitted there was a "hole in my heart" where he felt broken, empty, and he wasn't sure how to fill it. I told him about the loneliness I'd carried, all the pain I was in that I tried to push down, and the way the silence almost swallowed me whole. Together, we realized we didn't have to take it alone anymore.

Our bond became a quiet rebellion against everything that tried to tear us apart. In a house built on fear and control, we carved out a space of safety. Not perfect, not always easy, but ours.

Sometimes, when the world was too heavy, I'd catch Caleb watching out for me in ways small but authentic — a look, a touch on the shoulder, standing close when the past felt too near. And I learned to do the same for him.

It wasn't the fairy-tale "perfect sibling" love you read about. He inflicted trauma on me, in fact. But that was when he was entirely out of his mind, and I forgave him. Our bond was messy. Raw. Wounded. But it was real. A tether strong enough to hold us through the storms Nathaniel's shadow still cast.

That summer, we became not just siblings bound by blood, but partners in survival, guarding each other's scars, and holding space for the hope that someday, maybe, healing was possible.

The days after that phone call felt like walking through smoke — like I'd escaped a burning building but hadn't yet realized what I'd lost in the flames.

I moved through camp in a fog, a ghost wearing my skin.

I smiled when I was supposed to. I clapped during worship. I bowed my head when they prayed.

But inside, I was gone. Detached. Hollowed out like someone had scooped all the soft parts of me away and left only ash.

No one talked about what happened.

It was as if we had all silently agreed to pretend it never happened — to tuck the broken pieces under the rug of righteousness and keep singing worship songs like nothing had cracked open.

But something had.

Something permanent.

And no one came looking for the girl buried in the rubble.

I stopped asking for comfort. Stopped hoping for answers. I didn't tell anyone else what had happened — not the friends I trusted, not the camp leaders, not even God. Because what was the point? If your own parents wouldn't believe you, who would?

Instead, I folded the memory down into something tight and small and swallowed it. I taught myself to smile with my mouth while my eyes said nothing. I let the mask become permanent.

But something had shifted in me that couldn't be undone.

I stopped being afraid of silence.

I started sitting in it — quietly, stubbornly, like a protest. While the other campers sang *"Oceans"* or *"How He Loves,"* I sat on the edge of the worship tent and stared at the sky, arms crossed, heart bruised and locked behind bone. I didn't want God to fix it. I didn't want Him to wash me clean.

I just wanted to be *heard*. To be *held*. To be *believed*.

And maybe… to be angry.

No one tells you how sacred anger can be. Righteous anger — not just a tantrum or a flare of bitterness, but the holy fury of finally realizing you *deserve better*. That your pain mattered. That what happened *wasn't your fault* — and pretending otherwise is a cruelty disguised as piety.

That was the summer I stopped being the girl who stayed silent to keep the peace.

I haven't become loud — not yet. But I began to wonder what it would feel like if I *did* speak, if my voice wasn't shameful. If my truth had weight.

It would be years before I fully unpacked what happened.

Years before I dared say the word *assault*.

Years before I found a therapist who sat across from me with soft eyes and said, "What happened to you was real." Years before I believed her.

But something started that summer — not healing, not yet, but the quiet defiance that healing *could* come.

And strangely, it came not through church, scripture, or sermons — but through the most minor things.

Like the child at the daycare who climbed into my lap without fear, baby fingers wrapped around my thumb, her heartbeat fluttering against my ribs like a hummingbird.

Like the moment a little boy with speech delays whispered "thank you" after I helped him tie his shoes — his first real sentence all week.

Like the baby girl who reached for me across the room, arms wide and face lit up like I was the sun.

They didn't know what I carried.

They didn't need to.

They just trusted me.

And I realized, in their wide eyes and open arms, that I could be safe now. Not just for them — but for *me*, too.

I didn't have to be who my parents said I was.

I didn't have to be broken to be valuable.

I didn't have to bury the truth just to be loved.

Somewhere between the sobbing and the silence, the betrayal and the beginning, I had survived.

My heartbeat, once shattered, was now a quiet drum — a steady rhythm of hope, pulsing beneath the scars.

And that was no small thing.

It was everything.

CHAPTER 10A
We Were A Poem, Once

I t's strange how hope can haunt you — sometimes more than fear. Fear is predictable — almost familiar. You brace yourself, clench your teeth, and tighten your chest. But hope? Hope slips in like a forgotten song, and suddenly your guard is down. It leaves you unarmored, quivering, undone.

Last night I didn't sleep. Not because of nightmares, but because I remembered something good. A moment, golden and untouched, just before the darkness crept in. And for once, I didn't shut it out. I let myself feel it.

[Age 18 – Getting to Know Evander]

How does one begin to speak of the man I once believed to be the love of my life?

He came into my world gently, not like a flame, but like light through an open window. A quiet warmth I hadn't realized I was cold without. Where life had shouted and shoved and left bruises in its wake, Evander offered a silence that didn't demand anything from me — a calm tide after a storm.

He wasn't dazzling. He didn't sweep me off my feet — and he didn't need to. He was steady. And after everything I had survived, *steady* felt like a miracle.

In the shadow of what Blake left behind — the bruises you couldn't see, the shame that clung to my skin — Evander became a kind of sanctuary. Not all at once. Not with grand gestures. But in the way he saw me... and didn't flinch.

He never tried to force my story out of me. He just existed beside me like a lighthouse — unmoving, quietly aglow, waiting until I was ready to turn toward him.

At first, I didn't know how to be around him. Every moment felt like walking on eggshells laid across the floor of my chest. I was afraid I'd step wrong — say too much, reveal too little. His gentleness disarmed me. His eyes didn't consume me the way Blake's had. They studied me, not as a possession, but as a person.

Even so, I flinched when he handed me a water bottle one afternoon after youth group, our fingers brushing. The contact was fleeting — harmless — but my body recoiled anyway, reacting before reason could intervene. I hated myself for it.

He noticed. Of course he did. But instead of shame, I found kindness in his eyes. He pulled his hand back slowly, respectfully. Gave me space.

"You don't have to be afraid of me," he said softly, voice like velvet pulled through gravel. "I'm not going anywhere. I know it's hard. I'm not asking for anything you're not ready to give."

And something in me cracked open at the edges.

For so long, I had only known attention with expectation — kindness followed by control. But Evander didn't hold out his hand to claim me. He held it out to *give me space*. That difference felt revolutionary.

Still, fear doesn't evaporate just because someone is kind. I carried my past with me like a shadow stitched to my skin. Trauma doesn't knock — it walks in, uninvited, drags its suitcase down the hallway of your heart, and takes up residence in your nervous system.

Every time someone raised their voice, I startled. Every unexpected touch made my heart race. Every long gaze felt like a threat, even when it wasn't. My mind knew Evander was different. My body hadn't gotten the memo yet.

But he stayed. Through the trembling silences. Through the starts and stops. He never asked for more than I could give. And in that quiet commitment, I began to heal.

Healing wasn't loud. It didn't come with trumpets or breakthroughs. It came in the way I breathed a little easier around him. The way I didn't flinch *every* time. The way I began to *look forward* to seeing him.

It came one evening, during one of our walks, when he said, "I don't need you to be ready now. I need you to know I'm not leaving."

No fanfare. Just presence.

* * * * *

[Age 19 – Falling in Love]

By the time I turned nineteen, something in me had shifted. Evander was no longer just a refuge — he was *home*. Not a perfect one. Not one without doubts or shadows. But a home I chose.

He became the person I could laugh with over tea, the one I could sit next to in silence without needing to fill it. Our relationship wasn't made of grand confessions or sweeping gestures. It was built in the pauses. The waiting. The quiet endurance of two people learning each other's rhythms.

But I was still learning how to carry softness in a body that had only known defense.

One evening at our regular coffee shop, the words just fell out of me like rain through a cracked roof. "I don't know how to be around you sometimes," I said, "I'm not sure how to trust you. Every time you're kind, I think it means something I'm not ready for."

He didn't flinch. Just held my gaze. "I know. But I also know you're trying. And that's enough for me."

The simplicity of it floored me. He didn't try to *fix* my fear. He didn't argue with it. He just accepted it as part of me, without judgment.

"I just... I don't know how to feel safe again," I whispered.

"You don't have to know yet," he replied. "You're allowed to take your time. I'll be here."

There it was again — not a promise to solve me, but a promise to *stay*.

That kind of love felt bigger than anything I'd known.

Not because it was intense. But because it was consistent.

He met me in the in-between — in the days I couldn't explain why I was crying, in the moments I pushed him away to see if he'd come back. And every time... he came back.

Maybe that's what real love is. Not the fireworks or the frenzy. But the hand that stays open, even when you don't know how to reach for it.

Maybe healing isn't about returning to who I was before the hurt — maybe it's about becoming someone new, someone softer, someone who finally believes she is worthy of being treated gently.

* * * * *

[Age 20 – Going Deeper with Evander]

It took time, but I started to change — subtly, quietly, in ways I didn't immediately recognize. There were moments when I wasn't on edge. When I didn't second-guess every glance, every conversation. Evander's kindness — so steady, so unassuming — began to feel like a shelter. In that space, I learned how to breathe again.

But guilt has a way of lingering, like a shadow at the edge of the light. *Could I have stopped Blake? Should I have said no more forcefully, seen it coming, fought harder?* The questions still clawed at me. The weight of my own imagined failure hung like a chain I couldn't shake.

Over time, though, something inside me shifted. I began to realize that healing wasn't about one big moment of clarity. It wasn't about waking up and suddenly being okay. It was about learning to live with the guilt, not under it, and learning to walk beside my pain without letting it swallow me whole.

* * * * *

One evening, after an especially hard day, I called Evander. I didn't even know why at first — just that I needed something steady, and his voice had always been that.

My parents had signed me up for a "single life workshop" at an out-of-state church, suddenly anxious that I was too distant from men, when just a year ago they'd been relieved I hadn't shown any interest. It triggered a storm inside me that I hadn't been ready for — panic in slow, suffocating waves.

Evander picked up quickly. "Hey, you okay?"

Just the sound of his voice almost made my eyes well. "I don't know," I whispered. "I feel like I'm not getting better. I feel... stuck."

"You're not stuck," he said gently. "Sometimes the hardest thing is just accepting that you don't have to be perfect. You don't have to have all the answers. You're doing the best you can, and that's enough."

I lay back on my bed and closed my eyes, his words echoing in the quiet. Maybe I didn't have to carry it all. Perhaps I didn't have to earn healing. Maybe I could take one small breath at a time — and that could be enough.

* * * * *

The following months felt like walking a tightrope — moments of clarity followed by days when the fear returned, fast and breathless. Sometimes, all it took was a man's lingering glance or a song I hadn't heard since that night to send me spiraling. But through it all, Evander stayed. He didn't push. He didn't rush me. He just held space.

And I began to let him in.

Not all at once. Not with dramatic confessions or sweeping gestures. But in small ways — quiet conversations, shared secrets, the kind of trust that grows like moss, slow and persistent.

One afternoon, as the sun dipped behind the trees and painted the sky in soft golds and purples, I turned to him and said, "You know, I never thought I could trust someone like this. I never thought I could feel safe again."

Evander smiled — a soft, almost sad smile, like he understood the cost of what I'd just said. "I think you're learning how. And that's enough for me."

And, for the first time in a long time, I believed him.

* * * * *

Our connection deepened over the months. Gently. Gradually. But with a quiet intensity that scared me differently, not because I feared him, but because I feared losing the version of myself I was starting to rebuild.

I told him things I'd never said aloud before. About my past — or the lack of it. How I didn't remember anything before I turned thirteen. How guilt sometimes felt like a stone lodged in my chest. He never wavered. Never recoiled from my truth. He just listened.

But... there were moments.

Small ones, subtle at first. Easy to dismiss.

I started to notice a faint scent on him sometimes, at youth group, or church, late in the afternoons. It wasn't strong, not enough to be obvious — just a trace of something off beneath his usual cologne. I wanted to believe it was nothing. My mind said I was overreacting, projecting old fears onto someone who had never given me a reason not to trust him.

And yet... a seed of unease took root.

He began to shift in other ways as well. His moods sometimes turned sharp, almost without warning. He'd go from calm and attentive to suddenly impatient, his words clipped. When I asked if something was wrong, he brushed it off — he was "tired", he said — "just had a bad day".

At first, I excused it. *Love,* I told myself, *makes room for flaws.* But the tension grew.

* * * * *

One night, about four months into dating, we sat at our usual corner table in the coffee shop. I had just told him about a difficult conversation with my mom — how she still couldn't seem to accept what had happened to me regarding both tormentors, how she shifted the blame or refused to talk about it altogether.

"You should just let her go," Evander said abruptly. His voice was low, but the edge in it was unmistakable. "She's not going to change. It's been how long?"

I blinked. The sharpness in his tone caught me off guard. "I — well, it's complicated. She's still my mom, Evander. I can't just shut her out."

He sighed, the sound heavy with frustration. His fingers tapped against the table — too fast, too loud. "Yeah, I get it. However, sometimes people don't deserve a second chance. You've given her enough."

His words weren't wrong. But something in the way he said them — so cold, so final — rattled me. It didn't sound like the Evander I had trusted with my most fragile truths. It sounded like someone else entirely.

Before I could respond, he stood up suddenly. "I need to get going," he muttered, already turning away. "I'll see you later."

I watched him leave, a strange hollowness settling deep. I didn't know what had just happened. But it wasn't the first time I'd seen that version of him. And it wouldn't be the last.

* * * * *

Over the following weeks, those moments multiplied. We'd go on walks, and halfway through, something would shift. He'd start venting

— too loudly, too angrily — about a coworker, a friend, a church leader. His tone would harden, his words becoming sharper, colder.

And after those outbursts, he'd withdraw. Silent. Distant. I'd try to reach him, to understand what he was feeling — but he'd just shut down.

Then there were the other signs. Empty bottles in his car — tucked away in the backseat, under the driver's seat, places I wasn't meant to find. When I asked, he laughed it off. "I'm not an alcoholic," he said. "I'm just a problem drinker."

I didn't fully understand what that meant at the time. I didn't know that 'problem drinker' meant that if he had one, he had to drink until he passed out. I wanted to believe he was being honest, that he had it under control.

But a quiet voice inside me — one I had spent years trying to learn how to trust — was starting to whisper: *this isn't nothing.*

And the most challenging part was knowing that the man who had once been my sanctuary... might also be the next person I had to protect myself from.

* * * * *

[AGE 20 –Evander's Apartment]

One night, after we'd spent a quiet evening at his place, watching a movie, I noticed a pack of drinks sitting on his kitchen counter, half-empty. He seemed off all evening, his eyes clouded in a way that wasn't just from tiredness. He'd leaned a little too heavily on the counter when we'd made dinner together, his movements slow, deliberate. And when we'd sat on the couch afterward, he'd pulled me in close, his breath a little too sharp.

"Hey, you okay?" I asked, a little uncertain, trying to steady myself as I pulled away slightly.

He gave me that half-smile, the one that didn't quite reach his eyes. "Yeah, just a long day. You know how it is." He went for a can as he asked, "You want some?"

I shook my head, a sudden unease creeping up my spine. "I think I'm good." I smiled, though it felt forced. "I just think we should take it slow. You know? Let's enjoy tonight."

Evander's smile faded, his eyes hardening for a moment before he sighed, setting the can back down. "Yeah, sure. I guess you're right."

That night, once I'd gone home, I lay in bed, staring at the ceiling, my heart pounding a little faster than usual. There was a nagging feeling, a whisper in the back of my mind telling me that I needed to talk to him — ask him about what was going on, about what I was starting to see.

But the truth was — I was scared. Not of him, not in the way I had been scared of other men in my past, but scared of the fragile, flickering thing we had created between us. Scared to name what I suspected. Afraid to pull on the thread that might unravel it all. I had seen the signs — the smell of liquor on his breath, the sudden distance in his eyes, the way his warmth would sometimes give way to an unspoken storm inside him. And I was terrified that confronting it would break the spell we had woven together so delicately.

I didn't know if I could handle the truth, whatever that truth might be. I didn't want to admit that Evander, the man who had become a haven for me in the wake of so much wreckage, might be carrying personal shadows too heavy for me to hold. I didn't want to acknowledge that the kindness he offered so freely came from a heart splintered in ways I hadn't yet seen. That underneath his soft-spoken reassurances and steady presence was a man still at war with himself.

And yet... maybe that was what drew me closer.

Because I had demons too — fears I still carried, wounds that flinched at the wrong tone of voice or a passing memory. I had spent so long trying to survive that I barely knew how to exist outside of survival. Evander had met me in the middle of that storm. He had steadied me when my voice shook. He'd never asked me for more than I was ready to give. And for that alone, I cared for him.

I loved this man, not just the version he showed to the world, but the broken, tired parts he tried to bury. He had taken up residence not just in my thoughts, but in the tenderest corners of my heart. He lived there quietly, like a melody I couldn't forget, like a prayer I kept whispering.

So I made a silent vow, the kind only the heart can speak, I would stay. I would help him the way he had helped me. I would pour into him what had once been poured into me. I had learned joy again — fought tooth and nail to reclaim it — and I had enough to share: enough hope, enough patience, enough love for both of us.

It didn't mean I was naïve. I knew that loving someone didn't erase their battles. But I had chosen him. I had elected to try.

So when he proposed — a long letter in a parking lot, eyes full of something too vulnerable to name — I said yes. Without hesitation, without pause.

Elated, I believed not that our future would be easy, but that in that moment, we had something real. I believed in the version of him that wanted to get better. I believed in the possibility of healing side by side.

But beneath the joy, beneath the rush of adrenaline and the warmth of his arms wrapped around me, a quiet part of me whispered: *Be careful.* Not because I didn't love him, but because I did. Because I knew what it meant to lose yourself trying to save someone else.

Still, I smiled into his chest, my heart full, my eyes damp. *Whatever comes next, we'll face it together.* Or at least, that's what I told myself then.

The days that followed Evander's proposal felt like living inside a dream made of sunlight and soft promises.

He'd asked me quietly, without fanfare. No fancy dinner, no orchestrated scene — just us, sitting in his car after a long, meandering conversation about nothing and everything. The kind of conversation that felt like security. Looked at me like I was the last safe place he knew. The car smelled faintly of cold air and his nervous cologne. And then, almost shyly, Evander pulled the heirloom ring from his coat pocket. His hands moved involuntarily, just enough for me to notice.

"I want to do this with you," he had said. "All of it. Life. Healing. Mess and all."

I didn't need time to think. I had already decided long ago, in the quiet hours spent watching him breathe beside me, in the way he always reached for my hand when I drifted into silence, in the patience he showed me on my worst days. I had already said yes in a thousand unspoken ways.

And now, I've made it real.

We began making plans, creating a registry, and rushed toward a wedding date. We had our commitment, worn soft and true like an old sweater. We walked through those early days of our engagement wrapped in a kind of shared hope, whispering dreams of a home with creaky floors and plants we'd probably forget to water. He talked about quitting "for good this time," and I let myself believe it — not because I was blind, but because I needed to think that love could be stronger than his addiction.

I wanted to believe in the man he was when he was sober. The one who smiled in the morning and made jokes about naming our future baby something absurd. The one who kissed my forehead when I woke from nightmares and left handwritten notes in my coat pocket, just because. That man, the Evander I loved, was real. He was here.

There were moments I caught glimpses of something more. At a church potluck, he wrapped his arm around my shoulder and called me his "future wife" with a smile that made me hopeful. We stood in line for lukewarm mac and cheese and store-bought brownies, laughing like kids. It was the kind of joy that made me forget to be afraid.

For a while, that was enough. Hope was enough.

But there were cracks, even then.

Little things I didn't want to look at too closely. How his moods would shift quickly if he hadn't eaten, or if he got overwhelmed. How sometimes I'd find him staring too long at nothing, lost in a space I couldn't reach.

I told myself he was trying. And I believed he was. Most days, he really was. He made promises. He said things like, "Maybe this time

I'll talk to someone." And I cheered him on like it was already done. Like wanting to heal was the same as doing it.

Maybe I wanted to believe that our love could carry the weight of both of us, even when I could feel the strain settling into my bones. Perhaps I thought if I could just hold everything together — stay kind enough, supportive enough, joyful enough — then the darkness in him would lose its grip.

And there were days when I almost believed that it had.

One afternoon, we lay on the couch in his parents' house, watching the light shift across the ceiling, neither of us speaking. His hand rested over mine. He hadn't touched a drink in over two weeks. He looked at me with eyes I'd memorized.

"I'm scared I'm going to mess this up," he whispered.

"You won't," I replied, without thinking.

He shook his head slowly. "I've never wanted something good this much. I don't know how to hold onto it."

I moved closer, resting my forehead against his. "Then let me hold it with you."

He didn't say anything, but I felt the way his hand squeezed mine. I felt the way his breath stilled in his chest for a second, like my words had startled something tender awake inside him.

I wanted to believe love could be a kind of redemption. That maybe the parts of him that were still afraid, still broken, could be soothed by the gentleness of being chosen.

Looking back, those early days were the most beautiful kind of ache. A season colored by quiet optimism, and by a love that truly meant something — but was not, and would never be, quite enough on its own.

We weren't just planning a future. We were trying to stitch two wounded lives into something whole. And while there was joy, and laughter, and the softest kinds of hope, there was also the truth we kept locked away: that no amount of love can heal a wound someone won't face.

Still, I loved him. Deeply. Fiercely. Maybe that was both our salvation and the beginning of the unraveling. Love, I was learning, can hold your hand even as it leads you into fire.

CHAPTER 10B
The Weight of the Dress

I married him anyway. Despite the whisper in my mind — *wait* — despite the silent warnings from friends, the empty promises, the hidden bottles, and slurred texts, I married him because I loved him.

I believed — bone-deep — that love meant staying when someone's knees buckled. He had held me when I couldn't breathe. I thought that if I remained soft enough, joyful enough, *good* enough, I could heal him. He wanted to be saved. I wanted to be the one to save him.

So I ignored the signs. The way his hands trembled slightly as he held mine during the vows we practiced aloud in the kitchen. The way he avoided my eyes when I asked him — again — if he was truly ready.

He said yes — as he always did. And I wanted, more than anything, to believe him.

* * * * *

[AGE 21 — Grace Harbor Fellowship (Wedding Day)]

The morning of our wedding was overcast. The sky hung heavy and gray, but I didn't care. I stood in my simple white dress with a hint of blue, my hands clasped tightly to stop them from shaking, my heart full of trembling hope. My friends fluttered around me, giving me compliments as Faith adjusted my veil, smoothing the lace at my shoulders, and Etta told me, "You're the prettiest bride I've seen... since the last wedding I went to!"

I smiled at her candor, then again at myself in the mirror, trying to believe it.

Trying to believe I wasn't afraid.

Until someone whispered that Evander hadn't shown up yet, until one of the groomsmen, pale and uncomfortable, quietly pulled me aside and said, *"He's... not himself right now. Just give it a minute, okay?"* My vision narrowed to a pinpoint. I asked to see him. Everyone said no.

And when the ceremony finally started — nearly forty minutes late — I knew before I saw him. I knew from the hush in the air, the look on his mother's face, the way the Pastor's voice — my father's voice, because he wouldn't let me only have the officiant I wanted — shook as he greeted the guests.

I knew before I turned the corner and saw him standing at the end of the aisle.

He was smiling.

Too wide. Too loose.

His eyes were red-rimmed and glassy. His tie hung crooked. He swayed — just barely — on his feet. I could smell it as I drew close enough to take his hand — something sweet, sharp, and unmistakable.

I thought I saw something else in his pupils, too.

Something more than booze.

Something vacant and strange.

But the music was playing. The guests were watching. And I was already walking toward him.

His fingers clenched mine so tightly my skin prickled, as if warning me to hold on — or let go. When he leaned in to kiss my cheek, he whispered, *"You look like heaven,"* his words thick and slightly slurred. I froze for half a heartbeat. Just half. Then I smiled, and the ceremony began.

I stood there, reciting vows to a man who wasn't fully there. A man I loved more than I feared. A man I hoped could one day become the version of himself he'd only shown me in fragments. The kind man. The sweet man. The one who'd once made me believe I was worthy of safety.

But I wasn't just marrying who he was that day. I was marrying a memory. A version of him I kept in my heart like a secret photograph, smoothed and idealized over time. I was marrying the hope that love could fix things. That *my* love could.

He slurred a few words when he spoke his vows, and I flinched — not outwardly, but deep in the part of me still hoping this could be salvaged. I saw our officiants — my father, because Pastor Nathaniel never gave up control, no matter how old I was, and the one I had actually wanted, Pastor Lyle — hesitate, then continue.

And then, we were pronounced husband and wife.

* * * * *

Later, at the reception, he started acting intoxicated. Everyone pretended not to notice. Some did — and looked at me with eyes full of quiet apology. I smiled and made excuses.

He's just overwhelmed. He needed a minute. Weddings are emotional, right?

But I knew.

Alone at the sweetheart table, my plate untouched, my dress heavier than dawn, my heart heavier still.

I stayed seated, hands folded in my lap, the ring on my finger pressing like a bruise. The reception blurred after that. A slurry of speeches I can't fully remember and laughter that never quite reached me. My cheeks ached from smiling. My feet throbbed inside borrowed shoes. Someone spilled punch on the tablecloth. The photographer kept circling like a bee around something that had once been sweet.

Then Caleb, now nineteen, appeared beside me, his usual easy confidence tempered by something softer now. "Hey," he said quietly, sliding into the seat next to me. "You doing okay?"

I nodded, but my smile felt brittle.

He glanced toward Evander, shaking his head just a little. "Look, I know this isn't what you hoped for. But we're here. We've got your back." Caleb himself was extremely high at the moment and very drunk, but even in his condition, he noticed that Evander was off.

Etta, seventeen, came next, flinging an arm over Caleb's shoulder, eyes bright but worried. "Seriously, Sis, you're not alone in this. Evander's so out of it... We all want you to be happy. We just don't want you to get hurt."

Faith stood a little apart, but even at fifteen, she was very headstrong, arms crossed and gaze fierce. "You've always been the strong one, Serenity. But even strong people need people. We get it — Dad's been poison for all of us. We all want out. But we want better for you. For your marriage."

Caleb nodded, catching my eye. "We all want you to be safe. To be loved the way you deserve. And we're here to help if you need it. No judgment. Just family."

For a moment, the weight lifted a little. In that crowded room full of polite smiles and forced cheer, their presence was the one honest thing I could hold onto.

I reached out, taking Caleb's hand. "Thank you. I don't know what I'd do without you all."

Etta smiled, eyes shining with tears she refused to let fall. "We're your sisters. Your brother. Your family — no matter what."

Faith's voice was low-pitched but steady. "We'll get through this. Together."

And maybe, just maybe, that was enough.

Evander showed up for the first dance — barely. His breath smelled like whiskey and vanilla cake. He pulled me in too close, hands too tight around my waist, and swayed off-rhythm while the song I'd chosen — slow, fragile, aching — played behind us like a private joke.

When he leaned down to whisper something, his lips missed my ear and landed on my neck. I flinched. He didn't notice. Or maybe he did.

And then it was time to leave. He insisted on driving. I told him no. Twice. But he'd already taken the keys, stumbling toward the get-away car like it was a victory lap. His groomsmen laughed. Someone whistled. Someone clapped him on the back.

I stood frozen beside the passenger door, one hand clutching my skirt to keep it from dragging, the other clutching nothing at all.

The drive started quietly.

Too quiet. Just the sound of tires on wet pavement and the faint metallic rattle of cans still strung to the bumper.

I watched the dashboard clock. We were supposed to be heading to the hotel. But the road didn't look familiar. We passed a gas station that wasn't on the map. I didn't say anything at first. Maybe I was wrong. Possibly, I didn't remember the directions right.

I reached for the console to pull up directions — that's when the flashing lights erupted behind us, red and blue painting the wind-shield, upping the ante on my fear. My core knotted like a child's shoelace, tangled and impossible to undo.

He swore. Loudly. Slammed on the brakes. His hands shook at the wheel.

I could barely breathe. My thoughts scattered — *he's drunk, he'll get arrested, we'll crash, we'll die, it's over, it's all over—*

But the sirens passed. The cruiser flew by us like we were invisi-ble. Sped off into the night and left us alone in the dark.

Evander laughed. Guttural. Unhinged. *"God's on our side,"* he said. I didn't answer. My hands stayed clenched in my lap, fingernails pressed into skin.

It only got worse from there.

He missed the hotel driveway. Twice. Drove in a wide, confused circle until the GPS gave up, and I told him to pull over. I said we'd walk. He slurred something about the fresh air being *romantic,* like we were in some indie movie, stumbling hand in hand toward a fairy-lit honeymoon suite.

Except it wasn't romantic. It was humid and hot. The sidewalk was uneven. My dress dragged through puddles, heavy with mud, the lace graying by the second. Mosquitoes swarmed around us, drawn to the heat and sweat and misery. My veil snagged on a bush. I left it there.

He stumbled more than once, nearly took me down with him. When we finally arrived at the hotel, we looked like survivors of a flood. His tux shirt was half-untucked. My dress had turned from white to ash-gray at the hem. A smear of mud streaked across the train like a wound.

And then came the final humiliation.

He collapsed in the lobby. Just crumpled onto the nearest bench with a grunt and a crooked grin. The concierge watched us with a look I'll never forget — professional concern barely masking judgment. I smiled. Said something about a "long day," trying to make it sound light.

But I had to ask for help.

Two hotel staffers helped carry him up the stairs. I walked behind them, numb and silent, shoes squelching with each step. They didn't ask questions. They didn't have to.

We all knew.

Candles flickered, rose petals scattered across the bed, and soft music hummed from a speaker. Precisely the kind of night I'd dreamed of as a girl. I stood at the edge of the bed and looked down at him. He was passed out across the comforter.

Shoes are still on. Mouth open. One hand limp on the pillow where I should've been. I sat beside him and stared at the wall. After a while, he stirred. Reached for me and slurred something I couldn't quite catch. His hand fumbled with the zipper at the back of my dress — clumsy, impatient.

I froze. My body went stiff with tension. His fingers slipped. He cursed. Tried again. I didn't know what I was doing. He didn't either. Or maybe in his alcohol-addled state, he didn't care.

He leaned over me, his weight too much, his breath sour against my cheek.

I let him try for a few minutes — fumbling, grunting, his shirt damp against my shoulder. I didn't move. I didn't say no. But I didn't say yes either.

I just stayed still. Waiting for it to feel like something other than this. Eventually, he gave up. Rolled over. Passed out again. This time for good.

I slipped into the bathroom. Closed the door. Sat on the cold tile floor with my knees to my chest, dress bunched around me like a discarded curtain.

I peeled off my shoes. Washed my face. Stared at myself in the mirror until the girl in the reflection stopped looking like a bride.

That night didn't end with passion. Or laughter. Or even sleep.

It ended with silence. The kind that hums beneath your skin.

The kind you carry long after the candles burn out. And somewhere in the quiet, I whispered the truth to myself:

Love isn't always enough.

But even before the silence, before the drunken stumble into our supposed new beginning, there was another ache twisting through me. A quieter kind of confusion. One that I was at a loss to name at the time.

Because I had grown up being taught that my body was dangerous.

That it needed to be hidden — shoulders covered, skirts past the knee, necklines high. That I was responsible not just for my own choices, but for the thoughts of every boy who looked at me, if they stumbled, it was my fault — for being "too inviting," for wearing something "too tight," for not guarding my purity like a glass vase balanced on a ledge.

I had spent most of my life dressing like I belonged to another century — loose, long clothing, layers upon layers, always modest, always careful. No low necklines. No exposed thighs. No bare shoulders. No attention. Ever.

So, how am I supposed to switch that off all of a sudden?

I was trained, in subtle and not-so-subtle ways, to believe that modesty was holiness. That any inch of exposed skin was an invitation. That my body didn't belong to me — it belonged to God until it belonged to my husband.

And now?

Now I was supposed to flip a switch. Go from modest to magnetic. From invisible to lingerie-clad to naked in a single day. My body, once a battlefield of restraint and shame, was suddenly expected to become an altar of desire.

No one prepared me for that whiplash.

They taught us how to say *no*. They never taught us how to say *yes*.

I had no roadmap — just a muddy dress, a passed-out husband, and a heart full of contradiction. I sat on the edge of the hotel bed, staring at the white lace garter still wrapped around my thigh — delicate, ridiculous, symbolic.

This was supposed to be the moment everything changed, when I became a wife. A lover. A woman.

Instead, I felt like a girl dressed up in someone else's expectations.

Alone.

Confused.

Still, somehow too much and not enough.

And as I slowly peeled off the layers of tulle, satin, and shame, I didn't feel beautiful. I didn't feel holy. I didn't feel like a woman stepping into the joy of sacred union.

I felt exposed — not just in skin, but in spirit, as if every layer I'd carefully worn for years had suddenly dissolved.

And I wondered — *how many other girls have been told to cover themselves for years, only to find that shame doesn't slip off as easily as a wedding dress?*

It clings. Even in candlelight. Even in a hotel suite lined with rose petals. Even when you love the person lying next to you.

Or think you do.

* * * * *

Evander lay passed out on what should have been our wedding bed in our hotel... and I cried.

Not quiet tears, but deep, wracking sobs from somewhere older than the moment itself. I cried because I felt like I'd done something wrong. Because everything I'd been told about this part of marriage — that it would be sacred, beautiful, even magical — had collapsed into something that felt dull and painful. Violent, even.

I had waited, just like they told me to. Saved myself, like chastity was a prize to be handed over. Followed the rules, kept the boundaries, wore modesty like a breastplate. And yet, none of it had prepared me for this.

Nothing about it had felt magical. It felt... humiliating. Confusing. And worst of all, wrong.

I kept asking myself if maybe I was the problem. *Did I fail somehow? Was I not holy enough, healed enough, good enough to experience what everyone else seemed to describe in such glowing terms?*

There was no guidance for the in-between space — the space where shame meets intimacy, where fear meets expectation. The church had drilled into me the importance of waiting, of staying pure, of protecting my body like a temple... but they said next to nothing about what came after.

No one told me what sex would actually feel like, what to do if it hurt. No one said that pain wasn't normal, or that trauma could live in the muscles themselves. All I was ever told was that it was my duty to please my husband. That once I was married, I was to give myself fully. That it would be "beautiful."

But it wasn't beautiful. It was horrifying. And I had no idea that wasn't how it was supposed to be.

If someone had told me the truth — had pulled me aside and explained what sex really was, what it was supposed to feel like, both emotionally and physically — I might have been able to recognize, even back then, that something was wrong with me. Horribly, medically wrong. I might have understood that I wasn't frigid, or broken, or failing spiritually — I was in pain. Real pain. The kind that doesn't go away with prayer or positive thinking or "just relax and breathe."

But instead, I stayed silent.

I cried behind closed doors. I smiled in front of people. I said I was fine when I was anything but.

And underneath all that silence, I carried a quiet, growing grief: that something meant to be revered had instead left me feeling ashamed and unknowably alone.

I sat on the edge of the mattress, the train of my wedding dress pooling like ghost-white water around my feet as I stared at the wall for a long time.

This is not how I imagined the beginning.

But I still believed, somehow, that it could get better.

This is just one bad day. My love, if I keep pouring it out, will soak into the cracks and hold him together.

I didn't process well. Not that night. I was too numb, too stunned, still wrapped in the shock of a choice I hadn't fully realized I was making.

I lay beside him and listened to his breath rattle and stutter as he snored. And I whispered, just once, "Please... get better."

He didn't hear me.

* * * * *

The next morning, I woke up not with the blissful sense of newly-wed peace I had expected, but with a dull, radiating ache — one that quickly turned sharp and consuming as I tried to move. The pain wasn't just uncomfortable — it was excruciating. Deep, raw, almost unbearable. I winced, breath catching in my lungs, as I slowly sat up in bed.

Something is wrong. Very wrong.

At first, I thought it might be normal. *After all, it's supposed to hurt a little. That's what I've always heard. That your first time might be uncomfortable, awkward, even,* but this wasn't that. This wasn't tenderness or adjustment. *This is agony.*

Evander noticed almost immediately. "Are you okay?" he asked, sitting up beside me, his expression shifting from groggy affection mixed with an intense hangover to concern. "You're shaking."

I tried to nod, to downplay it, but the words caught. I didn't want to make him feel bad. I didn't want to admit that what was supposed to be beautiful had instead left me feeling broken.

"Something's wrong," I finally whispered. "It... hurts. Bad."

His brow furrowed, worry settling into his features. "But... that's not normal, right? I mean—" He paused, rubbing a hand over his face, clearly struggling to make sense of it. "Why was it like that for you? You're—" He hesitated, as if afraid to say it out loud. "You're a virgin. There should've been... I don't know, blood or something. It was supposed to be different."

I didn't have an answer for him. I didn't have an answer for myself.

All I could think about was the pain. Not just physical, but emotional. Deeply psychological. I felt exposed in a way I couldn't explain, like something had been torn open inside me, and not just my body. My sense of self, my idea of what intimacy was supposed to be, was unraveling fast.

I wrapped my arms around myself, folding inward like I was trying to protect whatever part of me still felt intact. My skin felt foreign. My body, once a source of quiet confidence, now felt alien and betrayed. *I'm not supposed to feel like this. I'm supposed to feel close to him. Safe. Loved. Instead, I feel defective. Shattered.*

"Why do I feel so gross?" I asked, not expecting him to have an answer. "Why didn't it work? Why didn't it feel right?"

He didn't respond right away. And when he finally spoke, his voice was barely a whisper. "I don't know. It's like... like your body rejected it. Like it couldn't happen."

The silence that followed was deafening. I could see it on his face — the confusion, the frustration, the helplessness. He wasn't angry. But he was scared. And so was I.

He didn't mean it cruelly, but when he said I felt "broken and damaged," it sank into my chest like a shingle. Those words echoed inside me for years. Unfortunately, they still resonate to this day, something I have to fight against tangibly... *Broken, Damaged.*

I tried to tell myself it was just the shock, the inexperience, the stress. But deep down, I wondered if there was something fundamentally wrong with me. If all the trauma I thought I had outrun had somehow etched itself into my skin, into my bones, and was now punishing me for trying to be normal. To be loved. To be touched.

And perhaps the most disorienting thing of all... There was no blood.

Everything I had ever been told — about purity, about virginity, about how this moment was "supposed" to go — was collapsing under the weight of my reality. No blood. Just pain. No joy. Just confusion.

It felt like my body had betrayed me. Or worse, like it was still holding secrets I hadn't unlocked — memories, perhaps, or buried trauma I hadn't fully uncovered.

Evander tried to be kind. He held me close, apologized for what he couldn't fix, and said he still loved me. But I could sense the shift between us. A heaviness had settled into the space where joy was supposed to live. He didn't know how to help, and it felt impossible to ask.

We were two people lying side by side, both hurting, both confused, both wondering what this meant for the life we had just begun.

* * * * *

But any dreams of a peaceful beginning, of settling into our new life as husband and wife, including sorting out my medical issues, would have to wait.

Evander's body began to give out right as we were meant to be enjoying our honeymoon.

It started slowly — what I assumed were just hangovers or exhaustion — but quickly spiraled into something darker, something violent and undeniable. His hands wouldn't stop shaking. He couldn't keep food down. His skin turned a sickly, sallow shade I'd never seen on him before. Then came the sweats, the chills, the tremors that made him curl up on the bathroom floor and shriek in pain.

At first, I didn't understand. I asked questions, offered water, begged him to rest, thinking maybe he had the flu or something worse. But when I pressed him — gently, carefully, afraid of pushing too hard — he finally admitted it.

"I started imbibing when I was a kid," he murmured one night, his voice hoarse, barely audible through clenched teeth. "Like until passing out, sometimes even blacking out. I never really... stopped."

There was no drama in his tone, no self-pity. Just a fact. As if it were as ordinary as the weather.

Years of numbing himself, of pouring alcohol over every wound, every fear, every moment of self-loathing had finally caught up with him. And now his body, brittle from the abuse, was screaming for what he'd been feeding it for years. He was going into withdrawal. Severe withdrawal.

We found a treatment center — not a glossy, celebrity rehab, but a small, clinical place with pale blue walls and nurses who looked tired but kind. They admitted him that same day. I remember the way his fingers gripped mine, and how his eyes, wild with pain and shadowed by fear and shame, never left mine as they led him behind the frosted glass.

I stood there, empty and unmoored, fingers tightening around the ring as if it could anchor me.

Powerlessness clawed at me like nothing before — the desperate urge to fix what I couldn't.

All I wanted was to help him. To take his pain and wear it on my skin if I had to. I would have traded places with him in an instant if it meant sparing him even an ounce of that suffering. But I couldn't. I could hold his hand, whisper comfort, pray — but I couldn't fight his battle.

That was the most brutal truth of all.

Because love, deep and aching as it was, was not enough to stop the tremors, or purge the poison from his bloodstream, or quiet the screaming in his nervous system. My presence didn't stop his body begging for something, anything, to make it stop.

I remember sitting in the waiting room, hands clasped so tightly my knuckles ached, praying through clenched teeth. *God, help him. Please help him. And if You won't help him, help me stay strong. Help me not to fall apart while I watch the man I love unravel.*

I barely ate or slept. All I did was wait. Hoping and whispering encouragement every time I was allowed into his room. I became a witness to his suffering, and it nearly broke me.

How do you save someone who keeps setting themselves on fire?

* * * * *

[AGE 21 — Apartment]

Even as Evander fought his demons, I was battling my own: discomfort that wasn't just physical, but something more profound.

Months passed, and the pain didn't fade.

It wasn't just the memory of that night — it was in my body now, constant and pulsing. Even the idea of intimacy made me flinch. I began to dread Evander's touch, even when it was innocent. And I hated that. I hated how my skin had become a battleground, how even tenderness had turned into a trigger.

Evander noticed. He grew quieter around me, more careful. We still shared a bed, but it felt like a gulf had opened between us — one neither of us knew how to cross.

Eventually, I gathered the courage to make an appointment.

I didn't even know what to say. What was I supposed to ask?

Why does sex feel like knives and needles?

Why did I bleed nowhere but ache everywhere?

Why does my body feel like it's locking itself down when it's supposed to open up?

The gynecologist was kind, thankfully older, with a gentle voice and tired eyes that had probably seen far worse than a newlywed trying not to fall apart.

I explained what I could — awkwardly, haltingly. I kept apologizing for sounding dramatic, and she kept assuring me I didn't. That pain during sex wasn't something to dismiss; I wasn't alone.

After a brief, careful exam, she leaned back and gave me a name: *Vaginismus.*

I blinked at her. "What is that?"

She explained that my body wasn't broken — it was trying to protect me. That part hit me like a punch to the chest. "Your body isn't betraying you," she said gently. "It's reacting to something." I cried right there on the exam table—big, quiet, shame-soaked tears. I hadn't realized how badly I needed someone to tell me I wasn't crazy, that I wasn't defective. That there was a reason.

When I told Evander later, he squeezed my hand and said, "We'll figure it out."

And I think he meant it.

But I also saw something shift behind his eyes — a kind of weariness, or maybe disappointment. And it scared me. Because who knew how long he'd be willing to wait? I didn't know how far his kindness would stretch.

Still, for the first time in months, I felt something unfamiliar flicker beneath the grief — maybe not joy, but something like hope.

I have a name now. I have a reason. I'm not "damaged."

I am a woman with a body trying to survive something it hasn't even fully explained to me yet.

The road ahead will be slow. Healing will be complicated. Nonlinear. But it's begun.

Or so I thought.

CHAPTER 11
Fragments Returning

People think the worst day is when the trauma happens. But sometimes, the worst day is when you realize you survived — and the weight of it all finally crashes down.

[AGE 21 — Grocery Store Parking Lot]

It happened without warning.

My husband, Evander, and I were sitting in silence in a grocery store parking lot. I was twenty-one. A song played softly through the car speakers — something old and familiar, though I couldn't name it now if I tried. It wasn't the lyrics that hit me. It was the melody. A chord progression that sank into my chest like a tremor.

And then, I wasn't in the car anymore.

My body stayed in the passenger seat. But my mind slipped beneath the surface of something vast and hidden. My breath caught. My hands went cold. Nausea bloomed in me like I'd swallowed ice water steeped in dread. My vision blurred.

Then, the first memory hit.

Not like a dream. Not like a thought.

Vivid. Sharp. Real.

[AGE 3 — Shepherd House, Living Room]

I was three. I knew because everything around me was too big, too loud, too far away. The carpet was tan and scratchy. The room smelled like dust and something sour.

My father was behind me.

I didn't turn around. I didn't need to. I felt him enter the room — a shift in the air, like a storm coming. I froze. Stillness, like prey. He called my name, too sweetly like a trick.

I clutched the chewed stuffed animal in my arms tightly.

His voice was calm. Patient. Coaxing. And that was worse.

That was the moment my body learned to be silent. I dissociated for the first time, watching it all unfold as if it were happening to someone else.

And then it was over.

I don't know how it ended. Only the cold. The numbness. The shame I didn't yet have a name for.

Back in the parking lot, I gasped and came back to the present like surfacing from deep water. I couldn't speak. My husband glanced at me, confused, but I didn't explain. How could I? I didn't even have language yet.

I only knew something had broken loose.

[AGE: Unknown — A Sauna, or Maybe a Cabin]

Cedar. The scent clung to me like breath in winter.

Even now, it hits me unexpectedly — in antique stores, forest trails, the hardware aisle — *and suddenly I'm back in that room.*

Wood walls. Heat. Steam. Sweat.

His hand at the small of my back. Gentle. Guiding. "It's alright, just relax."

But I never did. I braced.

I remember the wet heat, the shadows, the press of wood, the whispers. "Be still. Don't make a sound."

Even now, cedar wraps around my throat like a hand.

[AGE 3–8 — My Bedroom / Later Caleb's Room]

The memories didn't stop after that parking lot.

They came in fragments. Smells. Songs. Sensations.

Sometimes they burst through — other times, they slid in sideways.

He used the Bible as a weapon.

Sat beside me, leather-bound scripture in hand, his voice syrup smooth. "Honor thy father and thy mother."

"I can do all things through Christ who strengthens me."

And I believed him. I just wanted to be good.

I learned rules no one ever spoke aloud:

How to lie still.

How to stop asking questions.

How to fold inward.

[Back to 21 — Apartment Bathroom]

The more memories surfaced, the more my body fell apart.

Crouched on the bathroom floor, my breath shallow and forehead pressed against the tub, I felt rashes flare and pain burn through me. Diagnosis piled atop diagnosis.

The OBGYNs were baffled. "It's like your body is sealing itself shut, it's fusing, and we don't know why." One said.

And I thought: *Of course it is. It's been trying to protect me for decades.*

I turned on Ren's *Seven Sins*, one of the most relatable songs I'd ever heard, as I sang/screamed each lyric. I resonated so profoundly with this heartbreakingly beautiful depiction of actual pain that some will never understand. I wish I didn't understand. Violet's tale came on next, also by Ren. It hit a little too close to home, especially regarding her shitty, abusive father. I hadn't expected to find solace in rap, but Ren's lyrics mirrored emotions I hadn't found words for. However, as I've grown older and unraveled the trauma and pain, I've learned new things about myself.

I need someone to help me untangle the web. Someone who wouldn't dismiss it. Someone who would hear me — and stay.

I whispered, "I can't do this anymore."

And I meant it.

Not life — just *this*. The half-alive limbo of smiling while screaming inside.

That night, I typed into Google: Trauma-informed therapist near me.

Then, I clicked on the link for Dr. Ellen Matthews.

* * * * *

[Therapy — AGE 21 1/2 — The First Session]

The room smelled like bergamot and lavender. She asked if I wanted tea. I said no, emotion thickening my tongue.

I didn't say much in that first session, just fragments.

And then: "It wasn't just one thing. It was everything. All the time."

She nodded. Not with pity. With understanding. "You don't have to rush," she said. "We'll unfold it together."

And I believed her. For the first time in my life, I felt someone could help me hold the truth without breaking me in half.

[Flashback — AGE 4–8, Bedroom]

Some nights were "normal."
Others...
The door creaked open.
Nathaniel would whisper my name. Pull the blanket down. "I'm here. Just relax."

I learned how to pretend to sleep.
Eventually, I stopped reacting.
That's what people don't understand: how quiet kids become. Not because it's okay.
Because pretending makes it pass faster.

[Back in Therapy — EMDR, AGE 23]

Dr. Ellen explained that EMDR (Eye Movement Desensitization and Reprocessing) would feel strange. "You might feel your body react," she warned.

And it did.

I was back on the staircase. Thirteen. Blood. The crack of bone.

Then younger — two or three. Yellow wallpaper. A children's Bible. Nathaniel's hands.

I left my body, staring at the picture of baby Moses floating in a basket.

That's where it really began.

Not at thirteen.

Earlier.

Before I could name it.

[Flashback — AGE 13 — Shepherd House Staircase]

I was thirteen, he'd suggested a walk behind an abandoned church — his idea of a "father-daughter date." But when he reached for my hand, I pulled away. "I'm not doing this anymore," I said, yet again telling him no, finally.

He went quiet, tight, smiling silence, then we turned back home without a word.

The front door stood open when we arrived. I dashed upstairs, desperate to reach my mom or siblings before anything happened. But I heard his heavy, uneven footsteps following me. I didn't stop. I didn't speak. I just kept walking.

Then he shoved me.

Hard.

I remember more the blur than the fall — the weightlessness, then a crack, like my jaw had split inside. My vision went white. Then red.

Blood pooled on the wall, the stairs, my shirt — it coated my hair. I couldn't scream. I could barely breathe.

My mother rushed in, gasping, stunned — but she didn't ask real questions. Nathaniel was already talking, his voice calm, practiced: "She was playing — wrapped in a blanket, slipped, tumbled down. It was an accident."

Mom nodded, never looking at me.

Nathaniel added with a forced chuckle, "She pretended to be a caterpillar — wrapped her legs up, hopped off the top stair 'cause she wanted to fly."

That became the story. The one they told the EMTs, the doctors, everyone.

When the ER doctor gently asked what happened, I heard myself say, "I hopped... I slipped." It was the only version anyone would believe. I was dizzy, bleeding, scared to lie — or say the truth.

That night, I needed about twelve stitches in my chin. The nurse held my hand and called me brave.

I didn't feel brave. I only felt broken.

After that, the house hushed — not peaceful, but ear-ringing silence, like the aftermath of an explosion.

No one talked about the fall — only Nathaniel's version. It was concrete, unchangeable. He told it before guests met us. Friends later mentioned how odd it was he'd share it so quickly. Mom glanced at me over her soup, seeing the bandage but not the pain. Nathaniel whistled, cooked breakfast, and asked about school, like nothing had happened.

But everything had changed.

I'd thought danger lurked in dark bedrooms, whispered behind closed doors. Now I knew it could strike in daylight, in stairwells, right in front of those who were supposed to protect me. I wasn't safe just because others were nearby. That lie broke too.

[AGE 21 1/2 — Doctor's Office]

I return to this moment often — not because it haunts me, but because it quietly changed everything.

It was just before I began therapy, after the first wave of memories surfaced. I was sitting in my longtime family doctor's office, the same one I'd visited for years with chronic symptoms — mysterious pain, fatigue, digestive issues, anxiety, PTSD, and a pile of diagnoses — all blamed on stress.

That day, something in his demeanor was different. He examined me in precise silence, his gaze searching mine not judgmentally, but with what felt like recognition. After a long pause, he sat back and said softly:

"Off the record — if you're open — I've suspected for some time that your father may be connected to what you've been through, emotionally and physically. Much of your experience doesn't add up unless we consider long-term trauma. I didn't want to lead you, but I see you starting to remember. I think it's time to say it."

His words landed like a tiny earthquake — subtle, but earth-shattering. I realized there had been a witness all along: someone who saw the signs not as isolated issues, but as symptoms of something buried deep.

He didn't push. He offered his insight calmly and respectfully, allowing me to receive it without shame.

And he was right. My father had been at the root of so much pain — the unexplained health issues, the psychological burden I'd carried since childhood. My body remembered, long before my mind could speak.

I left feeling both shaken and oddly relieved. It wasn't exactly the confirmation I needed, but it was validation from someone who had watched over me for years and seen something wrong before I dared to name it.

That moment gave me courage. It didn't undo the past or bring back what was lost — but it made me feel less alone. Less crazy. And sometimes, that's the first step toward healing: acknowledging your pain isn't imagined — that someone else sees it too.

That quiet confirmation — his unspoken knowing — was the first click in my bones whispering: *See? You weren't crazy. It really happened.* Once someone else named it, I stopped fumbling mindlessly through the dark. I had a breadcrumb trail, an answer for the hollow ache all those years.

It wasn't healing — it was devastation.

Because when the lies unravel, the carefully constructed image of "family" shatters too. I mourned not only what my father did, but the father I thought I had — stern but redeemable. The man I now knew he was wasn't redeemable. I mourned the stolen childhood, the false safety, the pretend protection.

I mourned the Church's silence: the betrayal of a man cloaked in the authority of a Pastor. People revered him. Trusted him. And he used that trust like a weapon against truth, against me, against the God he claimed to serve.

That cut deep. It twisted my faith and prayers into tension and bile. *If God is a Father — and my father was what he was — then what does that say about God?*

It took years of gentle untangling — therapy, silent walks, letting the quiet speak — for me to separate the twisted image of my father from a God who wept with me from the shadows. But trust... that's been the hardest to rebuild.

It touched everything: my spirituality, my marriage, my friendships, my sense of self. I second-guessed kindness and braced for cruelty — even from Evander, after a night when he wasn't himself.

And yet I wanted to trust. I was tired of suspicion as armor.

So, I started small: I let my therapist see my emotional release. I told Evander when something triggered me. I wrote letters I never sent — to my father, my younger self, to God. In them, I found fierce love for the girl who survived.

I don't know if I'll ever trust freely again — but I know this: I've learned to trust myself. To honor my gut. To believe my memories. To accept truth in fragments.

I discovered family isn't always blood. It's my therapist who held space when I couldn't speak. It's a friend who sat in silence when words failed. It's anyone who sees the broken parts and stays.

And somehow, through all this, Evander remained. Not perfectly gentle —but present. On hard days and harder nights, he tried to love me through the fire.

We both had ashes to sift through. Together, we're building something new; something honest, something sacred, not despite the pain, but because of it.

The truth explained more than I ever wanted it to. It revealed my fear of men, my body's recoil from intimacy, the pain I once chalked up to nerves. The health mysteries that plagued me for years. The pattern of men drawn to take pieces of me.

I thought those other predators caused my damage, but everything began earlier. My body knew first. And when the memories returned, I unraveled.

I couldn't sleep or eat. I dissociated mid-conversation.

But Evander didn't run. He stayed — even when I felt beyond repair. He admitted, once frustrated, that "most men wouldn't stick around." But he did, even when I couldn't stay in my skin.

He didn't attend any of the doctor visits. I wish he had. There were doctor-confirmed scars and another far more terrifying diagnosis: *infertile.* That hope of motherhood, my quiet dream, felt stolen again. There was nothing I wanted more than to be a mother. I spent all of my free time teaching and caring for other people's children... would I not be blessed with my own?

In my darkest moments, I leaned on him. He held me, stayed in silence, and tried to comfort me in ways he didn't fully understand. But he stayed — and that mattered.

Still, cracks remained. His humor sometimes masked fear, and his jokes about my trauma stung when he called them "just being flirty."

I asked him to stop. I told him how much it hurt. The jokes continued, sharp and unexpected, bruising my heart again. I clung to the loyalty, the presence, the comfort — but sometimes love is both balm and blade.

I'd grown up believing love meant accepting sharp edges. Evander wasn't like my father. He didn't intend cruelty. But gentleness has to be chosen every day.

So we carried on. Two wounded people, hoping love might hold together what trauma had splintered. Some days, it almost did.

* * * * *

[AGE 24 — *Therapy Breakthrough*]

As therapy progressed, other buried traumas surfaced — different faces, but the same quiet violence.

It wasn't cinematic.

There was no sweeping music, no single perfect tear sliding down my cheek like in the movies. No grand revelation screamed into the heavens. It was quieter than that. But somehow sharper.

Like a window slowly opening in a room I didn't know had been sealed shut.

I sat curled on Dr. Ellen's yellow couch, my legs tucked beneath me, a pillow clutched to my chest like a life vest. My palms were damp. My lips were chapped from gnawing. I had chewed off nearly all my nail polish in the session before.

Outside her office window, the late afternoon sun slanted through the blinds in golden stripes, casting warm lines across the wooden floor. The hum of the white noise machine ticked like a heartbeat. I could smell the faint citrus of her hand lotion — orange blossom and something herbal, grounding. Safe.

We were going back through something I'd mentioned offhand weeks earlier — something I thought I could keep at arm's length.

But memory doesn't always respect boundaries.

"I want to go back to what you said last time about Connor," Dr. Ellen said gently, folding one leg beneath her, notebook untouched on the table beside her. "If you're ready."

I hesitated, trying to force my voice to steady. "I don't even know if it counts," I whispered.

Her voice didn't change. "What do you mean by that?"

"It wasn't... I mean, it wasn't rape. Not really. Not in the way people expect. I didn't scream. I didn't fight. I just—"

I paused, a sick weight settled low, dragging everything down with it.

"I just froze," I whispered.

The words came out so softly, they almost evaporated.

She leaned forward slightly. "Serenity. That *is* a trauma response. Freezing is a response the body exhibits when it feels unsafe and powerless. That *counts*. What happened to you matters — even if it didn't look like what you thought it should."

I looked away. My eyes focused on the corner of the rug where the fibers had frayed. My fingers picked at a loose thread on the pillow.

I felt heat behind my eyes, the way a storm brews slowly over the ocean—pressure before the crack.

"I remember Blake's laugh," I said, voice cracking now. "The way he said I 'liked it' whenever he touched me inappropriately. Like I should be *grateful,* he told people. My brother laughed. Everyone at school knew. And no one said anything. They looked at me as if I had asked for it. Like I *deserved* it."

Dr. Ellen's face softened, but she didn't rush in. She didn't interrupt. She let the silence bloom, let the truth hang there without smothering it.

I was shaking now. I didn't know if it was rage or grief or both.

"You were failed," she said, her voice steady, strong. "By Blake. By Connor. By your brother. By your school. And by the people who were supposed to protect you, especially your parents."

The word *failed* hit something in me, not like a punch, but like a key in a rusted lock.

"That doesn't make you weak," she said. "It makes them wrong."

The dam broke.

I didn't weep beautifully. My whole body folded forward, sobs wrenching up from some place deep, primal. I buried my face in the pillow and let it come — the kind that isn't about one moment, but *all* the moments. Every time that I was told I was dramatic. The moments when I was touched and told to smile. Every time I flinched, but no one seemed to notice. Each occasion that I swallowed the truth like a stone.

Dr. Ellen handed me a tissue, not with pity, but with presence. She stayed quiet, but I felt her attention like a solid hand on my back.

"I believed them," I choked. "All of them. For so long. I thought it was my fault. I thought *I* was the problem. I thought I was crazy."

Her voice cut through the haze. "You were never crazy. You were surviving."

The words settled into my bones like warm light. And then — something shifted.

Something I hadn't even realized I was carrying... lifted.

It was subtle at first, like loosening the strap of a too-tight backpack. But then it was unmistakable — the weight, the guilt, the shame... they weren't mine to carry. They never were.

My breath deepened. My body softened. For the first time in years, I felt my shoulders drop away from my ears. I wasn't braced. I wasn't flinching.

I was *here*.

And I wasn't alone.

"I didn't do anything wrong," I whispered, mostly to myself, testing the truth like a tongue against a new tooth. "I was just a kid."

Dr. Ellen nodded, eyes kind but fierce. "Exactly. And I am so sorry that no one told you that sooner."

I looked up at her then. And for the first time in my adult life, I let someone see me without the mask. No armor. No filter. Just me: raw, trembling, alive.

And she didn't turn away.

She held my gaze with steady compassion, no pity, no panic, just a quiet knowing that felt like the answer to a question I hadn't dared ask:

Am I allowed to believe in myself?
Yes.
That was the moment the fog started to lift.
Not all at once. Not like sunlight breaking through clouds. But like dawn, slow, inevitable, healing.

* * * * *

[Later That Year — Malie]

I didn't plan to tell my close friend Malie. It just happened.
"I've been starting to remember," I whispered. "Nathaniel... he... did things to me."
She didn't pull away. She held my hand and said, "That's not your fault. You didn't do anything wrong."
It was the first time someone outside therapy said it plainly.
And I believed her.

[AGE 33 — Now]

Even now, the past creeps in — when cedar lingers, when a joke cuts too deep, when a song hits the wrong chord. That familiar feeling creeps in — the sense that I have no refuge, no truly safe space to lay down my burdens without fear. Back then, it was constant. I had no one I could trust fully, no one I could confide in without worrying that my pain would be weaponized against me. My trauma, I believed, was a liability — something shameful that, if spoken aloud, could be twisted, mocked, or used to discredit me.

Thankfully, that is no longer my reality. I've since built a circle of incredible people — my chosen family — who have never once doubted me. Their belief in me is a kind of healing I never thought possible. They listen. They hold space. They remind me, time and time again, that I am not alone. But they weren't there during the years I needed them most. I was a child when the silence began. And in the absence of support, I adapted.

I learned to become palatable. Smiling when I wanted to scream. Offering kindness when I felt invisible. Speaking softly, even when I was aching to shout the truth. I became a master of appearing delicate — of playing the part of the cheerful, well-behaved girl — while a storm churned silently beneath the surface.

The damage was done not just by the cruel words spoken, but also by the compassionate ones that were never offered. The silence of those who should have protected me spoke volumes. And then there was Nathaniel. You'd think by now I'd be numb to his sharp tongue, but some wounds resist scabbing over.

He would tell my sister and me that we looked like sluts if we showed even the slightest amount of skin, though he directed it more at her; I wasn't spared. I remember the few times I dared not dress like I'd just stepped out of an Amish community. He'd look me over with disgust and spit out words like "slutty" and "asking for something to happen to you," as though my body was inherently culpable for its violation.

He didn't stop there. He called me a *liar*, an *exaggerator*, a *drama queen*. And I believed him. How could I not? He was a man of God, a revered Pastor, an adored Evangelist. If he said I was overreacting, then surely I must be. Surely I must be the problem.

That's what abuse does — it rearranges your sense of reality. It silences your instincts. And for a long time, I wore his words like name tags. I didn't question them. I just lived under them, like a ceiling too low to stand up straight beneath.

But I've built something more substantial.

I trust myself.

I trust the fragments.

I honor the truth — even when it hurts.

Because I was never broken, I was wounded. And I survived.

Now, I'm learning to live — not despite the fragments, but because of what they taught me.

CHAPTER 12
What It Costs to Breathe

If there was anyone I felt an unshakable need to protect in my twenties, it was my sisters. They were my heart outside my body — but none more so than Faith, the one I shared the most profound, most unspoken bond with. From the time we were little, there was a rhythm to us, a closeness that didn't need words.

I remember giving her a choice between two nicknames, one summer afternoon when the world still felt simple: Ladybug or Butterfly. She chose Ladybug without hesitation, wrinkling her nose at the frilliness of the other. And just like that, it stuck.

She was small then, with wide, curious eyes that saw far more than they let on. Even now, I can still see that little girl in her — the one I promised myself I'd shield from everything cruel in the world.

I would have done anything for Faith back then. The truth is, I still would. That kind of loyalty doesn't fade. It deepens — with time, with memory, with everything we've been through.

* * * * *

[AGE 25 — Weber Home, Early Afternoon]

One afternoon, as I sat at home, my phone buzzed with a message that would change everything. It was from Faith.

"Serenity, I really need your help."

Dread pooled like cold oil — thick and spreading. The urgency in her words made it clear: something was wrong. Another message followed, the desperation pouring through the screen.

"I'm not safe here anymore. Dad... he's been getting worse, and Mom is always on his side. I can't stay here. Please, I don't know what to do."

I stared at my phone, my mind racing. I knew exactly what she meant. The tension in that house had been building for a long time. Faith told me for weeks how Nathaniel's behavior was growing erratic. His Parkinsonism had only magnified the worst parts of him. I couldn't sit by while she was in danger.

My fingers trembled as I typed: *"I'm coming. Hang tight. We'll figure this out. I'll get you out."*

She responded instantly. *"Thank you. I don't know how much longer I can take this. It's not just the yelling anymore... It's like he's snapped. I'm scared."*

Heat flashed behind my eyes. That fear? It wasn't the usual teenage drama. It was raw, honest, and I felt it cut through me.

I called Evander immediately.

Before he could even say hello, I blurted, "We're going to get Faith. Now."

"Where is she?" His voice went serious.

I told him everything — how Nathaniel and Mom were making Faith feel trapped and unsafe, how it had escalated beyond shouting matches.

No hesitation.

"I'll pack. We leave in fifteen."

* * * * *

[AGE 25 — *Shepherd House*]

When we arrived at Faith's — our childhood home — the air hung thick, sour with unspoken words and clenched jaws. My breath came in short, jagged gasps, as if I were drowning in open air, as we walked to the front door. Evander knocked firmly, his military bearing impossible to miss. Faith opened the door almost immediately, glancing nervously over her shoulder before stepping outside.

She pulled me into a fierce hug. "I didn't know who else to call. Dad's lost it, Serenity. I can't do this anymore."

"You don't have to. You're safe now," I told her, pulling her tighter into my arms.

But I knew that was only half true. Nathaniel wasn't going to let her go without a fight, and I was terrified of what that fight would look like.

Faith always had fire. She was a vegetarian from the heart — loved animals more than people sometimes — and Dad always tried to force her to eat meat. He had his ideas about how girls should dress and act. Faith pushed back hard, and it blew up into shouting matches that echoed through the house. She needed out. We all did. When she asked for help, I didn't hesitate. Evander came too — partly to protect me, but mostly because I wasn't taking no for an answer.

Here's the thing about that day: Nathaniel's version twisted everything, claiming we took Faith by force, that Evander brandished a gun, even that we worshipped him. None of it was true.

Evander told his side — how Nathaniel attacked first, how he restrained him. He said Nathaniel told Mom to grab a gun, and that she reached for one on the counter.

Evander later told me he'd grabbed me by my ponytail to drag me out — something I had no memory of until he said it. I still don't understand how I could forget something so violent, only that in that moment, it blurred into panic. He said it was to protect me. But no part of me felt protected — only yanked, controlled. For years, I hadn't let myself name it, but now it wouldn't stay unnamed.

Here's what *really* happened:

Faith had asked us to help her move out. She didn't feel safe, and truthfully, I never had either. Faith timed it so both our parents would be out, and her boyfriend waited outside to load her things.

But nothing about it went as planned.

Martha and Nathaniel showed up unexpectedly. Nathaniel was livid. He and Evander exchanged heated words — Evander made it clear he didn't believe in their "happy family" act. He said things to provoke Nathaniel, and Nathaniel's fury escalated.

Despite his illness, Nathaniel's speech was sharp. He shoved some bags out of my hands and said awful things, accusing me of letting Evander "steal" me and now take Faith too. Evander tried to de-escalate, saying Faith just needed help and this wasn't about them. But Nathaniel lunged. He came at Evander so fast that, despite Evander's training, he ended up on the floor. Nathaniel was choking him, screaming, *"I'm going to kill you!!"*

Evander broke free and got Nathaniel into a hold. That's when Nathaniel started yelling for Martha to get the gun. Evander told him he had a weapon too (he says it was in the car). Nathaniel kept shouting. My mom laughed — maybe in shock, maybe from disbelief — but she didn't help us. She never did.

Nathaniel screamed at Evander, saying he had "ruined this family." Then, suddenly, he lunged for the wall where he kept hidden guns. He'd always bragged about them, especially when feeling threatened by men around me or my sisters. I'd never seen him move so fast.

Mom tried to stop him, but Nathaniel was determined. In the chaos, Evander grabbed me by my ponytail and dragged me out of the house and down the stairs. It was painful and humiliating. Once outside, Evander loaded his gun and pointed it at the door, watching.

Faith refused to leave without her dog. When Evander told her no, she stepped directly into the line of fire and went back inside. It was in that moment that I realized how dangerous both Nathaniel *and* Evander were. And I was terrified.

I worried Nathaniel and Martha might call the police. But Evander said if they did, I'd tell the truth about my childhood — and Nathaniel wouldn't risk that. Whether that was the reason or not, nothing came of it.

This all happened on June 11th, 2017 — a week before Father's Day.

The backlash? Brutal. Angry messages from people who bought Nathaniel's lies. Threats. Saying Faith was a minor, threatening to come after us.

A few months later, Nathaniel reached out from a different number, asking Evander to meet. Evander agreed — only if Nathaniel promised not to harm him. Nathaniel refused. That's what scares me most.

No matter what my mom says, this isn't about his Parkinsonism. That's just an excuse. The truth is, Nathaniel had a violent temper long before his diagnosis. It only got worse with time.

[AGE 25 — Late Night, Weber Home — After Faith's Escape]

The house was quiet except for the low hum of the heater, but my mind was a storm. I sat on the edge of the couch, staring at my hands, when Faith slipped in behind me.

She didn't say anything at first. Just dropped down onto the floor next to my feet, pulling her knees close. Her eyes caught mine — fierce, tired, but somehow still holding that stubborn spark.

"You did good," she said, voice low but steady. "I didn't think we'd get out of there without blood."

I tried to smile, but my muscles wouldn't cooperate.

"You scared?" she asked bluntly.

"Every day," I admitted.

Faith nodded, like she expected that answer.

"Me too. But we're still here. And I'm not going back. Not ever."

Her words hit me like a punch and a comfort all at once. I looked down at her troubled face, a silent badge of everything we'd survived.

"Thank you," I whispered. "For not giving up on me. On us."

Faith scooted closer, nudging my hand with hers.

"Don't ever forget," she said, "we've got each other's backs. No matter what comes next. Always." And for the first time in a long time, I believed it.

That night, once Faith had gone to her boyfriend's, I couldn't sleep. I kept replaying the moment Nathaniel's eyes went cold, the way Faith's hand trembled in mine. I had spent my life trying to hold the family together. Now I was the one tearing it apart.

But as I lay there in the dark, I realized something: I wasn't destroying a family. I was finally admitting we'd never been one.

[AGE 25 – Three Weeks Later — Weber Home, Evening Storm]

The rescue changed something in me and seemed to affect the very air around us as well. The storm rolled in suddenly, thunder cracking open the sky like a warning. Rain hit the windows in sheets, and I stood barefoot in the kitchen, watching the trees bend under the weight of the wind. Faith was curled up on the couch, reading one of my old novels, her dog asleep at her feet. From the outside, it could've looked almost peaceful.

But I was unraveling.

I pressed my palm to the cold glass of the window and tried to steady my breathing. Lately, the most minor things have started to shake me again. A car door slamming. A door creaking too slowly. The sound of someone raising their voice on TV. I'd come so far — yet the fear still lived just beneath my skin.

Evander walked in behind me, silent. His presence used to anchor me. Now, it flickered — like a lightbulb before it burns out. I didn't flinch — not outwardly—but I noticed how I shifted my weight, how I watched his reflection in the window instead of turning to meet his eyes.

"You okay?" he asked, gently.

I nodded too quickly. "Just the storm."

He came closer, placing a hand on my back. It was meant to be comforting. But I felt the tension in his fingers — just barely—and it made something cold crawl up my spine.

He didn't press. Just stood beside me, silent, like maybe he could sense the gulf opening between us.

"Want some tea?" I asked, already stepping away.

He didn't answer right away. Then: "Sure. That'd be nice."

We moved around each other in the kitchen like dancers who had forgotten the choreography. Polite. Careful. Avoiding the places we used to land so easily.

And I hated it.

But I didn't know how to fix it. Not yet.

[AGE 25 – Midnight, Bedroom —Same Day, After the Storm]

Even after the dust settled and Faith was safe under her boyfriend's roof, something in me stayed braced, not just from the violence behind us, but from the growing quiet between me and Evander.

Our cat snored softly next to my ear. Evander lay beside me in our bed, arm draped loosely over his eyes like he was trying to block out the world.

"I had a dream about Dad again," I whispered into the dark.

He didn't move.

I turned toward him anyway. "He was screaming at me. But I couldn't understand what he was saying. Every time I tried to get closer, his face kept changing and morphing into someone else's. My mom. Then Blake... Connor... then... you."

That got his attention. His arm lowered. He looked at me in the half-light.

"I'm not him," he said. "You know that, right?"

My breath caught. "I want to. I really do."

He sat up then, raking a hand through his hair. "You think I'd ever hurt you."

It wasn't a question.

"No," I said. "I don't think you want to. But that doesn't mean you can't." Silence. Heavy. Full of things neither of us was ready to say out loud.

"I'm trying," he said finally. "To be better. For you. For us."

I reached for his hand, my fingers brushing his. "I know," I said. "But trying doesn't make the fear go away. Not always."

And in that moment, I saw it — the guilt in his eyes. The shame he carried. I knew that look. I'd worn it too.

Maybe that's what made this so hard. We were both survivors. But survival had taught us to cope in different ways — him with withdrawal, with numbness, and sometimes control. I turned to silence and second-guessing.

We were trying to love each other through two different languages of pain.

And some nights, that love was fluent.

Other nights, it got lost in translation.

[AGE 25 — *The Next Morning, Around 2 a.m. — Kitchen Floor*]

After my husband went to bed, I stayed upstairs, sitting on the cold tile floor with a blanket wrapped around my shoulders. I couldn't sleep, so I texted Faith, just in case she was having the same problem. "You okay?"

I stared at the bubbles for a while, then she typed back: "No. But I think I will be."

I replied almost instantly. "Good. I'm here if you need. Just say the word."

For all the things that were breaking, maybe some things were still holding.

Maybe not all the love I had was slipping through my fingers.

Maybe some of it was finally starting to take root.

Right there — in the quiet, in the cracked places, in the soft promise of sisterhood — I let myself breathe.

Even if it still costs something. Even if healing meant walking forward with trembling hands and a heart half-mended.

I wasn't walking alone. And for tonight, that was enough.

* * * * *

In the days after Faith's escape, something inside me shifted. Not all at once — but like a foundation finally cracking under the weight it was never meant to bear. I had saved her. But I couldn't save myself by staying silent anymore.

I sat in my car outside the house where I'd grown up, engine running, hands shaking on the steering wheel. I could go inside. Pretend it never happened. Return to the careful dance of family peace.

Or I could choose something else.

Something harder.

Something true.

The truth explained more than I ever wanted it to. But knowing and healing, those were different countries entirely.

And I was about to discover that the hardest person to convince of my worth wasn't my mother or the church. It was the woman in the mirror — the one who still flinched at her own reflection, and some nights, forgot she was even allowed to breathe.

Part 3: Reconstruction

CHAPTER 13
The Mother I Needed Never Showed Up

The weeks after Faith's escape blurred together — adrenaline fading into something more challenging to name. Relief, yes. But also grief. I'd protected her, but in doing so, I'd finally seen the truth that I'd been avoiding — this wasn't a family worth saving. It was a family built on a foundation of shadows, not love.

As I began to regain my memories and a clearer picture of what had really happened emerged, I made a decision that wasn't easy but was necessary for my survival: I cut both my parents out of my life. This happened before Nathaniel passed away, around the time I was twenty-two. I sat down with my mother and told her the truth. I confided in her. I told her about the trauma.

There was no doubt in my mind — Nathaniel was a pedophile. I could never claim him as my father again. But what still haunts me, what I still wrestle with, is whether my mother knew.

I want to believe she didn't. I need to. But Evander, who saw a vastly different side of her, thinks she did. And sometimes it's hard not to wonder — *how could she have missed the signs?* When a child becomes meek, unnaturally eager to please, and constantly afraid of doing the wrong thing... something is wrong. Terribly wrong.

Still, I try to consider the other side. Maybe she blocked it out. Maybe her own mind buried it so deep she couldn't face it. Denial can be a powerful survival mechanism.

I'll never have the whole picture. But I know enough to try and move forward. Telling my story — sharing even pieces of it — has become a part of how I heal.

At the time, the safest thing for me was to walk away from both of them entirely.

My mother now insists I didn't tell her anything until after Nathaniel died. But that's not true. I told her that when I was twenty-two, over ten years ago, in a restaurant she had chosen. And her response? Cold. Dismissive.

* * * * *

[AGE 22 — Weber House Shower]

As I've touched on before, I was twenty-one when it all came back.

Not suddenly. Not like a movie reel snapping to life. It was slower than that. Crueler. A hundred tiny triggers I couldn't stop: an old hymn on the radio, cologne on someone's coat, the sound of a door clicking shut.

I had spent years locking the memories in a room I never visited. Trauma never stays buried. It waits for safety, for the chance to break free.

And then it floods.

The night more poignant memories came, I was twenty-two, in the shower. Water pounding, eyes closed. I don't remember what I was thinking about. But suddenly I was thirteen again — *blood in my mouth, chin split open, Nathaniel standing over me with that empty look in his eyes.*

I remembered the fear. The helplessness. The ache when my mother repeated his lie to the doctor.

"She was playing. She slipped."

I dropped to my knees in the tub. The memories wouldn't let go — flashbacks, panic attacks, sleepless nights.

I started writing again — this time not in code, like I'd done as a child. I wrote it all down. Every scene. Every feeling. I wanted it out of me. I wanted it to be *known*.

* * * * *

[AGE 22 — Restaurant]

Eventually, I called my mother.

We hadn't talked much in years — just brief conversations on holidays, polite distance. But a part of me still wanted her to see me. To say she was sorry. To say she hadn't known, but now she did, that she believed me. That it mattered.

We met for dinner at a dimly lit, half-empty restaurant just off the main road. Booths lined the walls like confessionals, shadowed alcoves that swallowed sound. The air was thick with the stale scent of fryer grease and old carpet, like time had settled into the fibers. My coat stuck to the vinyl seat as I slid in across from her. A ceiling fan ticked overhead, slow and uneven, stirring the warm air like an afterthought.

She was already there, already composed. Lipstick was a shade too dark for her skin. A coral scarf wound tightly at her throat like a lifeline or a noose — I couldn't tell. Her makeup was immaculate, sharp like armor — blush sculpted her cheekbones, mascara thick enough to cast shadows. Not a smudge out of place. She smiled too much. Laughed at nothing. Her fingers kept drifting to her wedding ring, spinning it, like she could anchor herself with its weight.

Her nervousness was loud, all in the small, constant movements. The tremor in her spoon as she stirred her tea, though it was already cold. The way her knee bounced beneath the table, hitting the underside every so often with a muted thump.

She was already unraveling before I even spoke.

I laid bare the whole story, every buried fragment, every shattered piece. From the first Bible story in Caleb's old room to the night Nathaniel shoved me down the stairs. I laid it all out in a voice I barely recognized — too steady, too flat.

My hands vibrated, a low hum of heat just under the skin beneath the table, clenching into fists in my lap. The condensation on my water glass left rings on the table and smeared wet lines on my fingertips. My mouth was dry, my tongue thick and parched, but I didn't stop, not even when my voice splintered. Not even when the pain swelled in me like something living, clawing to be let out.

Tears threatened behind my lids, but I blinked them back, holding on until the last word.

When I finished, she sat back — slowly — like I'd just told her a ghost story. Like I'd spoken in a language only half-familiar. Her eyes skimmed mine with the vacancy of someone trying to find the right station on a broken radio.

Then, she shook her head.

As if I'd told her the sky was green.

As if gravity had changed direction.

"That never happened," she said, just like that.

Her voice was flat. Final. Not angry — not yet—just exhausted. Like she'd been holding her version of the story so tightly for so long, it had fossilized inside her.

I waited. Waited for her face to soften. For her voice to waver. The "*Maybe I just didn't see it.*"

But it never came.

"I would've known," she added, her tone matter-of-fact, like she was explaining basic arithmetic. "I lived in that house. I would've seen something."

"You did," I whispered. It burned to speak, but I continued, "You helped cover it up. The stairs. The story. You told the doctor—"

"I told the doctor what I was told. What I saw," She snapped. Her smile was gone now, replaced by something hard and flat. Her fork clinked against the plate as she set it down, her hand twitching. "And if this really happened, why didn't you say something back then? Why wait until now?"

"Because I was a child," I said, the words tearing from my throat. "Because I was scared. Because I didn't even know how to name it. I was taught to obey. To forgive. To pray harder. You always said family came first — but you never meant me."

She scoffed. A bitter, wounded sound. "That's not true."

"It is," I said. "You taught me how to stay quiet without ever saying the words. You taught me how to smile through pain so no one would ask questions."

Her eyes narrowed. She sucked in a breath like she'd been slapped. "You don't know what you're saying."

"I do," I said. "I remember the way he locked the door. The way he smiled like God approved. I remember your heels on the floorboards. You stopped. You hesitated. And then you walked away."

Her gaze dropped. Jaw tight. Her hand wrapped around her water glass, squeezing like she wanted it to shatter.

"That's not fair," she said at last. "You don't understand the pressure we were under. Nathaniel was — he *is* — a good man. A father. A leader. Do you know what this would do to the church? To your father's legacy?"

I flinched. Her words hit like stones thrown through stained glass.

"There it is," I said. "You care more about the church than your daughter. About his reputation, than what I lived through — all the pain I still feel, that might ease if I stop burying it."

"He is a Pastor," she said, her voice rising, sharp and strained. "He lives to serve. People *look up* to him. He is above reproach. You don't get to tarnish a life like that without proof."

"I'm not trying to tarnish anything," I said, leaning forward, voice low and shaking. "I'm trying to survive it. You say he's above reproach — but what does that mean? That no one like him *could* do something like this? Or that no one would *believe it* if I spoke?"

She looked away. The lines around her mouth deepened.

"You were always so sensitive," she murmured, quieter now. "So impressionable. You had nightmares, remember? You used to wake up screaming. You said the shadows talked to you. Maybe your mind just... rewrote something. Maybe that's what this is."

"My mind didn't rewrite anything," I said. "I lived it. I bled from it. I lost years to silence. I have the scar tissue and constant, unending pain to prove it."

Her expression twisted — not with disbelief, but something murkier like fear curdling into defensiveness.

"Think about your siblings," she said suddenly. "Think about what this would do to them. To Caleb. To Etta and Faith. They adore him. They always have. You're not just burning a bridge — you're lighting the whole family on fire."

"I'm not the one who struck the match," I said. "I've just been choking on the smoke."

"You're confused," she whispered. Her voice shook now, barely audible above the clatter of dishes in the kitchen. "You must be. You have no idea what you're doing."

"Yes, I do," I said. "For once in my life, I do."

Her voice dropped again, calm and measured, like a courtroom verdict. "You're asking me to believe something that, if true, would ruin everything I've ever known. Everything we stand for. Everything he built."

I met her gaze, not with anger, but with unflinching clarity.

"Let it burn," I said, tears rising. "Let the whole damn legacy fall if it means I can finally breathe." Then, softer, as I felt my shirt soak through with emotion, I added, "Maybe it needs to be ruined," I said. "If it's built on this."

She blinked rapidly, as though the air itself had turned on her. Her napkin was in her lap, now twisted into a rope in her hands.

"I need proof," she said, crossing her arms like a gate slamming shut. "You can't just say things like this and expect me to turn my life upside down. Memory is tricky. You saw a — a shaman, right? Maybe he—"

"I've never seen a shaman," I cut in. "I'm seeing a *therapist*. No one gave me these memories. This is my life. My pain. My truth."

"I didn't say you were lying," she replied, voice icy again. "I said you were wrong. There's a difference."

"No," I said, standing. The vinyl seat squeaked beneath me, loud in the hush between us. "There's a mother who believes her daughter, and one who doesn't. That's the only difference that matters now."

She neither spoke nor met my gaze. Just stared through me, lips parted like she might say something, but never did.

I walked out.

The cold air hit like a slap, sudden and sharp. I didn't even make it to the parking lot. I leaned against the side of the building, the brick rough against my spine, and I cried.

Not because she didn't believe me.

But because some part of me, some foolish, flickering part, still hoped she would.

* * * * *

Therapy didn't fix me. Not in some movie-like, full-circle way. But it gave me *language*. Breath.

Dr. Ellen Matthews had a calmness that made me feel safe just being in her office. She never flinched when I told her the hard things, and she never looked away.

She told me I wasn't broken. That trauma rearranges the brain. Surviving is a strength. I didn't believe her at first. But I kept showing up.

I started building something that looked like a life, a real one. I found work I didn't hate. I made new friends, people who didn't know the whole story but loved me anyway. Faith and Malie were still my anchors. We led busy lives, but both my closest friend and my beloved sister always picked up.

And still... I kept trying with my mother.

It wasn't logical. Even Dr. Ellen said so.

But it wasn't about logic. It was about the small, desperate part of me that still wanted a version of her I never had. A mother who would say, "*I'm sorry. You were brave. I believe you.*"

But her face always tightened when I walked into a room. She never said it, but I could feel the disapproval in my lungs like smoke, cruel and suffocating.

* * * * *

[AGE 23 — Shepherd House]

The second time, almost a year later, I brought her a medical report.

It was from Dr. Harmon, who had paused mid-exam one afternoon, her latex gloves cold and clinical against my skin. She looked up gently and asked, *"Has anyone ever hurt you down there?"* She already knew. Scar tissue doesn't lie. She documented everything. It was all there, in black and white.

I slid the folder across the kitchen table. The laminate surface was worn, edges curling. A chipped teacup sat beside her, half full of tea gone cold. We were alone. No restaurant chatter to soften the edges. Just the hum of the fridge and the lemon cleaner clinging to the air like a memory no one asked for.

She didn't touch the papers.

"Scars don't name names," she said quietly, her eyes fixed on the dark swirl in her cup.

"They tell *my* story," I replied.

"They tell *a* story," she countered. "You had accidents as a child. I remember them."

"Do you remember who pushed me down the stairs?"

Her head snapped up. There it was — that flicker. Offense. Fear. Calculation. "Don't start that again," she said. "You wrapped yourself in a blanket. You wanted to fly. Your father helped you up. He held you all night."

"No. He cried for show. And you told the doctor I jumped."

"You did."

"I wasn't that kind of kid. I wasn't brave or foolhardy. I wasn't a risk taker. I had enough pain, even at thirteen, I never would have wrapped myself up in a blanket and hopped off the stairs. I even asked my sisters — they agree. That wasn't me."

Silence.

Thick. Unbreathable. The kind that fills your mouth with the taste of metal and fury.

"You wanted proof. My medical records show I was raped. I just wanted you to know that."

"I now believe *someone* did something to you," she said slowly. "But it wasn't your dad." Then, reaching unquestioningly for anything to hold onto: "Remember, there were a lot of pedophiles that lived around our home."

I stared at her.

Mouth agape.

"And <u>who</u> brought pedophiles into and around our home?! You and Nathaniel rented to felons. Abusers. You called it evangelizing. What about <u>protecting your own children</u>?!" I let out a sob, not bothering to soften my words like I had always done in the past. I felt an overwhelming sense of anger, and the sadness was seeping out of every pore of my body.

She stood abruptly, chair legs screeching across the tile. Walked to the sink. Picked up a clean glass. Rinsed it. Again. And again. Water poured over her fingers like absolution she hadn't earned.

"I don't know what you want from me." She said, her voice small. "If I say it happened, what then? The church falls? Your father's name is ruined?"

"I lose a mother every time you say it didn't," I whispered. "I just want you to stop telling me that you'll pray I find out who did this to me. It pierces my heart every single time."

She didn't turn around.

* * * * *

[AGE 24 — Coffee Shop]

The third time, after waiting a year, I brought her a letter.

We met in a coffee shop tucked into a quiet corner of town — the kind of place where the music played low, and people spoke like they were afraid to break something. Rain tapped at the windows, soft and persistent. Outside, the sky was the color of wet slate. Inside, everything smelled of cinnamon, espresso, and worn pages. The wooden chairs creaked beneath even the gentlest shifts, and the fogged-up windows held our reflections in soft blur, like half-finished memories.

My hands were cold. I gripped my mug like an anchor — chipped ceramic, warm beneath my fingers, grounding me in the present as a hollow ache bloomed behind my collarbone.

The letter was folded neatly in my bag. Handwritten. Ink smudged in places from where my fingers trembled. It was from Sister Geneva, one of the oldest members of our childhood church. Her handwriting looped like ivy across the page. Crooked, but careful.

"I always felt something was wrong with the way he looked at you," it read.

"I never said anything. I'm sorry. You deserved to be safe."

I passed it across the table like it was something sacred — a paper relic, a sliver of truth outside my voice. I didn't speak. Just pushed it toward my mother with both hands and held my breath.

She took it delicately, like it might stain her skin. She read in silence, lips pressed tight, her eyes flicking across the page once... then again. She folded it slowly — a practiced precision — and set it gently on the table between us like a receipt she didn't want.

"She's old," she said at last. "Probably confused. People want to feel useful again."

The Italian soda in my gut turned bitter as I processed her words.

"And people want to protect a lie," I said, my voice low, tight. "You cover his sins like it's holy. Like nothing rotten ever happened behind those sermons and Sunday suits."

Her nostrils flared. "Don't you dare talk about your father that way. He is a righteous man. A man of God."

"He uses God's name like camouflage," I said. "He wrapped his violence in scripture, and you helped him fold the edges."

"You're in pain," she said, smoothing the sleeve of her blouse like it was her only defense. "But that doesn't give you the right to destroy a man's name."

"I'm not destroying anything," I said. "I'm telling the truth. If that truth ruins him — that's on him."

Her voice cracked then, just slightly. "It wasn't him. He loved you. He would never—"

Each word landed like a slap.

Quiet. Icy. Final.

My throat ached with words I couldn't make her hear. The air between us thickened with things unspoken, years of silence compressed into one table-length of grief.

Still, I sat there. Silent.

Because this is the worst kind of pain:

When someone looks you in the eye and tells you the thing that broke you never happened.

* * * * *

[AGE 25 — *Shepherd House*]

The fourth time was the last.

No letters. No documents. No witnesses.

Just me.

We sat on the porch of the Shepherd house, the old retreat center they'd turned into a haven for "healing." The wooden planks beneath our feet moaned with age. A warm dusk settled over the landscape like a worn blanket. The sky had been bleeding out light for an hour, deepening from gold to bruised purple.

A single moth threw itself over and over at the porch light above our heads, spiraling in drunk, frantic loops, desperate for warmth that would burn it.

She sat with her hands folded in her lap, knotted like prayer. Her wedding band caught the fading light, dull and worn. She looked smaller than I remembered — not in body, but in presence. Like someone time had weathered thin.

My hands rested on my thighs, palms flat, and knees steady. I focused on the feel of the wood beneath me — the rhythm of my breath. The ache blooming behind my ribs.

"I just want you to believe me," I said. The words fell into the air like offerings. Simple. Bare. Nothing left to prove.

She didn't turn. Just kept her gaze trained on the tree line, on the slow unraveling of day.

"I believe *you* believe it," she said.

A pause stretched between us, long and aching. "That's not the same."

Silence settled like dusk.

Thick. Solemn. Final.

"Say it," I whispered. My voice was raw, a thread pulled too tight. "Say you believe me that it wasn't my fault. That you're sorry."

The moth struck the light again. The porch boards creaked.

Still nothing.

Then, quietly — so quietly I almost missed it: "I can't," she said. "If I believe you... Everything I've built falls apart. My faith. My marriage. My memories. I can't lose everything. I've already lost too much." Her voice broke there — just a crack.

I nodded. Once. Sharp and slow. I stood. My chair scraped against the wood, not loud, but loud enough to feel like something tearing open.

I didn't say goodbye.

I drove home with both hands locked on the steering wheel, knuckles white, mournful. The night swallowed the road ahead of me like it was trying to keep me from going forward. But I kept driving.

And when I got home, I didn't let it out right away. I brushed my teeth. Changed clothes. Fed the cat. Sat on the edge of my bed.

Then I lay down and cried into a pillow already soaked in a hundred other heartbreaks. Not wailing and not gasping. Just quiet, gutted sobs that shook my shoulders and dampened the silence.

After that, I walked away from both Pastor Nathaniel and Martha. Stopped calling them 'Mom' and 'Dad.' Each time I slipped up and said their parental titles when talking about them, it felt like a jagged knife wound that never healed. I needed to step back from both of them.

Walking away wasn't just survival. It was reclaiming myself from the shadows they cast.

For my health.

For my safety.

For my life.

CHAPTER 14
The False Prophet's Funeral

[AGE 27 — Weber House]

Then Nathaniel died two years after I shunned them. Complications from Parkinsonism. Quick. No time for goodbyes — not that I wanted one.

When I first got the news, relief washed over me. Then guilt followed — sharp and nauseating. I felt wrong for feeling relief, the same way I had when Blake died. It's a horrible thing to feel when someone passes, but I couldn't help it. The weight he had placed on me, the fear he had instilled in me, was finally gone.

But then came the shame. The internal struggle. *Am I a terrible person for not mourning my father?*

I prayed. I asked for peace. And eventually, I realized it was okay to feel what I felt. He had been a monster in my life — the "big bad," like the villains on TV. Of course, I felt relief. He couldn't hurt me anymore. Not again. Not ever.

Still, I didn't want to be seen as someone *glad* he was gone. I didn't want to be the one to shatter the image others had clung to. It was easier to keep that part of me locked away.

I hadn't seen Martha in two years — not since I laid my truth bare before her for the last time, and she refused to believe it. And now, I was about to see her... at *his* funeral.

* * * * *

[AGE 27 — *Grace Harbor Fellowship – The Funeral*]

I shouldn't have gone.

The moment my hand touched the cold brass handle of the church door, something in me recoiled — like a wire drawn too tight. The smell of old hymnals and polished wood crept out into the morning air like a warning. It was the same smell from my childhood: dust and lemon oil, coffee in Styrofoam cups, the faint sting of bleach from the bathroom sinks, and something else; something more sour, more human, something that clung to trauma like mildew to damp walls.

If it happened today, I wouldn't have gone. Or maybe I would — but I wouldn't go quietly. I'd walk in like a storm breaking across the sea, fists clenched around truth like shattered glass. I'd rip the illusion apart.

But instead... I sat. Silent. Still.

The sanctuary was cloaked in a hush too reverent to be real. Mourners moved like shadows through the soft amber light filtering through stained glass — blue and blood-red panels casting holy shapes on the floor tainted by the shadow of memory. Every word spoken hovered in the air too long, suspended like incense smoke — gentle, fragrant lies curling up toward a ceiling that had seen too much.

People whispered about how great he had been. How much he had done. For the church. For the community. For them.

I wanted to scream.

I wanted to claw their words out of the air and crush them in my hands — show them the man beneath their golden image, the one with breath that stank of rage and sweat, whose kindness was currency and cruelty, indistinguishable from one another.

He had worn his mask so well, smiling, benevolent, measured, that it had hardened into legend. To them, he was a monument. A patriarch. A shepherd of souls.

To me, he was a wound that never scabbed over.

Each praise — "His generosity," "His wisdom," "His steadfast faith" — landed like a slap across my face, so sharp it nearly turned my vision white.

The funeral was a contradiction wrapped in tradition: sacred silence and polished lies. It didn't matter how many therapy sessions I had survived, how much distance I had placed between then and now — no mental preparation could have braced me for this kind of unreality.

Outwardly, Nathaniel was the celebrated Pastor, the stalwart of Grace Harbor Fellowship, the smiling man in every photo who "touched so many lives." People loved him. They adored him in a way that made nausea claw up my esophagus, a furious, choking presence I couldn't swallow back.

Their voices echoed through the sanctuary like hymns, thick with devotion.

And me? I was just one more figure in the pews, a ghost in a black dress, clutching the armrest to keep my hands from shaking. I listened as layer upon layer of admiration was stacked like bricks — a mausoleum of myth, sealing him in reverence forever.

But I had seen what they hadn't.

He wasn't just flawed.

He was dangerous.

Predatory. Manipulative. Controlled by a fury that was never loud in public, but always near. A man who knew how to weaponize charm and wrap his violence in scripture. Nathaniel did what he wanted because he believed God approved of it.

They didn't know about the bruises — the kind you couldn't see — or the real ones, either. They didn't know about the nights I locked my door and still didn't sleep. Or the times I had to smile while eating meals I'd been screamed into preparing. They didn't know about the cars he had illegally flipped to sell, or the toxic waste he had dumped in ravines, or the things he said when no one but I could hear him.

They didn't know the venom behind his "love." They didn't know love shouldn't hurt that much.

None of that made it to the pulpit.

None of that stained the eulogies.

They praised a fiction, and I was the only one awake in a dream made of soft music, florals, and lies.

From the pew beside me, I heard the low grumble of Caleb's voice.

"Saint my ass." My brother's tone was rough, bitter, barely contained. The sharpest edge of his pain cut through the quiet. He had been in jail for months now, caught in a spiral of drugs and a violent episode that nearly ended in tragedy. Attempted murder, they said, but I knew the darkness he'd fought beneath it all. His trauma had swallowed him whole. He was allowed to attend the funeral, but then it was right back to jail… for at least another thirty or so years.

Etta's hand found mine, fingers tight and trembling. She leaned in, voice low, steady in a way that grounded me. "He wasn't a saint. But he was our father. And I don't know how to feel about any of this." Her words were careful, vulnerable. Etta, always the peacemaker, caught between love and pain, truth, and grace.

Faith, sitting close by, whispered fiercely, almost like a prayer turned weapon. "He hurt us all. In ways no one else saw. And he still holds us hostage, even now." Her eyes burned bright — a mix of grief and fury, raw and real.

I swallowed hard. "Yes," I said quietly. "He was a false shepherd. Not the man they pretend to mourn. But this place… this silence… It's what lets the story stay buried."

Caleb shifted, voice cracked but loud enough for the nearest pews to catch,

"I tried to fight the shadow he left behind. Got lost instead. Maybe that's what happens when you grow up in his house — the only way out is to go through fire." He looked away, voice softer now. "I'm still fighting."

Etta's breath caught, tears welling. "We all are. In our ways."

Faith reached over, her small hand covering mine again, fierce in its tenderness. "But we're still here. And we're still standing."

The minister's voice rose again, offering prayers and scripture that felt hollow. I glanced around — the faces glowing with grief and reverence — and felt alone in the middle of a crowd.

But at least, I wasn't alone here.

My siblings were with me, wounded, fragmented, but unyielding.

And together, we held onto the parts of ourselves that Nathaniel had tried to break.

* * * * *

I couldn't speak up. Not there. Not in that church — a place that had stifled me at every turn. A place that had fostered its own share of abuse, from Sunday mornings to high school hallways.

What would it even change? The people there had already built their image of him. And shattering it would only bring more pain to my siblings, to my mother, even to my unborn son, and it was such a miracle that I was pregnant at all.

So I sat there as my body clenched and refused to let go with each heart-breaking lie that washed over me.

"He was a man of God."

"He was a saint."

"He was a pillar of the community."

To me, he was the man who had torn my life apart, shaped me in disfiguring ways that caused almost all, if not all, of my very intense medical issues, even to this day.

* * * * *

They didn't know the version of Nathaniel I knew.

They never saw the monster.

His cruelty wasn't confined to me. It bled into everything he touched. His "help" always came with strings. His "faith" was a weapon. His presence was suffocating, his silence loud with threat. Even his love was just control dressed in benevolence.

People praised him as generous, wise, and godly. They said he was always there to help, just a call away. That he "sacrificed" for his family. That he "kept the faith."

And all I wanted to do was scream, *"No. You didn't know him. You didn't see what he did to me!"*

I remember someone saying, "Your father was a good man. A devoted husband and father."

Devoted? To *what*? To keep me in line? Making me afraid of my own shadow?

"Such a wise man," another said. "He always knew what to say."

Yes. He did. That was the terrifying part. He knew *exactly* what to say to twist your thoughts, to make you doubt yourself, to keep you quiet. That wasn't wisdom. That was precision; cruelty in disguise.

Each word they spoke was a dagger.

The room felt smaller by the minute. Shrinking. Walls closing in as the panic hijacked even my smallest movements. The gnawing returned.

No one in that room had ever seen him lose control. No one had seen the hours of silent rage, the threats, the punishments, the half-naked "practices," the stare that could make your blood freeze.

I had.

And yet they kept talking.

"He helped me fix my car."

"He gave so much."

"He was a man of honor."

"A reflection of Christ."

Christ? Christ didn't terrorize his children. Christ didn't wrap cruelty in prayer.

* * * * *

The minister's voice softened as the hymns began again, gentle and practiced. But the words felt distant, like echoes behind a thick glass.

Caleb shifted beside me, eyes scanning the room like he wanted to tear it all down. "I don't get it," he muttered low. "How can they just sit here, pretending none of it happened? Like, Dad was some man of God. Like we're the bad ones for breaking."

Etta squeezed my hand. "It's the story they want to tell, Caleb. It's easier for them to believe the mask."

Caleb's laugh was bitter. "Easy for them, yeah. Not for us. I got locked up trying to escape it. Tried to drown the pain in whatever I could find. Almost lost me forever."

Faith's voice was sharp, cutting through the quiet. "You weren't lost. You were fighting. And you're still fighting." She glanced at Caleb, her eyes fierce but full of something soft beneath it all. "We all carry scars. Yours just got louder."

Caleb's gaze dropped, voice raw. "Sometimes I wonder if that's what Dad wanted. To break us. To watch us fall apart. To prove he was the only one who mattered."

"That's the worst kind of cruelty," I whispered. "To turn your family into enemies, to use fear like a weapon."

Etta's eyes glistened. "I used to pray he'd change for years. But it never came. And now, here we are — pretending to mourn a man none of us truly knew."

Faith swallowed hard, voice trembling just a bit. "I don't think any of us can mourn the man he was. But we can mourn what we lost because of him. Our childhoods. Our innocence."

Caleb nodded slowly, almost in agreement. "And whatever chance I had to be different got swallowed up by that house. I'm sorry I wasn't stronger. For all of you."

"No one's blaming you," I said, voice firm. "We all made it out in our own way. And we're still here. That counts."

The final hymn wrapped the room in a soft, somber melody. The Preacher's voice rose again, blessing the congregation, speaking of peace and forgiveness — words that felt far away.

Faith whispered, "Maybe forgiveness is for us, not him."

Etta exhaled deeply, a fragile smile breaking through. "Maybe it's how we finally heal."

Caleb wiped a hand across his face, a glint of something like hope breaking through the haze. "I want to believe that."

I looked at my siblings — battered, bruised, but unbroken. For the first time in years, I felt a flicker of something I thought I'd lost: belonging, not to a family of saints, but to a family that survived.

I then glanced around at all the faces of those who didn't have a clue; all the people smiling, mourning a man they thought they knew. And all I could see was the mask — the flawless, polished mask he had worn his whole life.

They never saw the cracks.

Never saw what hid beneath.

But I had. I still did.

I wanted to rip the illusion apart, to make them see. But I couldn't, not without tearing apart what little was left of my family, not without burning everything to the ground.

Let them grieve the man he *pretended* to be.

I didn't weep for Nathaniel.

I cried for the little girl who had to stand there in silence.

For the woman who still bore the weight of his shadow.

And as the final prayer was said, as they honored a man who never deserved it, I made a silent vow: *I know who he really was. And I will never forget.*

Let them keep their stories.

I have mine.

* * * * *

[AGE 33 (Now) — Grocery Store]

Even years after the funeral, people still approached me, in random grocery stores and such, with the same stories — reverence for the man I had known as a monster.

"Your father was a saint," they would say. "A man of great faith."

Each time, it felt like a new wound, a fresh stab. It enraged me, but there was nothing I could do about it. Speaking out would tear everything apart. It would hurt people I loved. So, I held my tongue, let them believe their lies, and carried the truth alone.

I couldn't change how the world saw him. But I knew who he really was. And in the end, that had to be enough.

Over the years, I've learned it's okay to grieve the father I should have had — the mother I needed. A long time ago — around the time I finally grasped the full extent of what had been done to me — I chose not to tell everyone. I shared my story only with a few trusted friends, my husband, and my therapists. Not for Nathaniel's sake — I owed him nothing. But Martha was my mother. And I loved her, despite everything.

Even when I didn't know whether she had known about Nathaniel's abuse, I still felt compelled to protect her. All she had left was her family and her reputation. If I had gone public with what Nathaniel had done, it would have destroyed her. She would have been labeled the wife of a pedophile, and I knew that would break her more than his death ever could.

The cost of exposing him felt too high. So I kept quiet for her.

I thought his death would end my trauma, so that I could finally breathe. But I was wrong. People still recognize me. Nowadays, they even say, "Your son looks just like him."

No, he <u>doesn't.</u>

It takes everything in me to will the tears away when well-meaning people speak of Nathaniel's generosity, his joy, his faith. Every compliment is a fresh laceration.

Sometimes, I blame myself. I could have spoken out earlier — when I first started remembering, or after he died. But what good would it have done? It wouldn't undo the past. It would only bring more pain to my mother, to my siblings, and to my child, who would grow up with the legacy of those revelations. It seemed easier to keep it contained. I confided in those who could handle the weight.

Eventually, medical records, evaluations, and therapy confirmed everything. The memories weren't false. The evidence was indisputable. I could stop pretending.

But that's when it started.

"I need to say something," my mother told the Pastors at the church Nathaniel once led. "People are trying to destroy a good man's name. My husband was a man of faith. A man of honor. I won't let him be remembered as a monster."

My friend, who was present, almost rolled her eyes but stayed to listen.

"There's so much talk about 'trauma' and 'false memories' these days," my mother went on. "The devil confuses people. It's in the Bible. Even family can be used to destroy. We need to pray for those who are lost. Pray they come back to the truth."

By the end, she was crying. The kind of tears that win sympathy. The kind people believe. Maybe she couldn't admit the truth — because if she did, she'd have to reckon with her silence too.

It seemed some in the church did believe her.

One woman messaged me directly. She asked how I could do this to my mother — how I could tarnish a good man's memory to "make a name" for myself.

I didn't respond. Not right away.

For a while, I wanted to hide. It's one thing to be disbelieved in private. It's another to be discredited publicly. To watch your pain become slander. To see a community gather around your abuser's grave and call him holy.

But then, something unexpected happened.

People began to reach out.

Not everyone. Not loudly. But some — quietly. Carefully.

"I believe you."

One woman sent an email late one night. She'd always felt something was off. She'd seen things she couldn't explain. She was sorry.

Others followed. Slowly. Gently.

And I realized something: I didn't need everyone to believe me. I didn't need my mother's permission to tell the truth.

Because I survived.

Because I knew.

Because the truth doesn't require validation to be real.

At first, I didn't expect the Pastors to listen. This was the same church that once called Nathaniel "a man of God." The same pulpit where my mother had wept for him, her grief polished and rehearsed.

But time had passed. A new generation had come. Some elders had quietly stepped away. And when I asked to speak — really speak — they didn't shut the door.

They listened.

It wasn't easy. They asked hard questions — not to challenge, but to gain a deeper understanding. They didn't offer sermons or easy answers: only silence, and grief, and a readiness to hear the truth. Not just for me, but for others they now suspected might be sitting silently in their pews, hiding invisible wounds.

I left that night feeling sick from everything I had relived — but also with a strange, new clarity. A sense that true healing might be possible. Perhaps I can help others as I have helped myself.

I found a women's group that met quietly in a different church. No titles. No pressure. Just tea, chairs, and a box of tissues that we kept refilling. At first, we were few. Then more came. Some spoke loudly. Others barely whispered. Some didn't speak at all — not at first. But we all came with stories etched deep in our bones.

We talked about trauma — how it rewires your brain. We talked about survival as something sacred. We read scripture — not the verses used to shame, but the ones that gave breath: *You are fearfully and wonderfully made. The truth will set you free. The Lord is close to the brokenhearted.*

I began to share my story there.

Not to shock. Not to preach. Just to be heard. And in speaking, I found peace — not the kind that comes from forgetting, but the kind that comes from being known.

They never asked for proof. They didn't need it.

And each time a woman came to me afterward — shaking, tearful, whispering, "Me too" — I began to understand:

This wasn't just survival.

This was calling.

Not the calling Nathaniel had claimed for me. Not his twisted legacy. But something that belonged entirely to me.

I started writing again. First blog posts, then essays; next, a book proposal. The more I wrote, the more I healed. My voice, once silenced, grew strong — and it didn't just belong to me anymore. It belonged to every woman who had ever sat in silence, thinking no one would believe her.

I made boundaries with my mother after one final attempt to rewrite history. This time, I didn't explain. I didn't beg. I let the silence stand.

Because I didn't need her to know who I was.

I knew.

I was a survivor: a truth-teller. A woman who once locked the door against monsters — and now opens it for others trying to escape.

And every time I sit across from another survivor and say, "Me too. I believe you," I feel it again:

Not shame.

Not fear.

But purpose.

Now I use my voice for more than just remembering. I use it to protect.

To expose.

To teach.

I speak at conferences, at women's retreats, and at trauma-informed churches. I sit on panels about PTSD, medical trauma, the long tale of abuse, and how it hides in bodies for decades. I discuss how healing is not a linear process. That forgiveness doesn't mean silence. Parenting yourself is brutal when the people who raised you taught you shame, not love.

I speak about flashbacks in grocery stores. Panic attacks in bathrooms. About how your body keeps the score even when your mind tries to forget.

I use my life as a cautionary tale — not to scare, but to wake people up.

Because predators don't always look like danger.

Sometimes they wear collars.

Sometimes they carry Bibles.

Sometimes they call themselves *father*.

And titles mean <u>nothing</u>.

I say this boldly now with my whole chest.

<u>"Pastor" is not a free pass.</u>

<u>"Evangelist" is not a shield.</u>

<u>"Father" is not always a protector.</u>

A title is not a soul. It is not character. And it does not make someone worthy of trust, especially not with children.

I discuss the dangers of relying on blind faith, charisma, and how communities circle the wagons around charm instead of asking hard questions. I speak against the silence that kills — the silence I lived in for too long.

I speak for the girl I used to be. The one who thought she was alone. The one who blamed herself. The one who sat in the ER with a bleeding chin and told a lie she'd been taught, because the truth had no safe place to land.

Now, I make space for that truth.

I make space for others to speak.

And I shine a light into the darkness. Not to stir shame — but to drive it out.

To make sure no one else has to live in the shadows of someone else's sickness. To ensure that when the next child says, "This happened to me," someone is there to say, *"I believe you."*

I don't do it because it's easy.

I do it because it's right.

Because silence almost killed me. And now, I hope my voice helps save lives.

CHAPTER 15
Light Amidst the Darkness: The Birth of My Son

Now this chapter is far easier to write! There's nothing that gives me greater joy and pride than my sweet little love, my Noah.

[AGE 27 — Hospital Delivery Room; during Pandemic]

The day my son was born, something in me softened that hadn't softened in years — maybe ever.

It was like ice cracking after a long winter, like breath returning to lungs that had only ever half-filled.

Doctors dismissed the possibility. I barely dared to imagine it myself.

They'd told me my body was *inhospitable*. Inhospitable. That word haunted me like a cruel prophecy. It echoed in sterile exam rooms, in whispered conversations, in my midnight thoughts. I began to believe it — that I was a house with broken windows and buckled floorboards, unfit for life, unfit for softness. That nothing would ever grow in me, that no one would ever stay.

I tried to come to terms with it. I told myself I didn't need motherhood to be whole: a womb didn't measure that strength. But beneath that logic — beneath the grief that had turned itself into armor — a tiny hope still flickered.

Small. Soundless. Persistent.

And then, somehow, there was Noah. A pink plus sign blooming on white plastic.

A heartbeat flickering like distant starlight on the ultrasound screen.

A tiny blip of defiance that slipped through the cracks I had sealed shut.

He was my miracle. Not loud. Not flashy. But holy. The kind of miracle that walks softly. That enters in silence and remakes everything without fanfare.

But miracles, I learned, don't come easily.

Noah was born in the thick of the pandemic. Masked nurses, hushed hallways, fear thick in the recycled hospital air. The scent of antiseptic and latex gloves clung to everything. People moved like ghosts, wrapped in PPE, speaking in muffled tones behind fogged face shields.

Evander hadn't been allowed into the room at first.

We were waiting on his COVID-19 test results.

So I labored alone.

Six hours.

Six hours of masked breathing, white-knuckle contractions, and the sterile silence between surges of pain. My knuckles whitened as I gripped the bed's edges, palms raw, fingers cramped, every breath a battle.

I wasn't trying to prove anything to the world.

Not even to the doctors.

I was trying to prove something to him.

Evander.

He had once scoffed at my pain, called me weak. "Pussy," he said, when I cried during cramps. "You could never survive real labor." He laughed when he said it, but it sliced something in me — left me bleeding invisibly.

So I made a vow:

No pain medication.

No epidural.

Just breath, blood, and grit. I would bring our son into the world without flinching.

By the time they let Evander in, I was soaked with sweat, my gown sticking to my back, my body spiraling inward. I had already reached six centimeters. My pain was no longer a sharp edge — it had become a rhythm, a tidal wave crashing through me in timed intervals. I breathed through it like a mantra, like a prayer.

Ten hours in, something shifted.

The monitor beside me began to beep — faster, then erratic, then a flatline of chaos.

It didn't scream — but I did.

A nurse rushed in, checked the screen, went pale, and disappeared.

Seconds later, the room filled.

Five people — gloves snapping, scrubs rustling, voices clipped and fast.

"Noah's heart rate is dropping," someone said. "We need to get him out. Now."

Time warped.

I was still in the room, but not in it.

The overhead light felt too bright, blinding, surgical. I squinted against it, blinking through sweat.

Hands moved around me, lifting my legs into stirrups. Instruments clanged — metal on metal. I heard Evander's voice, somewhere near my feet, urgent and unsure. The pain was no longer rhythmic. It was white-hot. Unrelenting. "Push," my husband shouted.

I did.

But Noah wasn't coming.

Then came the cone — a vacuum extractor, long and medieval-looking, clamped to his tiny head. It was clinical and terrifying, and I screamed. A sound ripped from me that I didn't recognize — primal, ancient, full of fury and fear and the desperate hope that I could keep him alive.

I pushed like my life depended on it.

Because it did.

Because Noah did.

And then — like silence after a storm, like the pause between lightning and thunder — he was there.

A slippery, howling miracle was placed on my chest.

Noah Weber.

His name was a benediction on my lips.

Tiny. Warm. Real.

His skin was slick, red, and wrinkled — like he'd been swimming through stars.

His mouth opened in a cry that sounded more like protest than fear, and his eyes, oh God, his eyes fluttered open just long enough for me to catch a glimpse of the entire cosmos inside them.

And in that instant, everything dissolved.

The pain.

The pandemic.

The noise.

The fear.

Gone.

There was only him. I remember the moment the doctor placed him on my chest. It was as if time stopped — or perhaps time had opened. A thin, sacred veil lifted, and I glimpsed something eternal.

The fluorescent lights dimmed behind my tears. The hospital faded to the edges. The room hushed.

He looked up at me with those cloudy newborn eyes — unfocused but knowing. And for the first time in my life, I felt something more profound than hope.

I felt redemption.

Like all the years of pain had cracked open just wide enough to let this light in.

Like all the "inhospitable" places in me had become holy ground.

He didn't know my history. Didn't know the weight I'd carried. Didn't know the abuse, or the shame, or the silent screams in the night. He only knew one thing.

My heartbeat.

And he had followed it home.

I couldn't stop crying. Not the crying that heaves or wails. Just tears — constant and unstoppable — sliding down my cheeks, soaking the inside of my surgical mask until a nurse gently, quietly, pulled it down so I could breathe him in.

Skin to skin.

Heart to heart.

And just like that, he stopped crying.

Like he knew me. Like he always had.

The monitors beeped. Nurses moved. Evander spoke. The world returned.

But I didn't move.

There was only Noah and me.

My body was wrecked — aching, shaking, stitched, and sore. My hair plastered to my skull, salt-damp and tangled. But I was whole in a way I had never been before.

Motherhood didn't just arrive. It wrapped itself around me like light. Soft, steady, unshakable. And for the first time in my life, I didn't feel like a fractured thing trying to be loved.

I felt chosen.

Claimed.

Transformed.

Noah was not just my child. He was my resurrection. The proof that even the most wounded places in us can bloom again.

That life — true, sacred life — can emerge from ashes. From trauma. From places we were told could never hold brightness again.

He is my light. Born in darkness. And bringing me home to myself.

One heartbeat at a time.

* * * * *

The hours and days that followed were strange and dreamlike. I hardly slept. I didn't want to. I just watched him — watched his tiny hands curl, his lashes flutter, his chest rise and fall with impossible grace.

When he latched for the first time, I wept again. Not because of the pain. Because of the wonder.

"I want to be a good dad," Evander said, rocking Noah with trembling arms. I wanted to believe him. For Noah's sake. For mine.

But I'd learned not to trust words. Not unless they were backed by action.

Still, motherhood has had an impact on me. It healed parts of me I didn't know were wounded. It made me brave. Soft and fierce all at once. It taught me that I could be the safe place I never had. That I could be enough.

Even if no one else showed up, even if Evander never became the man he promised to be.

Noah was here.

And with every breath he took, I remembered: *My body is not broken. It has made magic.*

For all the warnings and heartbreak I'd carried about my fertility, for all the late nights I'd wept quietly into my pillow believing I'd never get to hold a child of my own, there he was. Tiny. Fragile. Fiercely alive. My son.

A blessing wrapped in pink wrinkled skin and impossibly small fingers that curled around mine like he'd been waiting for me his whole life.

* * * * *

[AGE 27-28 — Weber House, Noah 0-1]

The first months to a year were a blur of late-night feedings and sunrises through half-closed blinds. My world shrank to the size of Noah's face — his sleepy sighs, the tiny grip of his fingers around mine, the sweet, milky scent of his head pressed against my chest. Time moved differently. Softer. Slower. And every moment with him felt sacred.

I'd wake before dawn, his warm little body curled against me like a comma in the middle of my sentence. Sometimes I'd stare at him, this little gift who had chosen me. His eyes would open and search for mine — not with desperation, but with trust. Complete, wordless trust. Like he knew I'd always be there. Like he believed I could hold the whole sky up if I had to.

And the strange thing was, with him in my arms, I could.

I talked to him constantly. About the dishes I needed to wash. About the book I was reading, about the dreams I used to have, and the ones that were reshaping themselves now around him.

He'd coo and babble in response, a little symphony of sound that became our private language. I sang to him, too — old hymns, lullabies, whatever I could remember through the haze of exhaustion. Sometimes, just humming, my lips pressed gently to his forehead.

He was my joy. My purpose. My tether to the present moment when everything else felt like it was fraying.

Evander tried.

In his own way, he tried.

He'd bounce Noah on his knee for a few minutes in the evening, call him 'buddy' and 'little man,' try to make him smile. He'd make a bottle once in a while — usually after I asked three times. Sometimes he'd come into the nursery while I rocked Noah to sleep and say, "You're such a natural," with this glazed smile like he was observing a scene from a movie instead of living in it.

But when Noah cried at 3 a.m., it was I who rose from bed.

When Noah was teething and feverish and wouldn't sleep unless he was on my chest, it was I who paced the living room floor, whispering soothing nonsense into the dark.

When I hadn't showered in two days, when my body still ached from labor, when I just needed fifteen minutes to breathe, Evander was busy. With work. With errands. With himself.

He loved Noah, I know he did. I think he may have even loved the idea of being a father. But the doing of it? The daily, thankless, sacred work of raising a child? That was left to me.

At first, I made excuses for him. He didn't know how. He wasn't raised with softness. He needed time. But the truth crept in, quiet and sharp: he was choosing not to show up. Not fully. Not when it was hard. Not when it was inconvenient.

So I carried it. All of it.

I didn't resent Noah for that. Not even a little. If anything, I loved him more fiercely. Because I knew what it felt like to be unwanted. To be a burden. And I would never let him think that — not while I was breathing.

He'd fall asleep with his hand tucked into the neckline of my shirt, like he needed to make sure I wouldn't drift too far. And I never did. I was always right there. Watching over him, loving him more with every heartbeat.

I had a village of friends – I didn't get the chance to see them often, but I knew I had support. What saddened me is that I didn't have a partner in the ways that mattered most.

But I had Noah.

And Noah had me.

And for a long while, that was enough.

* * * * *

[AGE 28-30 — Weber House, Noah 1-3]

Noah grew in quiet marvels.

First, the slow, sturdy crawl — his palms slapping against the hardwood as he made his way toward me like I was the only lighthouse in his stormless sea. Then came the wobbly steps, arms out like tiny wings, giggling when he fell because it meant I would swoop him up and kiss his knees like they were made of gold.

His first word was "Mama."

His second was "book."

He'd toddle into the room holding a board book upside down, plop himself into my lap without invitation, and demand, "Again," before I'd even started reading. We read *Goodnight Moon* until I knew it by heart. *The Very Hungry Caterpillar. Owl Babies.* Dozens more, all soft-edged and slightly sticky from little fingers covered in peanut butter or jelly.

As his words came clearer, his thoughts came faster, and he had questions about everything. "Why do bees buzz?" "How come rain falls down and not up?" "What happens to shadows at night?" He asked each with wide, unblinking sincerity, as if the world were a puzzle he was sure I could help him solve.

And I tried. I always tried. Because being his mother wasn't just a role, it was the best part of me. He made me softer and firmer in the same breath. I was never more grounded than when I was curled next to him under a blanket, tracing the curve of his nose while he told me his dreams.

When he got upset, we worked through it together.

Sometimes he'd scream because his sock was "too itchy," or because his banana broke in half. But I didn't laugh. I knelt, eye to eye, and helped him name the feeling. "You're frustrated, huh?" I'd say gently. "That's okay. Let's breathe together."

And he would. At barely three years old, he'd pause, close his eyes, and take those big, dramatic breaths kids take when they're trying so hard to be brave. Then he'd whisper, "All better now," and fall into my arms like I was the safest place in the world.

But even then, he knew.

He knew.

Evander loved him. I don't doubt that. He lit up when Noah walked into the room, always ready with a silly nickname, a snack, or a new toy he'd bought on a whim. They'd sit side by side watching cartoons, sharing trail mix from a mixing bowl. Evander would ruffle his hair, laugh too loudly at things a three-year-old didn't understand.

But he didn't play with Noah. Not really.

No pillow forts. No pretending to be dinosaurs. No messy painting in the yard. He wasn't the one who read the bedtime stories or wiped the tears after nightmares. He wasn't the one who noticed when Noah had outgrown his shoes or needed a haircut.

Evander was the fun parent — the vending machine for toys and treats.

And the older Noah got, the more he noticed. Not the absence of presence, but the presence of absence.

* * * * *

[AGE 32 — Weber House, Noah 3 ½]

One afternoon, I found him in the kitchen stacking soup cans. He looked up and said, "Are we getting Daddy's medicine at the store today?"

I froze. "What do you mean, sweetheart?"

He pointed to an empty can on the counter and said, "Daddy drinks, he sa-did."

My heart cracked, quiet and clean.

A few days later, we passed an Oaken Keg on a grocery run, and he tugged at my sleeve. "Mommy, daddy drinks! Helpin' daddy feelin'?"

And there it was — bare and unfiltered in the way only a child can say it. I crouched down in the middle of the store, next to the display of seltzers and wine bottles, and pulled him close.

"No, baby," I whispered. "That's not real medicine. And you don't have to worry about Daddy's feelings, okay? That's not your job."

He looked up at me with those wide, gentle eyes — the same shape as mine — and nodded slowly. But I could tell he didn't understand. Not fully. Only that something was wrong. That sometimes Daddy was loud when he shouldn't be, or quiet when it felt scary. That Daddy smelled different at night than he did in the morning. That Daddy was here... but not here.

I cried in the car with the groceries in the trunk and Noah asleep in the backseat, his stuffed giraffe tucked under his chin.

Because I had tried so hard to be the buffer. The translator. The shield. And still, still, the cracks had reached him. My bright, curious, kind boy. My small wonder. My heart with legs.

I didn't know how to fix it all.

But I knew this: Noah would always have me. For every scraped knee, every complex question, every moment he didn't have the words — I'd be there. I'd hold the line. I'd keep the door open, the light on.

Because I couldn't keep Evander from slipping away.

But I could keep Noah close.

And I would.

* * * * *

[AGE 32 — Weber House, Noah 3 ½ - Divorce Discussion]

It was late — past midnight — when I brought it up. The house was quiet, lit only by the soft amber light over the kitchen stove. I sat at the table in an old hoodie, sipping tea that had gone cold in my hands.

Evander came in from the living room, beer in hand, half-finished. His eyes were tired. So were mine.

"I think we need to talk," I said softly.

He groaned, but not cruelly — just weary. "Love, can it wait? It's been a long—"

"No," I interrupted. "It really can't."

He sat down across from me, rubbed his face, and leaned back in the chair. The silence stretched.

I swallowed hard, twisting my wedding ring with my thumb. "This isn't working. We both know it." I wanted to believe we could rebuild, but deep down, I knew some cracks ran too deep.

Evander didn't respond right away. His jaw tensed.

"I'm not saying you're a bad dad," I continued, gently. "And I know you love Noah. But what we have right now... this version of us — it's not healthy. For any of us. Especially him."

His fingers tightened around the neck of the bottle.

"He's already noticing things, Evander. Your escape mechanisms. The tension between us. He's learning what love looks like by watching us... and I don't want this to be the love he imitates."

He looked at me then — really looked — and I saw it land. The truth of it. The sadness. The defeat.

"I don't want to fight with you," I said, my voice softening. "I don't want to pretend we're okay when we're not. We aren't happy. We haven't been for a long time. We care about each other... but that's not the same as being in love."

Evander stared at the floor. "So what? You want a divorce?"

I nodded. "I think it's what's best for Noah. And for us. So we can both have a chance to improve — individually, perhaps even as co-parents. But not like this. Not under the same roof, walking on eggshells."

He exhaled, long and ragged. "... I never thought we'd be one of those couples."

"Neither did I," I whispered.

"But you're right," he finally said, voice hoarse. "I don't even recognize us anymore."

We sat in silence for a while. Not angry. Not accusatory. Just... mourning. The quiet death of a dream we'd clung to too long.

* * * * *

[AGE 33 — Mediation Office, Noah 4]

Mediation was painful.

Not in the way screaming matches are painful. But in the way sitting across from someone who used to feel like your entire world — and realizing they don't anymore — is agony.

We met in a small, neutral room with tissues on the table and a white noise machine by the door. The mediator's voice was calm, firm, and practiced. We discussed assets, parenting time, and communication plans.

"I want 50-50 custody," Evander said. "I'm not perfect, but I want to be there."

I nodded. "That's fair. He needs both of us. But he needs us whole, not pretending for his sake."

We decided on a two-week rotation, with one week with me and one with him. Noah would stay at the same school and daycare. Holidays split, birthdays shared. We mapped it all out: bedtime routines, school pickups, medical decisions. The logistics of love that's been divided.

We agreed to family counseling. To help Noah adjust. To make space for his questions, his grief.

And when it was all signed and stamped, I sat in my car and cried.

Not because I regretted it.

But because I knew it was right — and sometimes, that's the hardest thing of all.

* * * * *

[AGE 33 — Weber House, Noah 4]

Telling Noah was delicate.

We sat on the couch, Evander on one side, I on the other, Noah nestled in the middle with his beloved stuffed giraffe.

I kept it simple. "Little love... Mommy and Daddy love you very much. That's never going to change. But we've decided that we're going to live in different houses. You'll have two bedrooms. Two homes. And two people who love you more than anything in the whole world."

His face scrunched. "Did I do something bad?"

I felt my heart crack open. "No, sweetheart. Not even a little. This is a grown-up decision, and it's not your fault. Okay?"

He nodded slowly, fingers tightening around his giraffe. "Will Daddy still tuck me in?"

"Every time it's his week," I said. "And we'll still talk, even when we're not together."

He looked between us, then rested his head on my lap. "Okay. Can we read a story now?"

And just like that, life moved forward.

* * * * *

I didn't know what the future held, but I knew what I wouldn't do anymore.

I wouldn't live in a house where love meant silence or sacrifice.

I wouldn't teach my son that enduring pain was proof of strength.

I wouldn't forget myself for the sake of appearances.

Instead, I'd raise Noah to know what kindness sounds like. To trust the shape of honesty. To grow up in a home — two homes — that might not look like a fairy tale but would always feel like safety.

And maybe, someday, he'd look back and say, "My parents didn't stay together — but they stayed honest, loving, and always mine." And maybe, just maybe, he'll remember that even when everything else fell apart, there was always light in the room because he was in it.

CHAPTER 16
What I Buried Now Blooms

[AGE 33 — Prophetic Dream, Noah 4]

My turning point truly happened last year, in 2024, through a prophetic dream. In the dream, there was a mirror. I expected to see her — the woman who bends, who breaks, who says yes to survive. But the face looking back was different: still me, but firmer and softer. She held the gaze of someone who gives, not from fear, but from fullness.

The dream began with my ribs feeling too small, a cold, sharp fear that gripped me tightly. Blake and Connor were coming after my childcare. I could feel their presence, dark and threatening, like shadows creeping into the light. Everything sped up, each thud of my pulse pounding in my ears. I didn't have time to think — only to act.

I grabbed the nearest child, scooping them into my arms, their little body warm and soft against mine, the scent of their shampoo filling my senses, mixing with the smell of fresh grass from outside. "We have to go now!" I urged, my voice shaky but firm. I couldn't afford to hesitate.

I turned toward the other children, their eyes wide with confusion and fear. "Follow me, quick! We're going to be safe," I said, pushing the terror down and trying to sound brave, even though my very being was thrumming with dread. We hurried, my feet slapping against the ground, the gravel crunching beneath them. It was as if the air itself was thickening, making each step feel as though invisible chains weighed it down.

I gathered all of them — children and parents alike — into a small group. Among them were my boyfriend at the time, his kids, my mother, and others who were faceless but familiar, like people I should know but couldn't quite put a name to. They all looked to me, expectant, as if I held the answers, though I was just as lost as they were.

As I glanced around, the world felt distorted, as if it were twisting and folding in on itself. My legs wobbled from the effort, but somehow, I managed to keep it together. "We have to leave — now," I said again, though I could feel the words trembling on the edge of panic. My voice was a strange echo, muffled by the chaos around me.

And then, a voice, soft and calm, cut through the noise, stilling the panic inside. It was a motherly voice, warm and steady, like the embrace of someone who had seen the storms of life and knew how to weather them.

"God has prepared a house just for us," Lila said, her tone unwavering, as though she had already seen the end of this journey. "All we need to do is go there and accept our true identities."

Her words struck a deep chord within me, reverberating through my soul, grounding me amid the storm. The tension in my body eased, as though a weight had been lifted. I felt the pull of something greater than fear — something serene, yet powerful. We began walking together, our steps slower now, as though we were walking towards something that would change everything.

The house appeared before us, looming large on the horizon. It was magnificent — more glorious than any building I had ever seen. It seemed to shimmer and glow with a soft, welcoming light, standing untouched by the chaos that surrounded it. The scent of fresh wood mingled with blooming jasmine filled the air, carried gently on a crisp, cool breeze. The sound of birds chirping nearby seemed to echo with a soft, celestial harmony. The house felt like a place of refuge, a sanctuary from the darkness.

As we neared the entrance, I saw two doors. The door on the left was grand and polished — a path of least resistance, wide enough for anyone to walk through without challenge.

But then there was the door on the right. It was small, so small that I could barely make it out. Its roof sloped down at a severe angle, so steep that a person would have to crouch to even approach it. I felt an instinctive hesitation, my mind pulling me toward the larger door. It was obvious. It was the right choice.

But Lila, the motherly figure — a stranger radiating wisdom and calm — stopped me with a gentle touch on my arm. "That's not the right door," she said softly, her voice filled with the quiet strength of someone who knew what was coming.

I blinked, confused. "But... It's so easy. Why not go through the door right in front of us? It's the right one, isn't it?"

Lila's eyes met mine with a knowing look. "It's not the one for you."

I stared at her for a long moment, uncertainty swirling in my veins, before nodding. Reluctantly, I turned to the tiny door. The air around it felt heavier, like the very atmosphere was pushing against me. But I couldn't ignore Lila — something about her words rang true, even if I couldn't fully understand it.

"Come on," she urged, her voice steady and sure. "This is the path for you. Trust it."

So, I bent low, my knees creaking, the ground beneath me rough and uneven as I crawled forward. The children and adults followed suit, crawling on hands and knees as we made our way toward the small door. The air was thick with the scent of damp earth and pine, and my hands scraped against the cold, smooth walls of the narrow passage. Each step felt like a struggle against my doubts, but still, I kept moving.

We reached the door, and I could feel the weight of it, like it was locked in place by some invisible force. My fingers brushed against the cold, worn surface. With a deep breath, I pushed it open.

Inside, it was darker and cooler. There was no immediate light, no welcome — just a series of doors — one after another, each barely bigger than the last. A heavy, almost oppressive silence filled the space. The scent of ancient wood and a faint metallic note lingered in the air. I reached for the next door, tremors fluttering beneath my skin, involuntary and unrelenting. Each door was a little different from the last, yet they all shared one thing: they were impossibly small.

One by one, I opened them, only to find another, each growing just a fraction bigger than the last. The physical effort it took to crawl from door to door was exhausting. My body ached, and I began to wonder: *Why am I doing this?*

Turning to the group behind me, I caught their eyes. My voice came out as a hoarse whisper. "Why are we doing this? Why not just go back? Why not just go through the left door? It's right there, so easy..."

Lila, her voice still unwavering, stepped forward. "Because, my dear, that door is not for you. This is your journey. These doors are for you to discover who you are, piece by piece."

My boyfriend, standing beside me, placed a hand on my shoulder. "You've got this. It's worth it."

I nodded, not fully understanding, but knowing that there was something deeper at work here. The door in front of us opened, revealing yet another passage. This time, it felt different. The air was lighter, and the walls seemed to pulse with a kind of rhythm, as though the house itself was alive, guiding us forward.

After what felt like an eternity of crawling, I finally reached a door that stood apart from the others. It was tall and grand, yet something about it was humbling. I hesitated, my hand hovering over the handle. And when I opened it, something astonishing happened. The walls around us seemed to shift, and the doors we had passed through clicked into place, becoming part of the structure, as if they had always belonged. Each one was now part of the design, no longer just a struggle, but a piece of the whole.

Inside the house, the hallways stretched out before us, lined with doors — each one adorned with intricate pictures of people I knew: my students, my friends, my family. Each door felt like a canvas, a unique representation of the individual standing before it. Above each door was a banner that read, "Choose Your Personality/Identity."

The space was warm and alive with possibility. I could hear the gentle hum of voices behind me — children laughing, adults conversing, the air filled with the soft rustle of movement. There was a sense of peace here, as though each of us was meant to find our true selves.

I stepped back, observing, unsure of what to do. The children approached their doors without hesitation, each one finding the right fit. I watched in awe as my closest friend, her face serene, approached her door. She chose 'Prayer Warrior/Empathetic,' and the door opened easily. My boyfriend at the time picked 'Leader,' a natural fit for him. Lila chose 'Mother,' and it was clear, as if the door had been waiting for her.

But when it was my turn, I stood frozen. I had always been labeled a people pleaser. That was who I thought I was. I reached for the door marked 'People Pleaser,' confident that it would be the one I could walk through. But when I touched the handle, an error message flashed across the door: "This is not your identity. You will have to pay for this identity or choose another."

I blinked in confusion. *But that's me. That's who I am,* I thought. *Why isn't it opening?*

I stepped back, my core jackhammering. I saw my mother struggling in front of her own door. She was trying to open one marked '00 Virgin,' and the error message kept appearing. She refused to let go, even after multiple attempts had failed. But after a long time, she finally stepped back. She turned toward the left door — the easy one. I felt a pang in my chest, the sadness of seeing her leave without a word.

"You can't go back," I whispered under my breath.

Then, I saw a child — a boy, no more than seven — approach his door. He picked it confidently, and it opened easily. But instead of entering, he turned away and left the house, exiting through the left door without a word. I watched him go, confused by the finality of his choice. He had chosen correctly, yet he still left. Not out of rebellion — but perhaps he didn't yet know how to receive what was his.

Alone now, I stood before my door again. The pictures on it — images of my students, friends, and family — seemed to beckon me. I scanned the options, each one carrying its weight. Then I saw it — one word: *Nurturer.* A soft peace washed over me as I chose it. The door opened.

As I stepped through, I felt a warmth, a peace unlike anything I had known. It was like stepping into my true self, who I was always meant to be. The world around me felt lighter, my heart fuller. Joy bloomed within me, and I knew without a doubt that this was my identity, my calling, my place in Christ.

When I woke, the echo of that peace stayed with me, and I felt the Lord's voice clearer than ever:

- *Why choose a door anyone can walk out of, when I have one just for you, perfectly designed for every part of who you are?*
- *The doors you opened grew larger because they reflected your growth — from childhood to adulthood, from confusion to clarity.*
- *The identities you sought in the world were appealing, but they were not yours to claim. Some were godly, but they were not meant for you. Only the one destined for you will open.*
- *This journey with your mother may take time and space to unfold. You cannot force what isn't meant to be, and sometimes, distance is necessary for healing.*

The message was clear, and my heart was full of peace. This was more than a dream — it was a call to step into my true identity, to embrace who I was always meant to be.

In the dream, I had met a stranger who felt familiar. She didn't rush to fix. She didn't shrink to fit. She knelt beside pain, held it without fear. "I am you," she seemed to say. "Not the you shaped by fear.

The you before the pretending began." I opened my eyes and printed her name: *nurturer*. It wasn't just a dream — it was a reckoning. A vision of what I would be if I stopped living through others' expectations. I saw the truth like a film unspooling:

I was not born to please. I was born to nurture. But no one ever told me I had to nurture *myself* first.

* * * * *

When I awoke from the dream, tears were already on my cheeks — not the frantic kind, but the type that stream slowly, as if the soul itself is exhaling. The light in the room was soft and gray, dawn beginning to brush against the blinds. I lay still for a long while, my body quiet, my breath steady. The dream still wrapped around me like a blanket. I could feel it, not just remember it, as though I had returned from a place more real than anything I had lived in years.

It didn't vanish like other dreams. It stayed.

In the weeks that followed, something inside me began to shift — not loudly, not all at once, but like winter softening into spring. Quietly. Persistently. My mind kept returning to the doors. To the woman who touched my arm. To the choice I made.

Nurturer.

That word didn't just fit — it anchored me. For the first time, my identity wasn't about compliance. It wasn't about managing perceptions, diffusing other people's anger, or earning space in a room I was already standing in.

It was about becoming.

That dream was the first time I saw myself apart from my survival tactics. For so long, I'd equated kindness with submission, caretaking with worth, and patience with silence. I gave and gave and gave — until I bled dry — because somewhere along the way I had learned that was the only way to be loved. But the woman in the dream — the one who met others with compassion without losing herself — she was me. She is me.

And I think part of me always knew she was in there, buried beneath the rubble of years spent in fear, confusion, and self-abandonment.

Healing, I've learned, is not a single moment.

It's not an altar call or a sunrise or even a dream, though all of those things can be starting points. It's a thousand tiny choices. A quiet refusal to live afraid. A decision to put down the false names I was given — too emotional, too sensitive, not enough, too much — and pick up the name God whispered to me in the dark:

Nurturer.

That changed everything.

I began to rebuild.

Not perfectly. Not quickly. But faithfully.

I started with my mornings. Instead of waking up in panic, I permitted myself to wake slowly, to light a candle, to speak gratitude aloud even when I didn't feel it. I stopped starting the day with shame and began starting it with presence.

I chose to treat my body like something worth keeping. I walked gently. I fed myself real food. I let myself rest. Not collapse-from-burnout rest, but intentional rest — rest as protest. Rest as worship. Rest becoming a declaration that I am no longer a machine for other people's needs.

I opened old journals and let myself weep for the girl who wrote them. I held her words with tenderness. I didn't correct her anymore. I just listened. And in that listening, she softened. She grew quiet. She no longer needed to scream to be heard.

Therapy felt different after the dream as well. I didn't sit in the chair to recount pain — I sat in the chair to reclaim myself. I wasn't just working through trauma. I was re-parenting the child in me who had been taught to flinch from her feelings, to never name them so as not to give the devil a foothold. I learned to say no without guilt. I began noticing when I was about to change myself, and instead, I chose to stay whole.

I prayed with a different posture.

No longer begging.

No longer bargaining.

Now, simply being and sitting in the presence of a God who sees beyond the performance. Who considers the parts of me that I forget. Who whispers, "You were never too much. You were always mine."

I stopped trying to force my mother to understand. For years, I'd wanted to pull her through her own locked door, tried to shape her into someone who could name what we both lost. But the dream showed me: I can't choose her door. I can only select mine.

That realization hurt. But it also set me free.

Love doesn't always look like closeness. Sometimes, it's letting someone go, not in anger, but in peace. I'm still learning how to hold that distance with grace, to stop trying to fix what isn't mine to fix.

The healing didn't erase the past.

But it reframed it.

I stopped asking, "Why did I go through all of that?" and started asking, "What can grow from it now?"

What I buried in those years — the aching, the silence, the truth — has begun to bloom. And no, it's not always beautiful.

It's messy. Lonely. Terrifying — to live without the armor of performance. But it's real. It's rooted.

I no longer measure my worth by what I do for others. I no longer keep quiet to keep the peace. I no longer walk into rooms asking, "What do they need me to be?"

Now I ask: "What part of me gets to show up today?"

That's what the dream gave me. Not just clarity, but permission.

Permission to become.

Permission to bloom.

Permission to nurture — not just the world, but myself.

* * * * *

There are still days when I feel the old weight press in, where grief sneaks in through the seams. Moments where I want to crawl back through the easy door, to turn into the version of me that people found easier to love.

But I don't.

I remember the woman in the mirror — the one with kind eyes and a steady spine. The one who doesn't bend to be seen — she stands and sees herself. The one who gives, not from fear, but from fullness. The one who kneels beside pain and says, "You are safe with me."

That's who I am now.

And every day, I choose her again — the woman who blooms from what was once buried, fully and fearlessly.

CHAPTER 17
You Are Safe. You Are Loved. You Are Good.

If my life were a house, there would be rooms I'd rather never walk into again. But there's one room where the sun always rises. His name is Noah. Almost five years old and already teaching me what love looks like when it doesn't hurt. The first time he called me 'Mama,' something inside me broke — and healed. Not because I hadn't heard the word before, but because of the way he said it. Pure. Trusting. Like I was safe. Like *he* felt safe. In that moment, I swore to become the woman he already believed I was.

[AGE 33 — Our Home, Noah 4]

"Mommy, how come doggies got four feets but peoples only got two?"

I look up from the Lego castle we're building on the living room rug and smile. He's holding a tiny plastic knight upside-down, his hair tousled from a nap, his socks mismatched — one with dinosaurs, one with lightning bolts.

"Because if people had four legs, it would be hard to wear pants," I say.

He laughs — this high, pure, delighted sound that fills the whole room. "That's silly, Mommy! Pants would be sooo big! Like, like... elephant pants!"

We both dissolve into giggles. I grab a stuffed giraffe, his current favorite animal, and make it do a silly dance on his belly. He shrieks with laughter and curls into himself like a pill bug — safe and delighted.

My bright spot in life, my Noah. All legs and questions and peanut butter fingerprints. His laugh is wild and cheerful, like someone who doesn't know what fear is. Every time I hear it, something in me unknots.

"Mommy, look! I'm a cheetah now!"

He tears across the living room in his mismatched socks, growling through a paper towel roll, face smudged with marker whiskers.

"A very fast cheetah," I say, pretending to stumble as he zips past. "Too fast for me to catch!"

He skids to a stop, turning with wide, excited eyes. "You gotta try harder! Run fast like this!" He demonstrates in slow motion, arms flapping dramatically.

So I do. I chase him around the couch, both of us breathless and laughing, and when I finally catch him, I scoop him up and swing him high in the air. He squeals, little arms clinging to my neck, legs kicking wildly.

"I'm flyingggg!" he shouts.

"You're unstoppable," I whisper back.

We collapse onto the rug, his head resting against my chest, my fingers tracing soft circles on his back. I close my eyes and breathe. For a minute, there is no past. No echo of locked doors or bleeding chins. Just this boy. This heart. This moment.

"I like when you play wif me, mommy," he says suddenly. "You make the best voices."

I smile. "That's because I had to learn a lot of stories."

He thinks for a moment, then asks, "Can I have all your stories?"

"You can have the ones that are good for your heart," I tell him. "The ones that help you grow big and kind and strong, little love."

He nods seriously. "Okay. But I want the funny ones, too."

"Deal."

"Can we play again tomorrow?"

"Every mommy day, sweetheart," I say. "Every single mommy day."

He smiled, the kind that made his already bright blue eyes light up even more impossibly as he asked in true preschool fashion, "Do you want to guess what something? You're the beautifulest and nicest in this whole town. I want to clap you." He put his hand out for a high five, and I eagerly mimicked his motion, then pulled him into a long hug.

Because this is what healing looks like now. Not perfect. Not linear. But real. Tangible. Soft in all the places I was once hard to survive.

He is my bright spot.

Not because he saves me. I saved myself.

But because loving him is proof that it's possible to build something whole from the broken. To make a safe home. To raise a child who runs wild without fear because he's never been taught to shrink. He's witnessed a lot in his young life, but I hope and pray that the trauma will be washed clean, taking away any residual anxiety, so that he may never go through any of what I experienced, as a child and as an adult.

Every time he says Mommy, I hear it — not just as a name, but as a vow.

That the traumatic part of our story ends on a note of light.

And that it begins again, better.

My heartbeat. My safe place in motion.

Every day, I marvel at how much joy can exist in one small person. He gets up, triumphant. "See, Mommy? Told ya!"

"You are the fastest," I say, clapping. "And definitely the bravest."

He grins — vast, whole, untouched by anything dark. He has no idea how much that smile has saved me.

Later, he curls up next to me while I read his favorite book for the fifth time this week. Halfway through, he interrupts. "Mommy?"

"Yeah, sweetie?"

He reaches out and touches my cheek gently with his small, sticky fingers. "You're the best Mommy. Even when you get a little sa-did."

I blink, throat tightening. "Thank you, little love. That means everything to me."

"If you cry, it's okay. I'll stay wif you," he says, with complete, simple certainty. "Cuz you're my Mommy."

And just like that, the years fall off me. The shadows hush. I'm not the girl on the staircase, or the woman trying to convince her mother of the truth, or the survivor standing in front of strangers explaining the darkness she lived through.

I'm his mommy. That's the brightest truth of all. He reminds me, every day, that cycles can come to an end. That healing doesn't mean erasing the past, but rather ensuring it never affects the next generation. That softness is strength. That love can be loud and silly and covered in cracker crumbs.

We play. We build pillow forts and go on scavenger hunts in the backyard. We make up songs with ridiculous rhymes. I let him paint my face with washable markers and roar like a dinosaur under the dinner table.

And when I tuck him in at night, I whisper, "You are safe. You are loved. You are good."

Because no one ever said that to me when I needed it.

But he will grow up knowing.

And that, more than anything, is the proof that healing is real.

That love — true, safe, honest love — can grow in the very soil where someone once planted fear.

In a world where touch once meant harm, where love once meant control, Noah became my soft place to land. He reaches for my hand, not to take anything from me, but to hold it. To be with me. And that, more than anything, is what saved me. He was born into my brokenness, but he didn't inherit it. Noah arrived with a light so blinding it revealed every corner of the pain I tried to hide. And still, he loved me. His love didn't fix me. It invited me to start taking care of myself.

Before Noah, I thought love was something you had to earn. Something you gave in exchange for safety or a sense of belonging. Then he looked at me with those big, knowing eyes, and I realized — real love doesn't cost anything. But it gives everything. Some days, I still flinch at loud noises. Some memories don't loosen their grip easily. But when Noah laughs — from his belly, from his joy — it quiets every ghost. That sound is my sanctuary. My boy is my beginning again.

* * * * *

[AGE 33 — Our Home, Noah 4]

Motherhood became both a sanctuary and a battleground. Holding my son in my arms, I felt a profound sense of purpose and love that I had never known. His presence was a salve to my weary heart, a reminder that beauty and hope could emerge from the ashes of my past. Yet, the path to healing was yet again neither linear nor simple.

As a single mother, I faced the daily challenges of parenting while carrying the weight of my trauma. The exhaustion was palpable, and the emotional toll was significant. Yet, I found strength in the small victories: the moments of laughter, the quiet evenings spent reading together, the way my son looked at me with unconditional love. These moments, though fleeting, reminded me of my resilience and capacity for joy.

Healing was a multifaceted journey. I sought therapy, practiced mindfulness, and leaned into supportive communities. I learned to set boundaries, to prioritize self-care, and to forgive myself for not having all the answers. Slowly, I began to reconnect with the woman I could have been before trauma rewrote my DNA, rediscovering passions and interests that had long been dormant.

Divorce had shaken the very foundation of my faith. Raised in a religious community that emphasized the sanctity of marriage, I grappled with feelings of guilt and shame. I questioned God's plan for me and struggled to reconcile my experiences with my beliefs.

Yet, in the midst of my doubts, I found solace in the quiet moments of reflection. I began to explore spirituality on my terms, seeking a connection that was authentic and healing. I read spiritual texts, meditated, and engaged in conversations with others who had faced similar challenges. Through this process, I discovered a more compassionate and understanding relationship with the divine, one that embraced my imperfections and honored my journey.

The end of my marriage also meant the loss of a shared community. The church that should have been a place of comfort (though let's face it, it was more a den to house most of my trauma) now felt even more alienating. I struggled to find my place within a community that seemed to view divorce as a failure rather than a transition. "Why did you divorce him? After all, he never hit you." That hit harder than I thought it would and made me rethink going to church.

However, I discovered that community could take many forms. I found support in online groups for single mothers, in friendships with others who had experienced similar pain, and in new spiritual communities that embraced diversity and healing. These connections provided a sense of belonging and reminded me that I was not alone in my journey.

As I look to the future, I do so with a sense of hope and possibility. The road has been long and fraught with challenges, but it has also been marked by growth, resilience, and love. I have learned to trust myself, to honor my needs, and to embrace the unknown with courage.

My son continues to be my greatest teacher, showing me daily the power of unconditional love and the beauty of new beginnings. Together, we are building a life that reflects our shared values and dreams.

Healing is an ongoing process that requires patience, self-compassion, and a sense of community. I am learning to walk this path with grace, knowing that each step brings me closer to the woman and mother I aspire to be.

My relationship with my son during his toddler and preschool years was nothing short of transformative. He was my shadow, my echo, my greatest teacher. In those years, love didn't always look like warm hugs and lullabies — it looked like holding him through tantrums I didn't fully understand, carrying him on my hip while stirring dinner, singing silly songs in the car when I was too tired to speak, and laughing until tears streamed down our faces over spilled cereal or made-up words.

He was a whirlwind of life and feeling — untamed, honest, wide-eyed. And I adored him.

There was something profoundly healing about being so close to someone who hadn't learned to lie, who hadn't learned fear the way I had. He didn't shrink from me when I was quiet or distant. He didn't analyze my words or measure my worth. He just *was*. And he wanted me, no matter what version of me showed up that day. That kind of acceptance softened me.

He had this way of pulling me out of myself, even on days when the weight of the past sat heavy on my shoulders. He'd grab my hand with his tiny, messy fingers and pull me toward play, toward sunshine, toward the present moment. When I'd start to drift into old thoughts, he'd say, "Mama, look!" and point at something so ordinary it became extraordinary in his eyes — a worm on the sidewalk, a puddle shaped like a heart, clouds that looked like dragons. Through him, I began to see the world anew.

Those years weren't perfect, of course. They were messy. Sometimes painfully so. There were moments when he needed more than I felt I had to give. There were mornings when I struggled to get out of bed, and evenings when I'd lose patience more quickly than I wanted to admit.

But I kept trying.

In parenting him, I was parenting myself too, learning how to give the comfort and presence I had longed for as a child. I established routines, boundaries, and safety measures. I read parenting books and trauma recovery books side by side, scribbling in both. I apologized when I messed up. I told him I loved him a thousand times a day. I made it clear: *You are safe. You are loved. You are enough.*

And every time he rested his head on my chest and sighed with contentment, it was like a tiny piece of my soul clicked back into place.

As he grew into his preschool years, his vocabulary expanded, and so did his questions. "Where's Daddy?" "Why do people cry?" "Were you ever little like me?" Sometimes he asked hard questions without realizing it, and I had to take deep breaths before answering.

I never spoke ill of his father. That was a promise I made to myself early on. But I did talk honestly, in ways he could understand. "Daddy and I both love you very much," I'd say, "but sometimes grown-ups can't be happy together, and that's okay." And when the sadness flickered behind his bright eyes, I held him a little longer, told him he didn't need to carry any of it.

Because the truth is, I never wanted my son to inherit my trauma. I wanted to give him something better — a legacy of healing, of honesty, of emotional safety.

And I knew that began with me. There were so many moments I stored away like sacred relics:

- The way he'd fall asleep in my lap mid-sentence, trusting me completely.
- The time he brought me a wildflower from the yard and said, "It's for you, because you're my best friend."
- The morning I found him "reading" one of my therapy books, his face profoundly serious, as he flipped pages backward.
- The night he said, "I like it when you smile, Mama. It makes the room brighter."

Moments like that stitched up the holes in my heart. They were reminders that even though I hadn't chosen how my story began, I was now the author of how it would continue. And my son, my wild, thoughtful, endlessly curious little boy, was my co-writer in every sense.

* * * * *

[AGE 33 —Our Home, Noah 4]

Being a single mother felt, at first, like waking up on unfamiliar ground every day. Like I'd crossed some invisible border into a country where everything looked the same, but nothing felt the same. I still packed lunches. I still folded tiny clothes. I still brushed hair, sang lullabies, poured cereal, wiped counters, and tended to scraped knees.

But the silence after bedtime felt different. Heavier. Sometimes sharper.

Noah was almost a few months past four now — bright, imaginative, with questions that never seemed to stop and a heart as open as the sky. And while he adjusted to our new reality better than I'd expected, he still carried the confusion of it in the tilt of his head, the way his brow furrowed when he tried to piece it all together.

One night, while I tucked him in, he looked at me and asked, "Mommy... do you love Daddy?"

My airway felt narrow, but I kept my voice calm. "I love the part of Daddy that helped make you. And I always will. But sometimes, two people can care about each other and still not be good at living in the same house."

He blinked up at me. "So... you live here. Daddy lives at Daddy house. I live both?"

I smiled and kissed his forehead. "Exactly. You get the best of both of us."

"Mommy," he whispered, "I want mommy and daddy my house."

"I know," I said. "Me too, sometimes. And it's okay to feel that way. You can feel whatever you feel, and I'll always be there to listen. Always."

He wrapped his arms around my neck then and murmured, "I love our house. You the bestest mommy because you give me the bestest toys and yummy treats an' food."

I smiled, correcting gently, "Toys and treats are nice, but that's not why we love people. I love you because you're my son. I love building airports, making a fort, cuddling – I love you because you are Noah. No matter what."

After a beat, Noah beamed as he cupped my face. "I love playin' wit' you mommy. You are so beautiful, an' you play with me all day long."

And I held him like he was still newborn — because in that moment, he was. A new version of him was being born, too, just like a new version of me.

* * * * *

Single motherhood wasn't a punishment.

It was a rebirth.

Not just of my identity.

But of our bond — me and Noah, two hearts stitched together in a home where love didn't shout, or hide, or run.

It simply stayed.

And that, I realized, was enough.

* * * * *

[AGE 33 1/2 — Our Home, Noah 4 1/2]

The moment I decided to try dating again didn't feel monumental. There wasn't a sunrise or a sign from God or a dramatic pep talk in the mirror. It was quiet. Subtle. It came in the form of a single breath — one I took while folding laundry on a Tuesday night, four months after the divorce had been officially finalized. After Noah had fallen asleep, the house was dim and still. I sat there, surrounded by socks and storybooks and the faint hum of the dryer, and I just... wondered.

Was it time?

Not to replace anything. Not to chase down some fairy tale.

... to open the door a crack.

So I downloaded a Christian dating app.

And just like that, the world shifted a little. Pings. Messages. Profiles with Bible verses and awkward selfies in church parking lots. Men who called me "Queen" without ever reading a word I'd written. A few were overly bold, others painfully shy.

I was overwhelmed. Flattered. A little nauseous. But also curious.

I decided to be honest in my profile. Said I was a single mom. A teacher and writer. That Jesus mattered to me, but so did therapy, boundaries, and genuine apologies. I wrote that I'd survived things I don't joke about and was rebuilding a life that felt true. I posted a picture of me with ink on my fingers, Noah's hand in mine. I didn't try to sell a version of myself that wasn't real.

And maybe that's why the response surprised me.

Dozens of messages poured in, some thoughtful, others... not. I skimmed. Scanned. Laughed. Ignored. Replied.

When my book signing came up, I impulsively invited three men who had actually read my messages and seemed sincere. I figured it was a safe, public setting — no pressure. Just see what happened.

Two came.

One stayed longer.

His name was Micah.

He was a single father of two — an eight-year-old and a preschooler. He wore a button-down shirt that still had creases from the dryer, and he smiled like he hadn't smiled that way in a long time. His laugh was soft. Gentle. The way he looked at me when I talked about my writing made something flutter in my chest — something light, something hopeful.

During the signing, bravely in front of a group of friends, and even my mother and Faith, he asked shyly, "I hope this isn't forward, but... would you want to go get dinner? No pressure. ... you seem like someone I'd like to know."

I stood there, halfway through signing my autograph, hair frizzy from the long day, exhausted in that deep-soul way — and still, I found myself smiling.

I said yes.

Because for the first time in a long time, it didn't feel like a risk I was taking for someone else's benefit.

It felt like a risk for me.

He followed up. Respectfully. Kindly. He sent me a picture of his kids making pancakes and told me his daughter loves to read.

There was no love-bombing. No rush. Just something warm, cautious, and new.

And in that early shimmer of "maybe," I felt something I hadn't felt in a long time.

I felt ready.

* * * * *

It started like something sacred.

We waited months before introducing our kids — slow, gentle months where Micah and I met for tea on weekends or sat in his driveway talking while his kids napped inside.

We texted through preschool tantrums and middle-of-the-night wakeups. We didn't rush. We were intentional. Careful.

We discussed what kind of example we wanted to be, and how much we'd both seen go wrong. He said all the right things: that our kids deserved actual steadiness, that he didn't want to add chaos to my life, only kindness.

So when the time came — finally — I let Noah meet him.

* * * * *

[AGE 33 1/2 — Noah Meeting Micah, Noah 4 1/2]

The day Micah met Noah, after four months of us dating, felt like stepping into sunlight after a long, cold winter. Noah, four and full of questions, bounced beside me, his little sneakers lighting up with every step.

"Is he nice, Mommy? What's his name again? Does he got a beard? Is he tall? Will he like my trucks? I brought the blue one. And the red one too! Can I show him both?"

I smiled, trying to calm the flutter of nervous energy in my chest. "I think so, baby."

Micah arrived with his two kids — quiet Levi and little Emma, who clutched a Spiderman toy in one hand and a dragon in the other. She took one look at Noah and grabbed his hand without hesitation.

"Wanna play dragons?" she asked.

Noah beamed, eyes wide. "Yeah! I got a dino that *kinda* looks like a dragon. He goes *RAAAHHHR*! Wait — lemme get it from my backpack! It's the green one with the scratch on his tail — his name is Chompy!"

And just like that, they were off.

Watching them all together — kids giggling, running laps around the coffee table — felt fragile and precious, like holding something made of glass.

Micah was gentle. He helped build block towers, crouched to explain dinosaur roars, and laughed without condescension. I saw kindness in him, something I wanted so badly to trust.

That night, we ate spaghetti together — quiet talk of cartoons and school, sauce on cheeks, juice boxes emptied. Noah curled into my lap, drowsy and smiling. I caught Micah's eye across the table. And for a moment, I let myself believe *maybe this is the beginning of something good.*

* * * * *

It started like most hopeful stories do — with tenderness, with warmth, with the kind of slow-burning comfort that felt like a relief after years of turmoil. He was attentive in the beginning. Gentle. He asked about my day. Remembered my favorite tea. Complimented my parenting and said things like, *"Noah's lucky to have a mom like you."*

I believed him.

I met him during a period when I was beginning to believe in soft possibilities again. I had rebuilt so much of myself. I was standing tall in therapy, working hard, caring for my son, keeping our world stitched together with a quiet strength I'd earned the hard way. He didn't pursue me aggressively, which I appreciated. He listened. He gave space. He seemed safe.

And after all I'd endured, *safe* was seductive.

We dated slowly. He didn't push intimacy, didn't make jokes at my expense, didn't drink — at least not that I saw. My boy even began calling him "friend" and offering him his little Matchbox cars to play with. That meant something. I let myself believe again.

So when he suggested moving in together, it felt like the next right step in a growing relationship. I thought I'd finally found someone who wouldn't punish me for my past or see me as damaged. Someone who would help carry the weight of life instead of adding more to it.

* * * * *

[AGE 33 1/2 — Micah's Dynamic, 5 Months Into Relationship — Noah 4 1/2]

But as soon as the boxes were unpacked, something shifted.

He didn't raise his voice, not at first. He didn't need to. It was in the looks, the sighs, the thin-lipped silences. He started making decisions without asking. Which bills to be paid late. What to buy on the credit card I had — *my* name, *my* credit, without telling me when he'd pay me back. "It's for both of us," he'd say when I questioned it. "You'd spend it on the kid anyway. Why not help me and my kids, too?"

At first, I tried to rationalize it. Wanted to believe he was just under stress. Maybe he didn't mean to be so... *abrasive*. But soon the bank statements showed thousands of dollars in charges I hadn't seen a penny back from.

When I brought it up, he'd pivot so quickly it made my head spin. *"I've done everything for you. Do you have any idea how lucky you are that I love you?"* Guilt became his language. Gaslighting his currency.

And it was my son who paid the price, too.

It started small. Little barbs masked as jokes. "You're going for seconds?" he smirked. "You let Noah get away with too much," he said another night, after a meltdown. "He needs discipline."

Noah shrank at his words. So did I.

When I tried to speak up, Micah cut me down with sarcasm. "Oh, look at you, the perfect mom. Maybe if you weren't so soft, your kid wouldn't be such a mess."

Noah got quieter. More watchful. I saw confusion cloud his big eyes. When Micah raised his voice, even slightly, Noah would flinch. And something inside me — some primal, protective place — started to stir.

But I wanted to believe. I wanted love to win.

We kept going. One sunny Saturday, we met at a park with a wooden castle and a splash pad. Emma grabbed Noah's hand, said, "You be the dragon, I'll be the hero!"

He laughed. "I'll be both!"

Micah helped him down the slide, sunglasses pushed into his hair, laughing with the kids. That night, we had tacos on his patio under string lights. He held my hand under the table. In the car, Noah fell asleep on my lap, sticky with popsicle juice. I cried just a little. It felt like healing.

* * * * *

But then came the rot.

The man who once smiled warmly at my boy began growing cold and curt. The warmth faded to impatience. Then to disdain. "Why does Noah whine so much?" Micah would mutter under his breath, but loud enough for me and, worse, my son, to hear. "Maybe if you didn't baby him so much, he'd toughen up."

I caught him yelling at Noah multiple times. Loud and sharp. Cutting. My son had a hard time chewing with his mouth closed. He was four. But the way this man loomed over him, the venom in his voice... My son looked up at me with wide, frightened eyes. And something inside me snapped.

"Man, Noah cries a lot," he said one afternoon. "You baby him too much. Hope he toughens up."

"He's four," I replied, gently.

Micah shrugged. "Boys need grit."

I let it go until it happened again.

"You repeat yourself a lot. You like hearing yourself talk?" Micah snapped randomly.

I corrected Emma calmly later in the day — he muttered, "Control freak."

I showed up in a new sundress. He glanced at me and said, "That's what you're wearing? You look like a clown!" Then, with a laugh, "Kidding. You look fine. Just wasn't expecting... all that." I smiled through it. But I felt the sting.

Soon, the jabs weren't subtle anymore.

At a crowded restaurant, Noah clung to me, overwhelmed by the noise and movement. His fingers twisted into my shirt like lifelines.

Micah rolled his eyes. "Come on, champ. Mommy's not your emotional support animal."

He laughed.

Noah didn't. He looked up at me, his eyes wide, blinking fast, searching for something he didn't have words for yet. *Safety.* Understanding. Permission to feel.

That night, I sat in the car, stiff and silent, like a trapped animal caught between flight and freeze.

Noah's voice was soft from the back seat, thinner than usual, like it had curled in on itself. "Mommy?"

I turned slightly. "Yes, baby?"

"Why does he laugh when I'm sa-did?"

I stilled. "What do you mean, baby?"

"When I cry, he go, 'Boo-hoo, you want a bottle, baby boy?' Like that. Then he laughs. But I'm not bein' funny. My tummy was hurty and it was too loud and he said I'm... a-cous-tic. I bad?"

His voice cracked at the end, as if the word itself tasted wrong in his mouth.

The ground seemed to tilt beneath me like an elevator cut loose. *Autistic.* He meant autistic. And somehow, Micah had made it sound like a slur.

I pulled over, hands trembling, and turned fully to face him.

"You're not silly, love. Not when you're hurting. It's always okay to cry. Always."

He nodded slowly, staring down at his stuffed giraffe in his lap. "I don't like he call me names. It make me heart feel squish."

I reached back and brushed a curl off his forehead. "Your heart is perfect. And nobody gets to squish it."

He didn't smile, but his fingers found mine.

And I could feel it — the weight he had begun to carry. A weight too big for such small hands.

* * * * *

The first time Micah crossed the line, really crossed it, I felt it like a slap.

He wasn't just mocking me. He was belittling my son.

Noah clung to me on the couch that night, his little body trembling. And something in me cracked wide open.

The next time Micah raised his voice, I stood between him and Noah. "No," I said, calm but firm. "That's not okay. You don't speak to us like that."

He laughed. "Or what?"

I met his eyes. "Or we leave. For good."

The next day, Micah's older child was teasing Noah about being able to jump higher than Noah. My son tried to hit the eight-year-old, but the kid dodged, and my son ran into the road.

Voice strangled with emotion, I exclaimed loudly, "Noah, get out of the road! A car is coming!"

Noah yelled, "I want car to run me over!"

I couldn't breathe. The second Noah was safely in my arms, I held him like I'd never let him go. Micah called it manipulation, but I saw it as a desperate form of communication; he felt bullied, and didn't know how to make it stop. I made that clear to Micah, but he said I was blowing things out of proportion.

I also made it clear that my son and I needed a house with no more yelling and anger, where we could have respect. He acted like that was too much to ask for.

He didn't expect me to fight back. He thought I'd stay small. We were supposed to be celebrating exactly six months of dating, and instead, that was the day I walked away for good.

He tried to call.

Text.

Apologize.

Blame it on stress.

"You're blowing this out of proportion."

I blocked him after it became abundantly clear that he was not only not going to pay me back, but he weaponized my son, saying, "I don't love Noah."

A particularly nasty barrage of texts included, "No wonder your son was so f***ed up, because of your parenting."

I might put up with a lot of garbage, but no one gets to demean, belittle, and bully my son.

I looked at my little love — his sweet, resilient face — and I promised him this: *never again.*

CHAPTER 18
The Shepherd's Daughter No More

Starting over the first time had been like clawing my way out of wreckage — traumatized but hopeful. Starting over the second time? It was like stepping through the ashes of something I had *trusted* and realizing I was still standing, this time with armor.

But I was not bitter.

No, bitterness hadn't taken root — *wisdom* had.

After I left Micah, I didn't fall apart. I couldn't. My son needs me, and this time, so did *I*. There was a quiet fire building in me. Not a fire of rage or revenge, but of resolve. I stopped asking why I was a magnet for broken men and started asking what I *wanted* — not just for myself, but for my son. What kind of peace? What kind of life?

I cut my hair. Not dramatically, but enough to feel the weight of that past fall away in strands. I deleted every old message. Changed my phone number, address, and email. I met with a financial advisor. It took months to untangle the mess Micah had left in my name. I worked extra hours, sold a few things, and built slowly. Brick by brick. This time, I didn't make a home on borrowed trust — I built it on clear boundaries and an unshakable sense of self.

My son, too, carried scars from those months — scars that weren't always visible but surfaced in the ways he hesitated before speaking, or flinched when someone's voice grew sharp. I saw them. And because I had once been a child like that, I didn't ignore them.

We spent more time outside — just the two of us. Walks in the woods. Long car rides where we sang and talked about everything and nothing at all. I let him sob. I answered his questions honestly but gently. I told him, again and again, that none of it was his fault.

We began doing "brave check-ins" every week — a game where we each shared something brave we'd done or felt. His were sometimes small: *"I asked a question in class."* Mine were sometimes not: *"I said no to someone who made me feel small."*

And when he started to laugh more easily again — those pure, belly laughs that made his whole face light up — I counted that as my most tremendous success.

Trust didn't return easily, not in others, and not in myself. I second-guessed everything at first — how did I *miss* the signs? How did I let someone in who would hurt me and my child?

Therapy helped. My journal helped more. I learned that it wasn't naivety, it was *hope.* And there's no shame in hoping. But now, hope would have guardrails.

I didn't wall myself off, but I raised my standards. I learned to listen closely to how someone spoke to children, to cashiers, to servers. I trusted *actions* more than words. I practiced pausing before agreeing to anything, no matter how small.

Eventually, trust became something I gave in teaspoons instead of gallons — and I stopped apologizing for that.

I joined an online support group for women recovering from financial abuse and controlling relationships. At first, I just read. Then, I began to comment. Eventually, I started sharing my story.

Women began messaging me, asking for advice: *How did you know? How did you leave? What about the debt? How do you keep going?*

I didn't always have the answers, but I knew how to listen. I learned how to validate. I knew how to *name* what had happened when other women were still fumbling through the fog of denial.

Eventually, I started writing — just a small book. I named it *The Quiet Phoenix*. My first entry was raw and honest, about the day I left my ex-boyfriend. The second was about rebuilding my son's sense of safety. Then came the financial literacy posts, tips on spotting red flags, and emotional patterns of abuse.

I never shared names, never sought revenge. I simply told the truth. And the truth? It changed people. And it healed me.

I haven't closed the door on love. But I'm not chasing it either. If it comes again, I know what it will have to look like: respect, honesty, consistency, and kindness that doesn't dissolve once the front door closes. But if that does happen, it'll need to be years later. I need to take the time I never had before to learn who I am apart from what others say. To be with just my son, unapologetically having a good time, without fearing that someone will get upset or jealous because I want to spend quality time with Noah.

In the meantime, I will hold my son's hand when we cross the street, explaining it helps keep each other safe, instead of fear mongering. I'll teach him how to make Jalapeno Poppers. I read him stories at night, and sometimes, he reads them to *me* now. He tells me what he sees and what he remembers; that's beautiful. I make sure to tell him he is brave, good, and worthy, because I want those words carved so deeply into his soul that no one can ever take them from him.

And every so often, after he's fallen asleep, I stand in the doorway of his room and whisper:

"We made it. We're safe. We're okay. And we are not done becoming who we're meant to be."

There was a time when I measured my worth by whether someone stayed.

Now, I measure it by how deeply I have learned to stay with *myself*.

Being single isn't a prison sentence — it's become a sanctuary. A deliberate choice. A freedom I hadn't always known I could have. No longer chasing someone to rescue me from the ache of loneliness, I filled that space with something far more sacred: peace.

I am creating a life where the laughter of my son echoes through our small home like a hymn of healing. Mornings were slow and gentle. Cinnamon toast or a pop tart with some fruit, silly songs, and warm arms around each other before school. Evenings were spent reading, crafting, and sometimes dancing in the kitchen to music that reminds me how alive I am.

We have inside jokes. Secret codes. A rhythm that is all our own. He is my world — not as a substitute for love, but as a *manifestation* of it. The love we share is pure, honest, and so beautifully simple. It reminds me every day that *this* could be enough. Maybe I don't need to be someone's "other half" when I am already whole.

I have a wonderful group of people in my life, one of the most significant contributors being my younger sister, Faith, who has always been a quiet force — faithful, funny, and fiercely loyal. The kind of woman who showed up without needing to be asked. Who didn't just bring treats and hugs on hard days but could make me laugh until I forgot how heavy everything had felt moments before.

We've grown closer with time. Trauma had once created distance, but healing built bridges. My sister hasn't always understood what I've gone through, but she *never minimized it*. And that mattered more than perfect understanding.

Late-night phone calls. Spontaneous girls' nights. Long texts filled with "You've got this" and "Don't forget how strong you are." My sister is the kind of person who reminds me not just of who I am, but who I had always been — before the pain, before the fear, before the walls.

Together, we rewrote the narrative of what sisterhood could be.

I am not alone. That truth bloomed slowly but thoroughly.

Over the years, friendships had taken root — friends who weren't afraid of my messy days or complicated past. Women who let me release my pent-up emotions without trying to fix me. Friends who brought over soup when my son had the flu. Who sent me memes, articles, and love notes just because, and reminded me I didn't have to do this alone.

They had become my chosen family. My circle of truth-tellers, encouragers, prayer-warriors, and fellow survivors. With them, I could exhale. I didn't have to be strong all the time. I could be *real*.

And in those connections, I found parts of myself again — the playful parts, the creative parts, the parts that had once been silenced. They all came back like friends returning home.

For the first time in my life, fulfillment didn't have anything to do with being wanted by a man. It looked like:

- Waking up in a quiet house with sunlight spilling across the floor, my son tucked beside me.
- Watching him thrive in preschool, curious and kind, proud of his "for Momma" artwork.
- Writing posts that helped women I might never meet, but whose pain mirrored my own.
- Sitting in my backyard with a blanket and a book while the world softened around me.
- Laughing with my sister until our faces hurt.
- Saying no to people and situations that didn't bring peace, and not feeling guilty for it.

Love didn't need to be romantic to be *everything*.

I no longer waited for someone to choose me.

I chose *myself* — every morning when I got up, every night when I wrapped my arms around my son, every time I said, "I am enough, exactly as I am."

If love came again, it would have to *add* to my already whole life, not complete it. And until then? I am no longer afraid of the quiet. The quiet has become holy. I have made peace with my own company. With my scars. With my victories.

And in that peace, in that hard-won wholeness, I finally found what I had been searching for all along — not someone else to rescue me.

But the woman I had become.

* * * * *

[AGE 33 — *Our Home, Noah 4 3/4*]

Over the next month, after escaping Micah, I built walls. Boundaries that people couldn't cross without consequence. I protected our space and peace by breaking up and moving out, especially after an influx of even nastier texts came through. And I told Noah, every time:

"You are safe. You are loved. No one gets to make you feel small."

I found strength in Noah's hand in mine, in the way he began to laugh freely again, in the brightness returning to his eyes. I found strength in becoming the mother he needed — and the woman I had nearly forgotten I could be.

There were hard days — lonely ones. But every time I saw him smile, really smile, I knew I'd made the right choice.

I wasn't just protecting my child.

I was protecting the life we were rebuilding.

And that was a love neither of us would ever need to question again.

* * * * *

Noah was four going on five when I started to notice the change in him — not just the way he watched the world with sharper eyes, but how he seemed to carry a quiet weight, like he was trying to make sense of things no child should have to.

He'd ask questions that stopped me cold.

"Mommy... why does Daddy get mad with his *big voice* sometime?"

I looked at him in the rearview mirror, his face scrunched in confusion, fingers twisting the hem of his shirt.

"Why Micah so mean me? He say I a baby. He say I need a bottle. I wasn't playin'. I was cryin' for real life."

He paused, then added in a whisper, "He said I'm a... mani-plater."

(He meant *master manipulator*. Micah's favorite phrase each time Noah cried or had a meltdown. He'd mimic the noises, high-pitched, fake sobs, and laugh like it was all a joke.) It would be laughable if it weren't so damaging — a grown man accusing a four-year-old of manipulation. But the pain on Noah's face wasn't a joke.

Sometimes Noah's questions unraveled me more than anything else.

"Why you sad, Mommy?"

Just that — four soft words, said from the back seat while holding his plush giraffe to his cheek like a shield.

His innocence was starting to fracture, like glass catching a crack. And I hated that I couldn't protect him from everything. That my love wasn't always enough to keep the world kind.

But we were rebuilding — just the two of us — carving out a new kind of home from the wreckage. We had each other, and that was the start of something real.

But as we began healing emotionally, another form of trauma surfaced — one with interest rates and unpaid bills.

Leaving that relationship had its consequences. Mountainous debt was piled up in my name - a car loan in my name because I had excellent credit, two credit cards with balances that triggered my anxiety response, and rent owed on a place Micah had kicked us out of with just a month's notice. I hadn't been willing to stay there even a day longer, not after Noah had felt so mistreated.

I sat on the cold kitchen floor, tears blurring the numbers on the letters from the credit card company. The betrayal wasn't just emotional anymore — it was financial, legal, and suffocating.

Noah crawled into my lap, his small arms wrapping tightly around me. "Mommy, what wrong?" he whispered, sensing the storm even if he couldn't name it.

I kissed the top of his head and swallowed the lump threatening to take over. "We're going to be okay," I told him, more to convince myself than him. "We'll fix this. Together."

It was terrifying, but it also galvanized me. I reached out for help, talking to lawyers, police officer friends, credit counselors, and others who could guide me through the mess Micah left behind. He says he didn't mean to make me feel used, that financial abuse was not his intent, and that he will pay me back. I hope so, but for now, I have to act as if I won't be getting any of the over ten thousand dollars back.

* * * * *

[AGE 33 —Our Home, Noah 5]

Each doctor's visit added another name to my collection of pain. Endometriosis. Adenomyosis. Words I couldn't pronounce but felt in my bones. The doctors spoke in careful, clinical terms, but I heard only one thing: *Your body remembers*. Each diagnosis was both a curse and validation — proof that what I had endured left marks deeper than memory.

It left markers. It left scars.

My muscles were so tight they felt like stone — cords wrapped around my bones, bracing against a danger that had long since passed. My hips barely moved when I walked. My jaw clicked from years of holding back words I wasn't allowed to say. A serpent coiled in my gut, squeezing tighter with every breath. Some days, I felt like a haunted house — every nerve a doorway where trauma still lingered.

But somehow, my mind — the part of me that had once been just as rigid — was beginning to soften. Loosen. Open.

I no longer needed my mother's belief to validate my suffering. I no longer listened to those begging for proof. My body was the proof. Every inflamed nerve, every scarred organ, every fused inch of skin was a witness to what had been done and what I survived.

And even in that pain, I began to breathe again.

There was a night — I still remember it — when the silence in my bedroom wasn't hostile. Noah was asleep in the next room, his rhythmic breathing soft through the partially open door. Outside, rain tapped gently against the windowpane like a lullaby. And inside me, for the first time in decades, there was no screaming. No urgent survival plan. Just stillness.

I held the pill bottle in one hand, my journal in the other.

The ink bled a little as I wrote, the words shaky but sure:
"I choose the pen. I choose me."
I closed the bottle and slid it back into the drawer. Not because the pain was gone, but because I wasn't.
And because I still had a voice.
And I would use it for myself and for those who are still silent.
I don't want to be an angry victim. I'm committed to staying positive and using writing as a form of therapy. I won't let my past define me, and I refuse to remain silent. I'm learning to speak up for myself, even if it means facing judgment. If people don't like me or what I have to say, that's their right. But I'm done hiding.
The anger, the bitterness, the constant fear of rejection — those emotions no longer have a hold on me like they once did. I'm choosing not to let them. The stress of trying to make others understand, to force them to see me, doesn't define my worth anymore. Whether people believe me or not doesn't change the truth of my experiences. And, you know what? That's okay.
I don't need to contort myself to fit someone else's idea of truth. I don't need to exhaust myself to make others see my pain. There's an incredible freedom in that realization — one that fills me with a peace I never thought possible. It's like the weight of the world is lifting, one breath at a time.
I started letting sunlight touch my skin again, not just pass through the curtains. I bought fresh herbs — mint, basil, and rosemary — and grew them on the windowsill, watching them unfurl toward the light, just as I was learning to do. The smell of earth on my fingers became its own kind of therapy. Tiny roots. Tiny growth. Tiny hope.
I took baths in Epsom salts and lavender oil, letting my body float in warm water as if it were learning to be held. I let myself stare ahead, motionless, as tears leaked out with no ceremony — slow, uninvited, unstoppable in the tub. Let the heat soften the places that had gone cold.
I wore soft fabrics — things that didn't pinch or press or remind me of the rules I used to follow about being "put together." Some days,

I stayed in pajamas all day with Noah, making pancakes for lunch and turning the living room into a fort. I allowed joy to coexist with healing, not as a reward, but as a right.

I lit candles for no reason.

I played music — sometimes worship, other times Ren or Knox Hill, sometimes jazz, and occasionally just the sound of rain on a loop.

I bought myself flowers. I started asking myself, *"What do I need today?"* And then actually listening.

* * * * *

In the months that followed, something subtle but sacred began to shift; I started saying no.

No to guilt.
No to obligation.

No to the version of myself others still tried to hold onto — the silent daughter, the compliant church girl, the "forgiver" who carried other people's shame in her lungs.

Each "no" was a fence post in the garden I was learning to tend. Not a wall. A boundary. One that kept the toxicity out and the beauty in.

I cut contact with relatives who preferred denial over truth — the ones who called for 'unity' but ignored the harm.

I no longer walked into rooms where I had to hide to be allowed through the door. Their rejection no longer rearranged my self-worth.

With friends, I was gentle but firm. I no longer carried other people's feelings above my safety. I stopped overexplaining, mostly. That's a work in progress. I stopped apologizing for being sensitive, for canceling plans, for needing space. I let go of anyone who flinched at my truth and chose not to want to walk beside me. They are allowed to make their own opinions and choices, but I was no longer allowing others' opinions and beliefs to define my own.

And when people asked about relationships — romantic ones — I told the truth:

I'm open, someday. Maybe. But I'm not waiting. I'm not building my life as a placeholder for someone else to complete. I am whole with or without a ring, a partner, a shared mailbox. If love comes, it will come with care, with deep listening, with steady patience and reverence. And if it doesn't, I am already enough.

I have Noah.

I have peace.

I have my voice.

I have me.

For a long time, I wrestled with the name I was given — one that carried Nathaniel's shadow. One that I couldn't say without feeling the weight of what he did. So I changed it.

Not to hide.

To reclaim.

I became Serenity Lawson. Serenity, for the stillness I fought to find after chaos. For the quiet I earned. For the peace I built with my own two hands. Lawson — a name of my choosing. A name with no ghosts in the syllables. A name that says: *I am not who you said I was. I am who I choose to be.* I signed it for the first time on a rental agreement, our first little place for myself and Noah. I signed it again on medical forms, essays, articles, and the cover page of the book that carried my story out into the world.

Now, when I introduce myself at speaking events, I say it with calm conviction:

"My name is Serenity Lawson. I'm a survivor of childhood abuse. I'm a mother. A writer. A speaker. And I am living proof that darkness does not get the final word."

I pause.

"And neither do the people who try to silence you."

Because they didn't.

Because I'm here.

Because I kept going.

And because now, I help others find their way back to themselves, too.

* * * * *

From those ashes, I didn't just rise. I rebuilt. Not armored against love, but open, wise, awake, and no longer willing to burn for someone else's comfort.

How did I choose to work through my trauma? The idea came softly.

Not in a lightning bolt or a dream or some dramatic moment of revelation — but one quiet night, long after Noah had fallen asleep, while I sat at the kitchen table in my softest sweater, a cup of cold tea beside a spiral notebook filled with half-sentences and raw memories.

I looked at the pages — some tear-stained, some angry, some so soft they read like lullabies — and I realized: *This is more than mine.*

This story. These wounds. This healing. They were never just mine to hold.

I thought about the girl who still lives in so many homes, who hears footsteps in the hallway and wonders if it's her fault. About the woman who's grown but still flinches when someone raises their voice. About the mother who wonders if she's enough. About the survivor who hasn't yet said the words out loud.

I wanted them to know they aren't crazy.

They aren't weak.

They aren't alone.

So I wrote. Not for revenge. Not for pity. But for the truth.

I wrote it all: the memories, the ache, the diagnoses, the stress attacking my body in a myriad of ways, the therapy, the Bible verses twisted and then untangled. I wrote about what it felt like to say no for the first time. About the stairs. About the stitches. About the silence and the scream beneath it.

And I wrote about Noah — my bright, wiggly boy, my heart's proof that healing is possible. I wrote about pillow forts and bedtime whispers and the freedom of giving a child what you never had.

I didn't write to stay in the pain. I wrote to shine a light through it.

The more I wrote, the more the shame peeled away. The more the power shifted. I was no longer the girl under someone else's control — I was the woman telling the story on her own terms.

I found a writing group. I shared a chapter. Then another. The responses were quiet at first — tears, nods, small brave emails from people who whispered, *Me too.*

That's when I knew. This wasn't just a story. This was a map.

A hand reaching back.

A lantern in the dark.

And I was ready to carry it forward.

What I buried in shame now grows in light. My story is not a scar — it's a seed. And I am still blooming.

Epilogue
Beyond Survival

Book Launch: "It Happens Here Too: The Shepherd's Daughter."

[AGE 33 (Now) — Bookstore, Noah 5]

The bookstore glowed. Not with spotlights or fanfare — but with something deeper. Something sacred.

Warm and golden under soft string lights, the air carried the scent of steeped cinnamon tea, beeswax candles, and something nostalgic — old paper, binding glue, and the faint sweetness of vanilla tucked between pages. It smelled like safety, like a story. Like home.

Paper stars floated from the ceiling, strung on fishing line, swaying gently in the breeze of the ceiling fans. Tiny white candles flickered on every table — intentional, steady, like all the quiet hopes that had carried me here. Hopes that once sat voiceless in the corner of my chest now shone gently, burning without apology.

Stacks of my book rested beside a wild bouquet someone had left anonymously: sunflowers, thistles, white lilacs, sprigs of lavender, and sage. I pressed my fingers to the stems as I passed, feeling the dewy softness, the velvet petals, the strength in their survival. I didn't know who sent them, but I knew the gesture. I knew the language of survivors — loud without volume. Bold without spectacle.

The place was alive. Every corner buzzed — folding chairs arranged in half-circles, people gathered shoulder to shoulder, the tea bar humming like a heartbeat in the background. Laughter swelled, soft and reverent. The whole room breathed as if it were holding something sacred in its lungs.

I wore a soft blue dress that day — a flowy, simple one, like ocean water against sun-warmed skin. It swayed gently when I moved, brushing against my calves like a reminder: *I am not made of stone. I can bend. I can dance. I can flow.*

I had survived, yes. But more importantly, I was living.

Noah sat front and center, juice box in hand, his tiny legs swinging in his favorite socks — dinosaurs and lightning bolts. When I stepped toward the microphone, he beamed like I'd just grown a cape.

And honestly, in his eyes, I had.

My name was on a poster. ***Serenity Lawson.***

The title gleamed bold and unapologetic in black serif: *"It Happens Here Too: The Shepherd's Daughter."*

For a moment, I just stood there, absorbing it all. The air. The love. The gravity. I looked at that poster and thought:

I never imagined this.

Not when I was thirteen and bleeding on the staircase, fingers jittering like static electricity searching for release as I cleaned up evidence.

Not when I was twenty-two, curled in the corner of a shower stall, whispering, "I'm crazy," over and over just to survive the flashbacks.

Not when I told my mother and she turned her back.

Not even when I wrote the first trembling sentence, heart thumping like it might knock the keys off my laptop.

But I was here.

And so were they.

Survivors — some trembling, some radiant, all brave. Friends who'd stayed. Counselors who'd listened. Bible study women who had cried with me and never asked for a tidy ending. Pastors who leaned in when the story got hard. Even a few quiet churchgoers who had once looked through me, now sitting with softened eyes, hands folded, nodding.

Faith, my sister in blood and spirit, sat beside Noah, his hand tucked gently in hers. Her mascara had run before I even spoke a word.

Malie sat next to her, clutching the wristband from our first women's retreat, a balled-up tissue in her palm.

Behind them: my tribe. Celeste, radiant in gold earrings, the ones she wore the day she said, "You don't need fixing — just space to bloom."

Jo, my midnight-text lifeline, her eyes shining, a chipped mug of sparkling cider in hand.

Dr. Ahlia sat in the front row with her hand pressed over her heart, just like she used to in group therapy when one of us said something unbearably honest. She had once looked me in the eye and said, "You don't have to be cleaned up to be worthy of love." I'd clung to those words like oxygen.

Just behind her, Pastor Lyle, the first to say, "I believe you," without asking for dates, details, or evidence. Just belief — quiet, holy belief that changed everything.

I stepped up to the mic.

My breath didn't shake.

My voice didn't stutter.

"Thank you for being here," I began, and my voice echoed softly across the room, threading into the candles, the pages, and the hearts that had gathered. "This book... this night... none of it is about who I was told I had to be."

I looked out at them — all of them — and let the following words settle like truth in warm soil.

"It's about who I choose to become."

* * * * *

I spoke of truth.

Of how abuse doesn't just happen "out there."

It happens in pews and sanctuaries.

Behind stained glass.

Under holy titles.

I said the words out loud: "Silence protects wolves in shepherd's clothing."

"Truth-telling is a form of worship." "Survivors are prophets."

And I did not flinch.

Not once.

I didn't wince.

I stood in my story, in my voice, in the fire that no longer burned me.

Afterward, people stood in line — not for autographs, but for moments.

Some cried.

Some whispered.

Some pressed the book to their chest like it had unlocked a door they'd been too afraid to knock on.

A young woman with trembling hands leaned in, voice barely audible: "You told my story. I thought no one ever would."

An older man with watery eyes and a church usher's badge clutched his copy and said, "I didn't know. I didn't want to. But now I do."

A teenage girl with eyeliner wings and combat boots asked, "Will you speak at my school? They don't discuss this topic there. But we need it."

A mother, fingers laced with her daughter's, whispered, "Thank you. You wrote the words I've never been able to say."

I hugged each one. Listened. Honored their stories like the sacred offerings they were.

I stayed until the last person had spoken. Hugged. Cried. Exhaled.

And then Noah climbed into my lap, warm, weighty, and perfect. He offered me a half-eaten, smushed sugar cookie, completely sincere.

"Mommy!" he said, eyes wide. "They clapped so loud! Are you famous now, Mommy?"

I laughed, kissed his curls, breathed him in — peanut butter and juice and magic.

"No, baby," I whispered into his ear. "But I'm free."

And that's better than famous. Because I never wanted to be known for surviving. I wanted to be known for healing.

For telling the truth. For lighting the path for others who still don't know if they're allowed to speak.

Now, I know I was never too broken. I was never too late. I am not what happened to me. I am who I choose to become.

* * * * *

After the last guest had spoken and the hugs had been exchanged, I stepped away for a moment to catch my breath. That's when the event organizer handed me a small envelope.

"It's from Caleb," she said quietly.

I recognized his messy handwriting immediately. My heart clenched.

I unfolded the letter, voice steady but full of emotion as I read aloud:

"Serenity, I can't be there in person, but I've been holding onto your words like a lifeline through these dark days. I'm proud of you — proud that you found your voice when it felt like silence was all we had left.

I'm working every day to find my own peace, to break free from the chaos that nearly swallowed me whole. Your courage saved me more than you know. Keep shining.

— Caleb."

Grief climbed my throat like ivy until Etta came up beside me, her eyes shining with unshed tears.

"Serenity, you have no idea how proud I am of you," she said, voice thick with feeling. "I watched you carry all of it — the weight, the pain, the fear — and still stand here. You gave all of us permission to heal."

Faith joined us then, her hand slipping into mine, grounding me. "You're the reason I finally stopped running from the past," she whispered. "I started therapy because of your book, because I saw it was okay to be broken and still fight for joy. We're all living proof that the story doesn't end with what happened to us."

I looked at my siblings, scarred but fierce, beautiful in their survival.

Caleb's words echoed in my mind: *Your courage saved me more than you know.*

Etta smiled, wiping a tear. "I left the church a year ago. It was terrifying, but I'm finally free from those chains. My life isn't perfect, but it's mine."

Faith squeezed my hand harder. "And I'm learning how to love myself, not the way dad said I should, but the way I deserve."

I pulled them both close, feeling the steady beat of their hearts against mine. "We did this. All of us. Not just surviving but choosing to live."

Noah's laughter bubbled up from my lap, reminding me why this moment mattered. I was not alone.

We were not broken beyond repair.

We were whole in ways that counted — in ways Pastor Nathaniel never could have understood.

And together, we were drafting new stories.

* * * * *

After the launch, the messages didn't stop.

Some came through my email — quiet, lowercase, raw. Others arrived handwritten, ink smudged with what I can only guess were tears. Each one a lantern offered into the dark. Each one a reminder: *truth never echoes in vain.*

Sometimes, Noah peeked up from his coloring pages.

"Are you helpin' someone again, Mommy?"

"Yes, baby," I'd say, scooping him into my lap. "I think maybe I am."

We read the kind ones together — notes from parents learning to listen. He didn't understand all the words, but he understood love. He understood showing up.

One afternoon, he handed me a drawing: a stick-figure of me, holding a book. Yellow sparkles all around.

A tiny version of him beside me, smiling widely.

Above us, in big kindergarten letters:
MY MOMMY HELPS PEOPLE BE BRAVE.
I didn't even try to stop the tears.
He patted my shoulder. "It's okay, Mommy. Brave mommies cry too."

* * * * *

Two nights later, my girls surprised me.
Faith, Jo, Celeste, and Malie showed up with Polaroids, Thai takeout, and a mini cake that read:

TO FREEDOM. TO FIRE. TO SERENITY.

In the backyard, under fairy lights we'd strung up months ago and never taken down, we cried and danced and laughed ourselves stupid.
Jo held my face as if she were praying. "You stood in the fire," she whispered. "And you didn't just survive. You sang in it."
Celeste raised her glass, golden and fierce. "You burned the whole damn silence down."
Faith was barefoot in the grass, hoodie zipped up to her chin, sipping Thai iced tea like it was whiskey. She blinked at me, deadpan.
"I mean, you're basically famous now. I should've made you sign my copy when you were brand-new."
Then she smirked, took another sip, and added: "But for real? Some girl out there is gonna read your story and go, 'Oh. I'm not broken. I've just been gaslit to hell.' And then maybe she gets out. Because of you."
She looked down for a second, mouth twitching like she was about to say something softer, but instead she said, "You broke the whole damn spell with, like, metaphors and backbone. So... Good job. Try not to cry or anything."
I burst out laughing — and then cried anyway.
We lit sparklers at midnight. Faith accidentally set her sleeve on fire, swore under her breath, and muttered, "Okay, symbolism, calm down."
Our laughter echoed into the stars.

And for once, the night didn't feel heavy.
It felt like freedom.

* * * * *

Later that week, Noah and I built a pillow fort in the living room.

"The *Brave Cave!*" he announced, crawling inside with a flashlight, three stuffed animals, and a granola bar he'd snuck in like contraband.

He peeked out. "Only brave people allow-did. And you, Mommy. Cause you the bravest."

Halfway through story time, his eyelids started to droop, and he looked up at me, voice thick with sleep.

"I like you *so much*, Mommy. More than dinosaurs. More than moon rocks. More than Pop-Tarts. Even the strawberry kind."

"Wow," I grinned. "That's a lot."

"I *know*," he mumbled, curling into my chest. "You're my best mommy. Forever, and always, and never not."

His words tumbled over each other — imperfect, but sure.

And I held him tighter, hoping the Brave Cave could keep the world away just a little longer.

His breath slowed. My hand traced soft circles.

This.

This was healing.

Not an award.

Not a speech.

Not applause.

But a boy who feels safe enough to fall asleep in my arms.

A body that feels like home again.

A voice that no longer shakes.

* * * * *

A few days later, I visited Pastor Lyle.

"I read your book," he said. "Every page. I'm proud of you, not just for speaking. For standing."

"Thank you," I said. "For believing me even back then. Without asking for evidence. I can't tell you how much I value that, and you."

He smiled, gently. "You needed someone to call the truth holy. I just called it what it was."

Tears stung. "You did. And I'll never forget that."

He placed his hand over mine. "Keep walking, Serenity. Keep writing. You were always meant to lead others out of the silence."

* * * * *

That night, I lit one more candle.

For the girl I used to be.

For the women still waiting to be believed.

For those flinching at words like 'father' and 'Pastor'.

For the joy reclaimed, one breath at a time.

For the life I'm building now — soft, strong, sacred.

I tucked Noah into bed and brushed curls from his forehead.

"Mommy?" he whispered.

"Yes, love?"

"When I grow up... can I help people too?"

I kissed his forehead. "You already do." He grinned, turned over, clutching his giraffe. His peaceful breath filled the room.

I stepped into the hallway, hand over my heart.

The nightlight glowed. The silence didn't hurt anymore.

Survival was behind me. Now, I was choosing joy.

And I was finally — undeniably — free.

* * * * *

Later that weekend, my girlfriends whisked me away to a tiny Airbnb with backyard string lights and a record player. We toasted with fizzy mocktails, danced barefoot in the grass, and cried happy tears under the moonlight.

Jo made a speech with crackers in her teeth. Celeste held my face in her hands.

"You didn't just survive," she said. "You resurrected."

That night, lying on the couch with Faith's head on my shoulder and Malie snoring in the next room, I cried — not from pain, but release. From joy. From awe. For the first time, my body didn't feel like a battleground.

It felt like mine.

* * * * *

A week later, the first story for my second book arrived: *A Mouthpiece for the Mute.*

A handwritten letter in soft blue ink ended, "I've never told anyone. But I want you to have my story."

Then more came — emails, poems, journal entries, voice notes; women who had never spoken out loud before.

They came from Texas, Ohio, Kenya, and Canada. Trembling voices, growing stronger with every sentence. I printed each one. Held them like sacred scrolls. Lit a candle for every story.

For her. For him. For them.

For the parts of myself I once thought unworthy of light.

* * * * *

[AGE 33 ¾ (Now) — OBGYN's Clinic, Noah 5]

I stepped into my OBGYN's clinic with a quiet dread curling in the pit of my gut, like a storm cloud pressing against my ribs.

Yet her brow furrowed — not with alarm, but confusion.

"You... you healed yourself," she said, her voice no louder than a whisper, as if the truth of it might vanish if spoken too forcefully.

"Last time, you looked like you were being eaten alive. How did you heal yourself?"

I stared back at her, equally stunned.

No sharp intake of breath. No horrified expression. No urgent recommendation for immediate surgery. Just baffled silence.

And just like that, everything changed.

There was no more talk of cutting, anesthesia, risk, or recovery. The long list of medications — more than a dozen bottles lined up like artifacts from a war I no longer had to fight on my bathroom counter — vanished from my daily ritual. No pills for pain. No capsules for anxiety or PTSD. No need to numb the panic, to dull the ache, to quiet the scream beneath my skin.

All of it... gone.

And what replaced it was not just the absence of pain, but the presence of something more powerful — hope. Real, tangible hope. The kind that anchors you when you're drifting and cradles you when you finally stop fighting.

The healing came not through scalpels or pharmaceuticals, but through the raw, vulnerable power of speaking and telling my truth. Giving voice to the shadows I had silenced for so long. With every word, I seemed to stitch my wounds back together, slowly coaxing life back into a body that had forgotten, or rather had never known, what peace felt like.

Now, for months, I've lived without pain.

No stabbing in my abdomen. No fire coursing through my nerves. No migraines splitting my skull in half. No burning. No stinging. Just... stillness. Sweet, astonishing stillness.

I can sit in silence without flinching. I can breathe deeply without fearing what will rise inside me. I've discovered the quiet beauty of existing without agony.

My only lingering challenge is an afternoon slump, like clockwork — around 3 p.m., my energy dips, a gentle wave that reminds me I'm still human. But that, I can live with. Gladly.

Because now, I *am* living.

Vividly, gratefully alive.

And not a day goes by that I don't remember the darkness I came from — the prison of chronic pain, the fog of medication, the endless string of appointments and procedures. I don't take a single pain-free moment for granted.

To wake up and not hurt is, by far, the greatest miracle I've ever known, with Noah being my only exception.

* * * * *

[AGE 33 3/4 —Backyard, Noah 5]

That spring, Noah and I wandered barefoot through the backyard, following scavenger hunt clues taped to trees.

"Mommy! This one says go to the *birdy feeder!*" he shouted, holding the crumpled paper like a treasure map.

We raced across the grass, laughter bursting from us like bubbles, scattering the sparrows into the sky.

That night, I lay beside him, tracing tiny circles on his back as his breathing slowed.

"Mommy?" he mumbled into his pillow.

"Yes, sweet love?"

"You're the *bestest* mommy. I think... I think even the *moon* love you."

I smiled, heart aching with something holy. "Thank you, baby."

He nodded against me, eyes half-closed. "Even when you get cry-did... It's okay. I still stay super close. Ever and ever. I not go nowhere."

* * * * *

The air was thick with the scent of moss and river mist as I held Noah's small hand, his fingers yet again sticky from the granola bar he'd half-finished on the hike up. The sound of the waterfall thundered ahead — not imagined this time, but in front of me. Loud, wild, and alive.

"Noah, look," I whispered, crouching beside him as we rounded the final bend.

He gasped, eyes wide. "It's *so big*, Mommy! It's like the sky's takin' a bath!"

His joy, unfiltered and full-bodied, echoed off the trees. The spray hit our cheeks, cold and exhilarating.

Decades ago, I used to go to a waterfall in my mind to feel safe. To feel loved. I didn't know what was hurting me then — not really. I just knew I needed to hide.

But here I was now, in the flesh, standing before the real thing, my son at my side. Our feet are grounded in the soil of a life that once felt impossible. The roar of the water, the shimmer of light caught in the spray, the soft squish of damp earth beneath us — everything said: *you made it.*

I watched Noah step closer to the edge, arms spread wide to feel the mist.

"I gonna catch the water with my *elbows!*" he shouted gleefully, spinning in the wind.

And I smiled. The ache was gone. The need to disappear — gone.

I had finally brought the child in me home. And now, as a mother, I get to show *my* child what freedom looks like: open sky, cold spray, safe ground.

* * * * *

The book was out. But I wasn't done.

That night, after tucking Noah in, I opened a fresh journal.

There were still stories to carry.

Still fires to keep lit.

Still women rising in the dark, whispering, *"Me too."*

But this time, I didn't dread the blank page. I welcomed it. Because the pen is mine now. And I know exactly who I am.

My name is Serenity Lawson.

And I am not the end of the story. I am the beginning of someone else's.

And the light? It's not at the end of the tunnel. It's in me now. And I carry it forward. Every day. For all of us.

I know who I am now:

Mother. Survivor. Author. Advocate.

Free.

To the ones still hiding in silence: You don't have to tell your story today. You don't owe anyone your timeline. Your truth is enough. You are enough.

Some days, healing will feel like forward motion. Other days, like stumbling in the dark. That's okay. But know this: *The darkness doesn't get the final word.*

You are allowed to walk away. To protect yourself. To take up space. To say, "This happened to me. But it doesn't own me."

One day, when you're ready, your voice will make room.

And it will matter. *You matter.*

You are not what was done to you. You are what you build in its aftermath. You are the beginning of something braver than the world knows how to measure; a revolution in motion.

You are the story that will help others find their way; the light that shines through the cracks. And when you rise, we will rise with you.

With love,
And with fire,
Serenity Lawson

The False Shepherd

What is a father meant to be?
A protector, a guide, and a mentor — all three.
And yet mine was none of the above;
I worked myself to sickness for his performance-based love.
I didn't understand why he made me physically uneasy.
My thought was that I was simply scared of displeasing.
And sure, he had a temper, like when he stripped us half-naked,
Spanking us until we cried, the way he felt that we had repented.
Yet the truth was, my sisters and I learned quickly to fake our tears,
While my brother was stubborn, and it only intensified over the years.
On multiple occasions, the one we called our dad,
Would spank him till the paddle broke, yet he'd say he "is not mad."
If that wasn't bad enough, his words formed around my heart and mind,
Shaping my thinking — defining what I was allowed to find.
I was taught I was a drama queen, an embellisher, and a liar,
I needed to be practically perfect, expected of the Pastor's daughter.
I was told no one would believe me when I recounted what was done,
Asked to search my heart and tell him if *I* was the one.
Had I invited that evil man to hurt me? Was the guilt mine to bear?

I learned never to speak about my trauma, even though silence was
a nightmare.
I now understand all these words were only just part of his ploy:
If I thought no one would believe me, he could still destroy.
Oh, how I wish I'd had a kind and loving father,
One who didn't judge and belittle, treating those he despised like fodder.
Especially the kind of father who never would have done,
What any father never should — what I blocked until twenty-one.
I spent over a decade unraveling my past,
Determining why I'd often felt so targeted and harassed.
It's clear to me now: you were the one who shaped me negatively.
And with you around, there was never any safety.
It's been a long time since you've passed — over six years already,
Yet when people say, "Sorry for your loss," my heart still goes unsteady.
What do I say to kind souls who don't know their words pierce my heart?
I can't exactly admit you were never a father, not even from the start.
So I smile graciously, thank them for their kind words,
I'm sure to them he was a Godsend, but to me he was absurd.
I won't discount what he did as a Pastor, Evangelist, and mechanic,
But when I recall who he was, I still feel residual panic.
I am grateful he touched many lives and helped so many out.
But as for me, he was not safe. Of this, I have no doubt.
If you don't like my story, we can agree to disagree.
But I am finally speaking out. I am finally becoming free.

Author's Note & Resources

I want you to know that I'm not a therapist, but I *am* someone you can safely confide in. I vow that anything shared with me will remain strictly confidential. I will never disclose your story, even anonymously, without your explicit consent.

Everyone needs at least one safe person to talk to, and I would be honored if you chose me. But whoever you confide in, please — I beg you — learn from my mistakes. Don't stay silent. Don't stuff it down, pretending you're fine while your insides are combusting.

If there's one thing I've learned while interviewing fellow brave survivors, it's this: **stress, trauma, and abuse live in the body** in unnatural and paralyzing ways. If voicing what happened can prevent future pain or medical issues, we owe it to ourselves to try.

And if you don't feel ready to speak to anyone just yet — I get it. Please, at the very least, write it down. The therapy that comes from metaphorically bleeding on the page is deeply personal and profoundly restorative.

Please don't suffer in silence. There's no medal for doing so. The only reward I received was a lengthy list of diagnoses from well-meaning doctors who couldn't fully understand what was happening to my body. I want better for you.

My inbox is always open: **Marissa.conklin24@gmail.com.** Use it when and if you feel ready. There are more of *us* than there are of those untouched by trauma or abuse. And yet so many still hide their scars, leaving the rest of us unaware of how common it truly is.

Resources:

- **National Domestic Violence Hotline:** 800-799-7233
- **National Sexual Assault Hotline (RAINN):** 800-656-4673 or www.rainn.org
- **Office on Violence Against Women (Survivor Resources):** 334-832-4842
- **Suicide & Crisis Lifeline:** 988
- **Women's Aid (UK):** www.womensaid.org.uk
- **Love Is Respect** (teen dating violence): www.loveisrespect.org
- **Financial Abuse Awareness:** www.purplepurse.com
- **PTSD & Trauma Recovery – National Alliance on Mental Illness:** 800-950-6264 | www.nami.org

I also highly recommend seeking out groups, meetings, or peer support communities tailored to your experience. You are strong. You deserve to heal among people who *understand* and who will walk with you toward peace.

About the Author

Marissa Conklin is a survivor, mother, and author living in Alaska with her five-year-old son. Born and raised in the rugged beauty of Alaska, she carries both the resilience of the landscape and the scars of childhood trauma within a religious community.

It Happens Here Too: The Shepherd's Daughter is her debut novel—a fictionalized account of her own journey from childhood sexual abuse and religious trauma to healing and voice. At her publisher's suggestion, she transformed her memoir into fiction, discovering that the creative distance allowed her to tell her truth more completely and powerfully than memoir could have.

As a survivor of childhood abuse by a pastor father, Marissa intimately understands the unique challenges faced by those wounded within religious communities. Her background in early childhood education reflects her commitment to protecting vulnerable children and creating safe spaces for healing—work that takes on profound personal meaning given her own experiences.

Marissa's advocacy extends beyond the written word. She speaks at conferences and support groups, sharing her story to help others find their voice. She has become a resource for those navigating religious trauma syndrome and childhood abuse recovery, offering hope to those who feel trapped by their past.

Writing has been both Marissa's refuge and her rebellion—a way to transform the silence that once protected her abuser into a voice that now protects others. Through fiction, she found the freedom to reshape her pain into purpose, her trauma into testimony.

When not writing or advocating, Marissa can be found exploring Alaska's wilderness with her son, reading voraciously, and building the kind of peaceful, safe home she always dreamed of as a child. She is living proof that healing is possible, that cycles can be broken, and that survivors can reclaim their stories.

Her journey from victim to survivor to thriver serves as inspiration for anyone who has ever wondered if their voice matters, if their truth deserves to be heard, if healing is truly possible after profound betrayal.